RUGBEIANS IN THE GREAT WAR

RUGBEIANS IN
THE GREAT WAR

DANIEL J McLEAN

Pen & Sword
MILITARY

AN IMPRINT OF PEN & SWORD BOOKS LTD.
YORKSHIRE - PHILADELPHIA

First published in Great Britain in 2019 by
PEN AND SWORD MILITARY
An imprint of
Pen & Sword Books Ltd
Yorkshire – Philadelphia

Copyright © Daniel J McLean, 2019

ISBN 978 1 52674 285 8

Typeset in Times New Roman 11.5/14 by
Aura Technology and Software Services, India
Printed and bound in the UK by TJ International

Pen & Sword Books Limited incorporates the imprints of Atlas, Archaeology,
Aviation, Discovery, Family History, Fiction, History, Maritime, Military, Military
Classics, Politics, Select, Transport, True Crime, Air World, Frontline Publishing,
Leo Cooper, Remember When, Seaforth Publishing, The Praetorian Press,
Wharncliffe Local History, Wharncliffe Transport, Wharncliffe True Crime and
White Owl.

For a complete list of Pen & Sword titles please contact
PEN & SWORD BOOKS LIMITED
47 Church Street, Barnsley, South Yorkshire, S70 2AS, England
E-mail: enquiries@pen-and-sword.co.uk
Website: www.pen-and-sword.co.uk

Or

PEN AND SWORD BOOKS
1950 Lawrence Rd, Havertown, PA 19083, USA
E-mail: Uspen-and-sword@casematepublishers.com
Website: www.penandswordbooks.com

Contents

Acknowledgements

There are many members of Rugby School whom I must thank, both pupils and staff. In particular I am very grateful to the Headmaster, Mr Peter Green, who has been a great support throughout my teaching career, and Dr Jonathan Smith, school archivist, for encouraging my interest in the school's wartime history and for allowing me access to the fascinating recesses of the archives. I must also thank Lieutenant General Tim Radford, Old Rugbeian, governor and father of another Rugbeian, whose encouragement and kind agreement to write the book's foreword were a great spur to actual writing. Father David Lawrence-March's invaluable proof-reading skills have also been, as ever, extremely helpful. Finally, I must thank the boys of Sheriff House, Clare Bowes the matron, and Maurice Monteith, housemaster, for enduring my interminable conversations on topics that they no doubt find very dull.

Foreword

Almost exactly 100 years after the guns fell silent at the end of the First World War, it's impossible to appreciate fully the scale, brutality, hardship and sense of loss involved. Much has been written about the political and military leadership of the time and, arguably, many lessons have since been learnt.

The walls of the Rugby School Memorial Chapel stand as a stark reminder of the part played by Old Rugbeians, and the staff, between 1914 and 1918. Yet, these beautiful, simple inscriptions to 687 ORs cannot reflect the pain of the remainder, wounded in body and mind, who lived through this terrible life-changing ordeal. Nor can they convey the deep sadness and suffering of the families of the fallen, all of whom will have been connected to, and influenced by, Rugby School.

Despite the considerable advance in technology between 1914 and 1918, warfare was then, and always will be, a very human endeavour. It is, at its core, a battle of wills, about human strengths and fallibilities, about courage and selfless commitment, about innovation, initiative, compassion, sacrifice and about love.

For ORs like Maurice Hankey, the Cabinet Secretary, the Great War was about influencing prime ministers at the grand strategic level. For others, arguably less well-known, like Private H.A.B. Donkin of The Queen's (Royal West Surrey Regiment), who died of pneumonia three days before Christmas at the Somme aged 19, I sense the war will simply have been about duty, loyalty and survival.

Between 1914 and 1918 ORs served throughout the armed forces in every rank. The majority served in infantry battalions from across the breadth of the British Isles and her empire. Others served, for example, in the Royal Artillery, the Royal Engineers or the cavalry. Some ventured into the Royal Flying Corps, the Royal Naval Air Service and later, when it was created in 1918, the Royal Air Force. Many however found themselves fixed in trenches on the Western Front for the duration of the war while others saw equally challenging service in Italy, Egypt, Palestine, Iraq, East and West Africa, as well as at Gallipoli. Campaign medals were hard-earned and, in many instances, were pinned next to British and allied awards for gallantry. Many were simply thankful to survive.

Dan McLean's brilliantly researched account vividly captures a flavour of the part played by ORs in the First World War. Some, like Rupert Brooke, are well known. Others, like Ernest Swinton, the inventor of the tank and author of the seminal *Duffer's Drift*, have since had a major influence on warfare and junior officers throughout the western world. So too the tactical vignettes of Sergeant Richard Tawney and the works of Charles Cruttwell whose accounts of the realities of conflict remained authoritative for decades. For several the war enforced a pause from playing international rugby. Tragically, for others, the pause was permanent. The wartime records of many other ORs were shrouded by wider achievements in academia, business, the Church or sport. As is the Rugbeian way, they served, quietly, made a difference where they could and then got on with the rest of their lives.

I've had the great privilege of commanding and serving alongside many ORs, on operations – most notably in Afghanistan. The qualities demonstrated by ORs in the First World War were unquestionably still being shown in the summer of 2009 in Helmand Province by former pupils of Rugby School. Men and women who, like their forebears from the Great War had, until recently, sung together in the pews of the magnificent Butterfield Chapel and who had idled to lessons, side by side, between the doctor's wall and the Close.

Warfare has undoubtedly become more technical, more sophisticated and more complex but the relentless assault on human emotions has remained constant. There are dark moments when soldiers search for solace. For me, on a number of occasions, as I know for others, memories of halcyon schooldays helped to provide comfort and ease the pressure – a match on the Close, a hymn in chapel, the peace of a Sunday afternoon; sentiments that were undoubtedly shared by those who fought on foreign fields between 1914 and 1918.

As an OR, soldier, school governor and parent it strikes me that the qualities of courage, quiet self-assuredness, humility, kindness, selflessness and a hint of rebellion, which carried ORs through the Great

FOREWORD

War, are still just as evident in the classrooms, houses, chapel and on the sports pitches today.

This outstanding book serves as a gentle reminder, in particularly to current pupils, of the immense sacrifices made by young men who, once upon a time, inhabited their bed-spaces. The accounts are humbling and inspiring in equal measure, and an entirely fitting tribute to a lost generation.

Lieutenant General Tim Radford CB DSO OBE
11th November 2018

Introduction

One hundred years have passed since three and a half thousand Rugbeians went to war at the call of their country, and as a teacher in the twenty-first century it is quite impossible to imagine my pupils doing the same, certainly on such an extraordinary scale. Rugbeians still join the armed forces, but not by compulsion, and we no longer have the almost daily horror of the lists of dead to be read out in chapel by the Headmaster. It is all the more important, therefore, that we remember those who, through nothing more than an accident of birth, lived and died in a time when they were compelled to join and to fight, many of whom still lie on the battlefields where they fell. The inspiration for this book came from a chance discovery in the archives of Rugby School in November 2017. A battered suitcase, covered with shipping labels, caught my eye on a shelf and upon opening it I realised that it was full of letters, the topmost of which were addressed to a young officer in France in 1916. These were the effects of Second Lieutenant Louis Stokes of the Royal Marine Light Infantry, killed leading his platoon into action at Beaumont Hamel on the 13th November 1916. The collection was meticulously collected by Louis' father after his death. With a little digging I realised that many of the letters had been published in the 1990s as the fascinating book *A Dear and Noble Boy*, edited by two members of Rugby School staff at the time, but I had the enviable task of cataloguing the rest of the huge collection of documents, including all of Louis' school reports, calendars, documents relating to his applications to the RMLI and University of Cambridge, and even the invoices for the equipment he took with him to the Somme. Louis sat in the same classrooms, the same chapel pews and at the same dining tables as Rugbeians do today. He too once enthused over the wickets he took in house cricket and the quality of the food at lunch, threw chocolate to his friends in maths, and rejoiced at a cancelled lesson, but now he lies buried in the Picardy soil, at Mailly

INTRODUCTION

Wood Cemetery. One hundred years appears to be a short period of time when set in such a context.

It is perhaps surprising that nothing has been published until now about those men from Rugby School who served in the Great War. The school may be best known for the sport which bears its name and which has spread gloriously around the world, but the influence of its boys and, for the past forty years, girls, has stretched into so many elements of society, including politics, art, literature, sport and, of course, the armed forces. In addition, as the vast majority of Rugbeians in the Great War served as junior officers, an extraordinarily high twenty-one per cent were killed in action, very much in contrast to the mid/late twentieth century stereotype of brave soldiers led by cowardly and incompetent officers. Rugbeians led from the front, and all too often suffered for that. In writing about each individual I have concentrated as much as possible on the elements of their lives that are concerned with the school and the war, occasionally to the detriment of fascinating later careers. Some of them have already been the subjects of detailed biographies and it is not necessary to cover the same ground once again. Of course, there were thousands more Rugbeians who served, and hundreds more who died; this book is something of a memorial to them all, not only to those who are the subjects of its chapters. They gave their lives, extraordinarily short though they often were, for the good that they perceived.

Sheriff House
Rugby School 2018

Rugby on the Eve of War

Much has been written on the Edwardian public school experience, some nostalgic, some satirical, but many accounts share the opinion that it appears to the modern observer, at least, to have been the very bedrock of British colonial expansion and administration. Whatever the strengths and weaknesses of such an impression, it cannot be denied that Rugby School in 1914 was typical of such schools in the education it provided and the young men it produced. Much of that typicality may be explained by the fact that many of the characteristics of English public school education across the country in the late nineteenth century had grown from the sweeping reforms of Dr Thomas Arnold, Head Master of Rugby between 1828 and his early death in 1842. His introduction of mathematics, history and modern languages to the school's curriculum, as well as boarding houses presided over by masters, was swiftly copied by most of the major schools in the country; further improvements were begun under subsequent head masters, such as the introduction of a scientific education under Frederick Temple, later Archbishop of Canterbury.

The school had been founded in 1567 as part of a bequest by Lawrence Sheriff, spice merchant to Queen Elizabeth I, to provide a school and almshouses for the people of the town and the neighbouring village of Brownsover. In order to support the foundation he also left to the trustees the ownership of several acres of pasture outside the City of London, whose rents at the time must have been a welcome support, but now that those fields have developed into a major part of Bloomsbury, the subsequent income provides a significant sum to the school to this day. It remained a small town grammar school for its first hundred years, partially because of the ongoing lawsuits brought by the Howkins family, descendants of Lawrence Sheriff's sister, who sought to overturn the terms of the will, but in the eighteenth century the school moved from the centre of town to its current location, thought to be near to the founder's birthplace. The new-found space meant that further expansion could occur, but it was Arnold's appointment which really set the school on the road to the great successes of the nineteenth century and beyond.

At the beginning of the twentieth century Rugby was a school of approximately 570 pupils[1], the largest it had been up to that point, and it remained at the forefront of British public school education. A fascinating first-hand account of a boy's life at the school between 1911 and 1915 may be gleaned from the letters of Louis Mander Stokes, the son of a Cambridge clergyman who was a member of School House and whose effects are held in the school archives. Many of his letters were published in 1995[2], but the battered leather suitcase of papers holds much more, detailing almost every detail of school and military life until Louis' death. It is from sources such as these that we may gain a fairly accurate picture not only of the state of the school, but also of the experiences of its members, on the eve of the war in 1914.

Houses

A boy's house was the centre of his existence in school. It was where he ate and slept, as it still is in such schools, but the independence of each house was much greater than could be allowed today; some houses, such as School Field, were even been built by their first housemasters, who then sold them on to the school upon retirement. The exception was School House which, until the 1960s, was the domain of the Head Master himself, until the challenges of modern headmastering made such an arrangement untenable and a separate housemaster was appointed. Consequently, boys outside School House saw little of the Head Master, and indeed Ernest Swinton declared that he and his contemporaries knew Dr Percival only by sight. Today, each house has a permanent name, often that of a memorable housemaster of the past, but before the Great War

---

1 HARDY, 1911, p31.
2 BARLOW & BOWEN, 1995.

they were all known by the name of the incumbent, and so would periodically change, though some stayed for an extraordinarily long time. The houses that existed in 1911 were (with their modern names in brackets where appropriate):

G.F. Bradby's (Kilbracken, though in a different location)
H.C. Bradby's (School Field)
Dickinson's (Bradley)
St Hill's (Michell)
School House
Stallard's (Tudor)
Steel's (Stanley)
Town
Whitelaw's
Wilson's (Cotton)

Some of these men loomed large in Rugby life for many years, indeed decades. G.F. Bradby, an Old Rugbeian himself, was described by one colleague as '…not only the strongest single influence at Rugby for thirty years, but [he] had a considerable effect on the public school education of his time.'[3] His erudition, humour, and integrity ensured he became something of an oracle to younger masters, and in spite of the fact that his career had never taken him beyond the Close, many of those to whom he was a mentor went on to be headmasters of major public schools. Robert Whitelaw was a considerable Greek scholar who taught at Rugby for 47 years, 37 of which were served as a housemaster. However, for all of their importance as the principal adult in a boy's school life, housemasters were also still somewhat distant figures who often remained in 'private side' outside meal times, leaving the daily operation to the Sixth (house prefects), who at the age of 16 or 17 could wield a great deal of power over the younger boys. Fagging was a recognised part of house life, and all boys who had not been in the school for at least three terms had to drop whatever they were doing to run towards the call of 'FAG' echoing down the passageways, for the last to arrive would receive the task, which could take him anywhere across the school. Corporal punishment, when it occurred, was also

---

3 SIMPSON, 1954, p117.

largely carried out by the older boys. Two or three younger boys were allocated to each Sixth, and took turns to clean his room for a week at a time. Another duty, explained by Louis to his father in one letter, was that of 'Toast Fag'; these boys, before tea, piled into the house kitchen to grab a toasting fork in order to make the Sixths' toast in front of the hall fire. The most coveted place was 'middle middle', in the centre of the fire, followed by 'left middle', 'right middle' etc. The toast was then taken to high table to be inspected by one of the Sixth and, if he chose, kept by him. Excess toast would be thrown the length of the hall to be scrabbled for by the younger boys. Other duties included 'Coat Fagging', entailing carrying the Sixths' coats out to them at the end of sports fixtures. That might be a few yards in the case of a football match, but several miles after 'Bigside Runs', of which there were approximately six each half term. Such a life may seem oppressive to the modern eye, but Louis loved every moment, writing to his father on the 6th October 1912:

> I am getting on rippingly here. I am very glad in most ways
> that I came to Rugby – and now I'm here I know that School
> House can't be beaten – it's ripping. I have no end of fun,
> and if it wasn't for the fact that I like a more what-do-you-
> call-it kind of existence but still it is grand here.

Sport

Rugby Football loomed large in school life during the winter. Since the laws of the game were first published by the boys of the school in 1845, they had developed in many ways, not least in that teams, which originally had no limit on numbers on each side, had been successively restricted until the number was set at fifteen in 1877. By the beginning of the twentieth century the 'XV' were major figures in school life, and became influential role models to younger boys. Many went on to international careers; some, such as Ronald Poulton, sadly cut short by the war. Their importance is made clear by the persistent mention of members of the XV in Louis Stokes' letters – very few boys from other houses feature at all. The Captain of the XV had a great deal more responsibility than simply leading his team on the field; he was also responsible for awarding the complex array of XV, 'caps' and 'bags', with their accompanying coloured hat bands, stockings and shorts, and even paid all of the team's bills, including the weekly fee to the head groundsman for the preparation of the pitch on the Close. Matches were usually internal, and between houses (for the honour of 'Cock House') or the XV against the rest. External matches were known as 'foreign' games and, though rarer than today, were major events; the entire school were expected to turn out to watch the XV play Cheltenham College, Uppingham School and the University of Oxford.

It is to be expected that Rugby Football should feature regularly in the life of the school, but that was by no means the only sport popular in Rugby at the time. Cricket, of course, was a significant part of the Trinity (summer) term, with a similarly complex system of coloured caps and blazers for the XI and XXII, but running and shooting were also extremely popular. The Ashburton Shield, the senior shooting prize for public schools, had been begun at Bisley in 1861 by Rugby, Eton and Harrow, and is still competed for annually today. Rugby won that first competition, and in the years before the Great War the Shooting VIII were very successful, though the number of schools entering for the Ashburton Shield had increased many times over. Such successes provoked great celebrations by the whole school, such as in July 1912 when Louis Stokes described the return of the victorious VIII from Bisley:

> During this match rumours, which towards the end became a certainty, that the VIII had won the Ashburton. I suppose you are not familiar with this name, but it is a shield competed for at Bisley by the Public Schools, and is considered the highest shooting honour a school can get. Of course everyone went wild with delight!! Also we knew we should get a half! The Corps went down to meet the VIII in the evening, there were flags in many windows in town – generally great excitement. At 10.5pm the Corps and the VIII paraded in the Close before the rest of the school.
>
> We were all drawn up in front of the Doctor's Wall; there were electric lights rigged up on this. After a bit the Corps arrived – and formed up. Then came the victorious VIII

(I should mention that O.G.J.F. Breul is in the VIII, he made 67 out of 70, getting the King's Cup). They stood out in front shivering. Then the Corps saluted them to the playing of the band. Then the Bidge made a funny speech. He said how awfully bucked everyone was. He had been told that he need not stay at Rugby (for he had an engagement elsewhere) as the Ashburton wasn't coming this way. But he had a presentiment, and was very glad to be there to congratulate them. He had seen that evening his old corps uniform, which reminded him of when he was as young as Mr Bonboli (roars) – and as innocent as Mr 'Podmore (bellows). "By the way" says he "before I forget, I think we will have a half tomorrow" (loud cheers) He then congratulated the VIII on behalf of the school. They responded by shivering, but Bonnerjee, the captain, made a witty speech in which he said that when the Bidge first came with his birds to Rugby - they brought him the Ashburton as a wedding present. This year they were performing a like benefit on Mr Hardy (cheers). They hoped, next year, they would be able to present Mr Mayne with the same present (loud laughter).

I may mention that we won it by 1 point.

Running had long been an important element of Rugby School sport; the 'Crick', the annual race from the village of Crick in Northamptonshire back to the school, is the oldest school cross-country competition in the world, having been competed for each year since 1837. It still takes place each March, attracting many parents and Old Rugbeians to compete, as well as current pupils. At ten and a half miles, the modern race remains an arduous task, even if it is two miles shorter than the original. As well as the Crick there existed a list of about a dozen other established routes around the town of Rugby, though not all began or ended at the school. These 'Bigside Runs' were open to older pupils, though by 1914 only thirty to forty boys entered regularly. They had originated as paper-chases, giving rise to the official title of the captain of running, 'Holder of the Bigside Bags', who would keep the bags used to hold the shredded paper marking the routes, but over time particular routes became favoured and, eventually, established fixtures.

The Officer Training Corps

Though there are mentions of a volunteer corps at Rugby during the Napoleonic wars, it may be said that the modern cadet movement dates from the 12th May 1859, the date upon which the War Office sent a letter to the Lords Lieutenant, authorising the formation of new volunteer corps to counter the threat of possible invasion by Napoleon III. Just under a year later Dr Temple raised the subject at a masters' meeting and found most opposed to the idea, but nonetheless concluded, 'Then we will try it.'[4] On the 9th May 1860 it was announced in Old Big School:

> …that the Rugby School Rifle Corps was formed and that
> the hours of drill would be announced as soon as the Heads
> of Houses and the Head of the Eleven should arrange them.[5]

Masters began to serve as officers in 1868 and the Corps continued to grow and develop over the latter half of the nineteenth century. By the turn of the century, under the command of C.E.M. Hawkesworth, the Rugby School Rifle Corps was a popular and efficient part of school life; Hawkesworth had been commissioned as a second lieutenant in 1895 and was appointed by the Head Master to run the corps in 1902, being promoted to captain on the 27th May 1903[6]. His reputation for discipline, initiative and hard work[7] had a great effect on the cadets under his command, and meant that in the years preceding the Great War Rugby School produced many excellent young officers for the British Army, including several of those included in this book. In 1907 the Corps moved to a new home: the Armoury, constructed as a memorial to the twenty-six Old Rugbeians killed in the Boer War. Captain Hawkesworth spoke scathingly of the move:

> A wretched fiasco. No notice given to Corps Authorities.
> No officers present except Lt Satterthwaite. Only one or two
> boys. But the building is satisfactory in every way.[8]

---

4 HARRIS, 1960, p1.
5 Ibid.
6 Ibid, p65.
7 Ibid, p64.
8 Ibid, p185.

The Armoury served admirably for many years, with some extensions and additions, until 2010 when modern security concerns prompted a move to new, larger facilities elsewhere in the school, and in 2017 the building was converted into three smart new drama studios.

The Haldane Reforms of 1906-12 had effects beyond the army itself, and in 1908 the Rugby School Rifle Corps became a contingent of the newly-created Officer Training Corps, though colloquially it has continued to be known for the majority of its history simply as 'the Corps'.

The outbreak of war in 1914 caused an exodus of masters, which had an instantaneous and terrible effect on the staffing of the Corps; a report in the school magazine *The Meteor* in the autumn of that year commented on a staff photo that had been taken at the preceding term's camp:

> …all have since been employed in direct connection with the war. Nearly all have commissions or are at military colleges. The O.C. is with the 8th Service Battalion of the Rifle Brigade, Mr Podmore with the Northamptonshire Regiment, Mr Thomas at the Depot, the Royal Warwickshire Regiment, Mr Kempson had a very strenuous six weeks at the same place. Mr Whitworth, after a short turn there, was at the Tidworth September camp with some 70 Rugbeians. Mr Bonhote was able to get to both Warwick and Tidworth before he sailed, reluctantly enough in the circumstances, for India.[9]

Regardless of staff shortages, it was inevitable that the corps should play a significant role in school life during wartime, and the preparation of boys for commissions through the instruction and examination in the 'Certificate A' syllabus was a great responsibility for all public schools, as part of their contribution to the national war effort.

The Bidge and the Beaks

The life of a Rugby master, or beak, in the years preceding the war was a somewhat single-minded one. On a starting salary of between £300 and £350 per annum[10], the unmarried masters were suitably remunerated,

---

9   Ibid.
10 SIMPSON, 1954, p112.

and worked in an atmosphere of stately security, with an extraordinary amount of freedom to choose what they taught and how they taught it, and the variety afforded by the school week guarded against any sense of boredom or repetition. That said, all lived in school, as indeed they still do, but there were few opportunities to socialise, with the effect that colleagues of many years could have a friendly acquaintance, but rarely close friendship. Even so, there was a distinct impression that their chosen career was one of schoolmastering, rather than teaching, which was usually understood to be the preserve of state schools, which necessarily had a far lesser emphasis on the development of a child's overall character than a boarding school. Dr Albert David, Head Master from 1910, quickly gained a reputation as a reformer, to the chagrin of certain elder elements of the Common Room. Though he had been a Rugby beak himself several years earlier, he had distinct ideas about what society would come to demand from public schools, and what they could best do for the boys entrusted to their care. J.H. Simpson, another Old Rugbeian, who returned to teach in January 1913 declared that Dr David's innovations were indeed one of the principal attractions of such an appointment, and that his time as headmaster of Clifton College had given him a greater context from which to judge the strengths and weaknesses of Rugby routines:

> He understood fully all that was best in the traditions of Rugby... but at the same time he saw far more clearly than most of his colleagues that society – including parents, industry, commerce and people interested in education – was making, or soon would make, demands of the public schools which could only be satisfied by discarding practices and beliefs which had long since served their purpose.[11]

These innovations inevitably ran up against opposition from the more entrenched beaks who, quite understandably, believed that the school was efficient and popular and therefore that change was unnecessary, but as Dr David's ideas took root, such as the abolition of the first lesson before breakfast and of top hats in chapel, the greater encouragement of science teaching and of informal relations between

---

11 Ibid, p105.

staff and pupils, the majority of the Common Room came to agree. Even so, in the first three years of Dr David's tenure more than half of the boarding houses changed hands, as the Victorian finally gave way to the Edwardian.

A further innovation was the new head master's concentration upon the progress and support of the boys of the middle, who neither excelled nor courted failure, and he began doing so by meeting and getting to know as many boys as possible outside his own house. Through such methods, which seem obvious today, he came to realise that the public schools of the late nineteenth century had done almost nothing to support their pupils through the turbulence of adolescence, and so he courted further criticism by engaging the services of professional psychiatrists to help those boys in particular trouble. Simpson, undoubtedly one of Dr David's allies in his reforming zeal, described the process charitably:

> ...the process that I witnessed was one of humanising and vitalising the life of a school; of making it less rigid and formal, without necessarily making it less bracing; of increasing the dose of happiness and spontaneity, without altogether eliminating the dose of austerity.[12]

Rugby School Terminology

All public schools developed their own local vocabulary, Winchester's being perhaps the most extensive, and Rugby was no exception. Some terms remain in use, many have been lost, but the list below gives an idea of the vocabulary of an average Rugby boy in 1914:

Bags – minor sports colours.

The Bidge – the Head Master, Dr David (most head masters were known as 'The Bodger' but Dr David seems to have been an anomaly).

Boys' Man – Butler.

Cap – to acknowledge a passing master (later changed to 'tick').

---

12 Ibid, p126.

Chortleswade – the fictional school whom beaks reminded boys they were not members of when behavioural standards flagged.

The Close – the principal Rugby Football pitch, where the sport was originally developed.

C.O. – Call Over: a house or whole school register.

Cock House – winner of the house football competition (the world's oldest Rugby Football tournament).

Con – Latin or Greek translation (from construe).

Copy – an award for good work, recommended by a member of staff and confirmed by the Head Master.

Cut - to miss a lesson (whether legitimately or not).

Dic/Dix – house prayers (from *dicere*)

Dished – defeated.

Foreign – a sports match against another school.

Fug – biscuit.

Fug out – to clean.

Had-over – to be beaten as a punishment.

Holder of the Bigside Bags – Captain of Running.

Imposition – to redo a piece of work as a punishment.

In Hall – a boy who had exceeded seven terms at the school. Only those in Hall and above could carry an umbrella.

Jerries, Blogs, Bilhams, Joes, Louts or Buggins – house servants.

Lamb Singing – the practice of making new boys sing to the whole house (see *Tom Brown's Schooldays*)

Levée - a meeting (now used to refer to school prefects)

Long List – revision.

Old Big Side – the principal football pitch on the Close, where the game of Rugby Football was invented.

Other place – prep school.

People – parents.

Pontines – the pitch next to Old Big Side on the Close.

Porridge – an area of gravel outside School House and the Chapel.

Puntabout – informal football practice.

Rustication – to be sent home as a punishment.

San – the school sanatorium.

School – classroom.

Scrummage – wrestling in house passageways.

Sixth – prefect (now used to refer to house prefects).

Sixth Licking – to be beaten in the presence of all the heads of houses.

Smoking – blushing.

Speckle – to remove the privileges of one of the Sixth.

Stodge – snacks or extra food (this name was later given to the school tuck shop when it opened in the 1920s).

Sweat – to work hard, or an arduous task.

Tolly – candle.

Topos – lavatory.

Tosh – bath or swimming pool.

Young'un – younger brother.

THE ARTS

Sub Lieutenant Rupert Brooke (School Field)

Rupert Brooke's childhood was in every way Rugbeian. He was born on the 3rd August 1887 at his parents' home, 5 Hillmorton Road; the house is next to one boarding house and opposite another, and the housemaster across the road, the classical Greek scholar Robert Whitelaw, was Rupert's godfather, so every element of his early years was intimately bound up with the life of the school where his father was a master. Rupert was the middle of three sons, and named apparently after the Royalist general of the 1640s, Prince Rupert of the Rhine.[13] Early in his childhood Rupert's father also became a housemaster, and so the Brooke family moved the short distance to School Field, the characteristically Butterfield boarding house that sits surrounded by Chestnut trees at the opposite end of the Close to School House and the Chapel. Its location was convenient for Rupert's prep school, Hillbrow, which was only a few hundred yards down Barby Road, and which is now the site of another Rugby boarding house, Kilbracken. The average life of a boy at Rugby in the first years of the twentieth century is examined elsewhere, but Rupert's existence once he left Hillbrow was rather different to most, since his father's position meant that, while he lived in a boarding house, he slept in his own bedroom on 'private side', not in the dormitories inhabited by his peers. His room, still preserved to a certain extent, is on the top floor, with windows facing both south and east, and provided a welcome refuge from the hectic life of school. Rupert's father, known to the boys as 'Tooler', was characteristically absent from the boys' side of the house, as were his colleagues in other houses, leaving the daily administration in the hands of the VIth, but Tooler was also well known for his absent-mindedness, often pausing half way across the road or on the threshold of a room to recall where he had intended to go. Even so, his life was entirely given over to the school, and his two sons, Rupert and Alfred, were also inclined to view him as a somewhat distant figure. His tentative character is perhaps summarised by his own observation that 'The life of a Housemaster is like living on a volcano.'[14]

---

13 DELANY, 2015, p12.
14 HASSALL, 1964, p38.

Rupert joined his father's house in September 1901, and his first report from the Bodger[15] simply said, 'Has begun well'. That was certainly the case; he had won a scholarship, and by the end of his second year played both cricket and football for the house, and had been promoted to lance corporal in the Corps. Academically, he lived up to his scholarship, and in 1903 he was promoted to the XX, a senior form under the tutelage of Robert Whitelaw, an extraordinarily long-serving master whose former house on Hillmorton Road still bears his name. His character, including a certain degree of savageness in his assessment of boys' abilities, as well as his longevity, turned him into something of a revered figure in the first years of the new century, and the cult of 'Bobbieship' was an established joke among the boys of the XX. Rupert wrote a somewhat vicious yet admiring epigram in one of his exercise books:

> Olim erat Robertus Alba Lex, Puerorum tyrannicus et saevus rex, O Bobbie horridissime![16]

In the spring of that year, at the age of 16, Rupert's nascent poetical abilities were first made apparent; his poem *The Pyramids* came second in the school's annual poetry prize, but his mother, convinced of its quality, had it printed by Mr Over, the school's printer in town. It attracted the notice of St John Welles Lucas-Lucas, now aged 25 and residing in Middle Temple, though he had lived in Rugby during his childhood, where his family, including his father, the painter H.E. Lucas, still resided. As a poet himself, Rupert's parents were no doubt grateful that he visited during Rupert's convalescence from a throat infection, which kept him away from cricket for most of the Trinity term, but the visit from the pince-nez-wearing Lucas, accompanied by the young dramatist Arthur Eckersley, was to have a distinct influence on the remaining years of Rupert's adolescence. Lucas was an aesthete, one who had in his own way managed to perpetuate the cause of *The Yellow Book* and *The Lily* after the social disgrace of its figurehead, Oscar Wilde, in 1895. He left with Rupert various volumes that were devoured as exotic and intoxicating – Dowson, Housman and Baudelaire – and though Lucas

---

15 The traditional Rugby nickname for the Head Master, in use from the 1890s to the 1980s.
16 HASSALL, p40.

3

remained something of a mentor for Rupert's remaining time at Rugby, the aesthetic pose could never be anything but a private love in the life of an Edwardian schoolboy, where the cult of games ruled supreme, even in the relative safety of life in private side, rather than the tumultuous dormitories of the boys' side.

On Christmas Eve 1904 Rupert again fell ill, and the doctor persuaded his mother that a change of climate was required to ensure his recovery, so it was decided that he would spend the next term with friends Doctor and Mrs Gibbons at their villa at Rapallo, near Genoa. He set off with his younger brother Alfred and two cousins, Margaret and Reeve, and a certain amount of work to be completed, though he complained of the lack of intellectual stimulation in the Gibbons household to a letter to his great friend Geoffrey Keynes at School Field:

> The only things to read this benighted place supplies are Tennyson's Poems and a London Directory of 1888. I've tried both and prefer the latter.[17]
>
> At intervals they drag me up to Genoa and round a picture gallery; which is wasted on me. I say "How beautiful!" at every fourth picture and yawn.[18]

Lucas's influence was certainly growing at the time, and during his time at Rapallo Rupert devoured his new copy of Wilde's *De Profundis*, which Lucas had sent him, making copious notes in the margins, and his poems of the time are full of notable aesthetic themes. School Field and Rugby were never far from his thoughts, however, and he had begged Keynes to send him all news of the place:

> Nay, dear Keynaanite, think of the innumerable benefits I have conferred upon you. Have I not introduced you to G. K. Chesterton? Did I not once lend you an H. G. Wells? Have I not often made you laugh? Have I not occasionally even made you think?[19]

---

17 Ibid, p52.
18 HALE, 1998, p11.
19 HASSALL, P56.

Upon his return Rupert continued his convalescence at Bournemouth and Hastings, but returned to Rugby in time to enter his poem *The Bastille*, begun in Paris during his return from Italy by train, in the 1905 school poetry competition. Before leaving in January he had been promoted to Upper Bench, the senior form of the school[20], taught by the Head Master himself, but had neglected his reading during his absence, and now continued to do so in order to finish his prize poem, which duly won on the 24th April, with Rupert being awarded volumes of Browning and Rosetti as his prize. At the end of a long summer by the sea, Rupert, having eventually decided to try for Cambridge rather than Oxford, visited his uncle, the Dean of King's, and when it was intimated that he might be suitable for a classical scholarship, a private tutor was engaged and installed in School Field. The term was a busy one for Rupert: he played for the school XV, spoke at debates, and found time to enter two poetry competitions in the *Westminster Gazette*, the second of which he won, and so saw his work published for the first time, even if it was under the pseudonyms of 'Sandro' and 'Teragram'.[21] Just before the end of term, at Christmas 1905, Rupert and two Rugby friends travelled by train to Cambridge for their scholarship exams, and all received rewards. This in itself was a great achievement for the young man, now 18, who had been dogged throughout his school life by masters' opinions that he and his work were 'vague' and lacked detail. Perhaps that was the case to a certain degree, and if it was it became more so now, as Rupert saw the scholarship as the summation of his academic efforts, and gave little time to them henceforth. The summer of 1906 approached, and with it his final term at the school he loved. The light blue ribbon on his plain white straw hat signified his membership of the XI, but in other respects the aesthetic tendency was allowed to emerge just a little more than before; his hair went uncut, and his tie, which had to be black, was of florid silk. Though he was to receive the King's medal for Prose at Speech Day, for an essay on England's debt to William III, his school work was somewhat neglected for the Debating Society and Eranos, the senior literary society, to whom he gave a good number of papers, the last of which was delivered on his final Sunday as a schoolboy, on the subject of the modern poets. Perhaps his

---

20 Named after its classroom, where Thomas Arnold had taught, above the gate to Old Quad.
21 HASSALL, p73.

choice of readings left little impression upon his audience, which included Robert Whitelaw and Parker Brooke, but the opportunity to read to them from Housman's *A Shropshire Lad*, first introduced to him by Lucas, was his one last act of aesthetic defiance to the strictures of public school life. His final report from the Head Master was a short but accurate summary of his abilities:

> His work is more uneven than that of any other boy in the form; he either dislikes details or has no capacity for them. But when he is good – on the purely literary side of his work and scholarship he is capable of very brilliant results, and in English composition he must make a name. Always a delightful boy to work with. I am very sorry to lose him.[22]

Rupert was very sorry to leave too; one of his final acts as a member of the school was to take two catches in the annual Rugby–Marlborough cricket match at Lord's (though he scored no runs), and of course he would be returning to his family in School Field during the vacations from Cambridge, but as the other boys streamed home at the end of term he was acutely conscious of the fact that in the summer of 1906 a very happy chapter of his life was at a close. In one of his last letters to Edward Marsh he wrote,

> I am infinitely happy. I am writing nothing. I am content to live. After this term is over, the world awaits.[23]

Rupert Brooke's life at Cambridge and Grantchester is well-known and widely recorded, but he was to return to School Field in a somewhat more formal capacity than he can ever have imagined. He had returned home for his first Christmas since leaving school, and in the second week of January was packing for his return when an urgent summons arrived from a doctor in Southsea. Rupert's elder brother, Richard, was working for an engineering firm there and had been taken seriously ill with pneumonia, so his father rushed to the south coast, arriving in time to be at his eldest son's side at the moment of his death, on the 13th January 1907. Parker Brooke never entirely recovered from the shock of the experience, and from that moment

---

22 Ibid, p95.
23 MARSH, 1918, p17.

his characteristic forgetfulness became increasingly apparent, coupled with neuralgia which was at times crippling. By the closing days of 1909 the problems were almost continuous, and after the New Year his eyesight also suddenly failed, leaving him sitting alone in private side for hours, unable to fulfil his duties as housemaster, and the new head master, Dr Albert David[24], asked that he leave School Field at Easter. The family doctor had little idea what to diagnose, and so Rupert returned to Grantchester, but on the 23rd January a telegram arrived asking him to return to Rugby as soon as possible as his father was close to death. He and Alfred took turns to sit by their father's bed through the night, but he died the following morning; William Parker Brooke was 49 when he died in School Field, and on the day that the boys of the house returned for the new term their housemaster was being buried in the Clifton Road cemetery. Though he caught influenza at the funeral, Rupert was asked by Dr David to take over the running of School Field for a term while a new housemaster was sought.

Such a task was immensely daunting, but one to which Rupert quickly found himself remarkably well suited. He had only two days to fetch his work from Cambridge, but with no teaching required there was plenty of time to work on an essay on portrayals of Puritanism in seventeenth century drama, which he intended to submit for the Harness Prize in Cambridge.[25] Perhaps conscious of the circumstances which had led to his appointment, the boys of School Field were amenable to his efforts, and he wrote to a friend in a bright tone only a few weeks later:

> Being a Housemaster is in a way pleasant. The boys are delightful; and I find I am an admirable school-master. I have a bluff Christian tone which is entirely pedagogic. Also, they remember I used to play for the school at various violent games, and respect me accordingly. Every night at 9.20 I take prayers – a few verses of a psalm and one or two short heartfelt prayers. I nearly had to prepare the lads for Confirmation, but I, rather pusillanimously, wriggled out of that. But a certain incisive incredulity in my voice when I mention the word God is, I hope, slowly dropping the poison of truth into their young minds.[26]

---

24 Bishop of Liverpool 1923-44.
25 Rupert's poem won and he received a prize of £70.
26 HASSALL, p217.

For ten weeks Rupert was Housemaster of School Field, and when the time came to pass on the reins it was of course an emotional wrench, as he was leaving his childhood home, the house in which his father had only recently died, and which had been the most stable centre of his life for as long as he could remember. The family furniture was piled in the hall and valued by a local dealer, his mother taking the few pieces that she needed to furnish her new, much smaller, home on Bilton Road. The family cat, Tibby, was poisoned; at 16 she was deemed too old to survive the move. Rupert wrote again to his friend Marsh:

> I wept copiously last week in saying good-bye to the three and fifty little boys whose Faith and Morals I had upheld for ten weeks. I found I had fallen in love with them all. So pleasant and fresh-minded as they were. And it filled me with purpureal gloom to know that their plastic souls would harden into the required shapes, and they would go to swell the indistinguished masses who fill Trinity Hall, Clare, Caius,… and at last become members of the English Upper, or Upper Middle, Classes. I am glad I am not going to be a school-master for ever. The tragedy would be too great.[27]

Rupert's well-known literary life continued, and when war was declared in August 1914 he had recently returned from Tahiti. His first thought was that he should perhaps go to France to help gather the harvest before any real fighting began[28], but it wasn't long before the national fervour made him realise that he was likely to have to fight:

> I've spent a fortnight in chasing elusive employment about. For a time I got drilled on the chance of getting into a London corps as a private, but now I really think I shall get a commission. Territorial probably, through Cambridge. The whole thing, and the insupportable stress of this time, tired me to a useless rag.[29]

---

27 Ibid, p221.
28 MARSH, P147.
29 Ibid.

By this time Marsh was serving as private secretary to Winston Churchill, First Lord of the Admiralty, and so Rupert was commissioned as a temporary sub lieutenant in the Royal Naval Volunteer Reserve, for service with the Royal Naval Division. These somewhat strange units, the result of a larger number of naval personnel than was needed to man the fleet, served ashore throughout the war, and indeed saw action early in the conflict, Rupert among them. He was appointed to Anson Battalion, and on the 27th September 1914 Marsh saw him off on a train at Charing Cross bound for a training camp at Betteshanger in east Kent before they proceeded to the naval barracks at Chatham for musketry training. Finally, on the 5th October, having marched to Dover, the battalion sailed from Dover to Dunkirk, and was quickly approaching its first contact with the enemy. They were informed that they were to travel by train to Antwerp and that their transport was likely to be attacked; while that didn't happen, upon arrival they could hear the German guns in the distance and imagined all sorts of terrible ways to die as they wrote letters to be sent home in the event of their death. Sleeping in the gardens of a chateau, Rupert was at first struck by the contrast of the beauty of the countryside with the ominous, menacing noises echoing across the fields from Antwerp.[30] At 0730 the next morning they left and approached the increasingly-besieged port, where the Belgian Army had emptied the shipping fuel tanks and set fire to the petrol, giving a hellish first impression to the inexperienced sailors of Anson Battalion, with the ruined houses, dead horses and endless procession of Belgian refugees lit by the red glare of the flames. It was this experience that resolved Rupert's uncertainty about military service; he had seen war with his own eyes, and the British response was now, to his mind, entirely warranted:

> …now I've the feeling of anger at a seen wrong – Belgium –
> to make me happier and more resolved in my work. I know
> that whatever happens, I'll be doing some good, fighting to
> prevent that.[31]

With their return to England the officers of the battalion were dispersed, but in December 1914 Rupert was reunited at Blandford Camp with

---

30 Ibid, p155.
31 Ibid, p157.

Bernard Freyberg[32], Denis Browne, a friend since their earliest days at Rugby, and Arthur Asquith[33], son of the then prime minister, in Hood Battalion. Christmas in Blandford Camp was not a particular jolly affair, as Rupert spent most of Christmas Day supervising drunken stokers, but for a while he had been working on a series of five sonnets, to be entitled *1914*, and they were finished in Rugby when he visited his mother on leave just after Christmas.

On the 29th January 1915 Rupert got the train to London; he was ill with influenza again and, through his friendship with the Asquiths, he was to recuperate at 10 Downing Street, but by the 25th February he was back at Blandford for the King's inspection, and was deliriously excited to have heard that the battalion was heading for Gallipoli. For a classical scholar like Rupert, the prospect of sailing through the Aegean, past the cities and islands of his childhood reading, was almost more perfect than he could imagine, regardless of the reason for their journey. He wrote to Arthur Asquith's sister:

> I've never been quite so happy in my life, I think. Not quite so pervasively happy, like a stream flowing entirely to one end. I suddenly realise that the ambition of my life has been – since the age of two – to go on a military expedition against Constantinople. And when I thought I was hungry or sleepy or aching to write a poem – that is what I really, blindly, wanted. This is nonsense. Good-night. I'm very tired with equipping my platoon.[34]

On the 28th February Rupert left England for the last time, sailing on the *Grantully Castle* from Avonmouth and thoroughly enjoyed the voyage. After a single day of sea-sickness he marvelled at the earthy smells off the coast of Spain, the tawny mountains and white villages of North Africa, and even the prospect of conflict at Gallipoli reminded him that they were to sail through the Cyclades in order to get there.

---

32 Later Lieutenant General Bernard Freyberg, 1st Baron Freyberg VC GCMG KCB KBE DSO and three bars, Governor-General of New Zealand.

33 Joining as a Sub Lieutenant in 1914, just over three years later Asquith took command of the 189th Brigade, in an extraordinarily meteoric rise.

34 MARSH, p168.

It was as though they were on a holiday tour of the Mediterranean. Such sentiment was only reinforced by their stops along the way; a trip to the opera in Malta and an excursion to the pyramids at Giza were diverting entertainments, but while they were in Port Said Rupert suffered from sun-stroke, from which he took a good deal of time to recover, writing that when they reached Gallipoli he should only be able to give the Turks 'at the utmost, a kitten's-tap'[35]. On the 19th April they reached the Aegean island of Skyros, which Rupert was destined never to leave. The next day, after a battalion field-day on the island, he felt dreadfully tired and retired to bed immediately after dinner. On the 21st he couldn't leave his bed, with terrible pains in his head and back, and a swollen lip, and by the morning of Thursday the 22nd his temperature had increased dramatically, the swelling had grown, and he was diagnosed with acute blood poisoning from an infected mosquito bite. There was little to be done, and so it was decided to remove Rupert to the French hospital ship *Duguay-Trouin*, anchored nearby, though Rupert at first protested that he couldn't leave his platoon. Once he was settled in the largest cabin on the hospital-ship's sun deck, Denis Browne sent a wire to the Admiralty informing Churchill of the situation, but despite the attentions of the ship's medical staff he was never to recover consciousness after Thursday evening. At 1400 on Friday it was clear that he would not last much longer, and Denis sat with him until the end:

> At 4 o'clock he became weaker, and at 4.46 he died, with the sun shining all round his cabin, and the cool sea-breeze blowing through the door and the shaded windows. No one could have wished a quieter or a calmer end than in that lovely bay, shielded by the mountains and fragrant with sage and thyme.'[36]

That evening Rupert's body was carried ashore in a steam pinnace, and the flag-draped coffin was carried up the steep and narrow way to his grave, which had been dug by his friends and members of his platoon in a quiet olive grove overlooking the sea. It was not an easy journey, and

---

35 Ibid, p173.
36 Ibid, p182.

men with lamps were posted to light the coffin on its way, as it took two hours to cover the mile from the landing place. The sad procession was led by one of Rupert's platoon, carrying a large white cross painted with his name, then the firing party and the battalion officers, led by General Paris. Behind followed Rupert's body in its coffin, borne by the petty officers of his company. In the light of the moon and lamps the coffin was lowered into the grave, a wreath of olive placed upon it, and the chaplain said the funeral service, accompanied by the shots of a rifle salute and the Last Post. Once the service was complete and the grave filled the procession slowly wound its way back to the sea, but Rupert's friends remained behind to cover the grave with the lumps of white marble that littered the olive grove, surrounded it with flowers, and quietly made an agreement to return after the war to build a permanent wall around the site. The ship sailed at 6am the next morning, and within six weeks Denis Browne was himself dead, killed leading his platoon into battle at the attack on Achi Baba on the 4th June 1916, an action which cost the lives of nine Old Rugbeian officers.

The effect of Rupert's death at home was profound; Churchill summarised the feelings of many when he wrote,

> During the last few months of his life, months of preparation in gallant comradeship and open air, the poet soldier told with all the force of genius the sorrow of youth about to die and the sure triumphant consolation of a sincere and valiant spirit. He expected to die, he was willing to die for the dear England whose beauty and majesty he knew; and he advanced towards the brink in perfect serenity, with absolute conviction of the righteousness of his country's cause and a heart devoid of hate for fellow men. The thoughts to which he gave expression in the very few incomparable War sonnets, which he has left behind, will be shared by many thousands of young men, moving resolutely and blithely forward into this, the hardest, the cruellest, and the least rewarded of all the wars that men have fought. They are a whole history and revelation of Rupert Brooke himself. Joyous, fearless, versatile, deeply instructed, with classic symmetry of mind and body, ruled by high undoubting purpose, he was all that one would

wish England's noblest sons to be in days when no sacrifice but the most precious is acceptable, and the most precious is that which is most freely offered.[37]

The nature of Rupert's war poems, and the contrasts to be drawn between them and those of poets who experienced the horrors of the Western Front has been much discussed elsewhere, but Rupert had indeed experienced the reality of human conflict, in Antwerp. Had he lived he might well have changed his approach, taking into account the terrible scale of death which he did not live to see for himself, but in his own time he wrote of what he felt, of the unfortunate necessity of war and the justice of the defence of Belgium. His work is certainly of its time, and of his class, but it is no less remarkable for that. His end was, perhaps, very much as he would have wished, had he known, but he had without doubt faced the possibility of his own death. Edward Marsh presented this most clearly in his own memoir, written soon after Rupert died:

> Here then, in the island where Theseus was buried, and whence the young Achilles and the young Pyrrhus were called to Troy, Rupert Brooke died and was buried on Friday, the 23rd of April, the day of Shakespeare and of St George.[38]

---

37 Memorials of Rugbeians who Fell in the Great War.
38 MARSH, p180.

13

Second Lieutenant Percy Wyndham Lewis (Tudor)

Percy Wyndham Lewis (he soon stopped using his first name) was born on his father's yacht *Wanda*[39], at anchor off Campobello, Novia Scotia[40], on the 18th November 1882, to an English mother and American father, Charles Edward Lewis, who had fought in the American Civil War and been a prisoner of the Confederates[41]. The mutton-chopped Charles had met Wyndham's mother, Anne, in London and they had married in Camberwell in 1876[42]; Charles was seventeen years older than the sixteen-year-old Anne, and proud of his war service with the 1st New York Dragoons and his commission signed by Abraham Lincoln. Wyndham spent an enjoyable early childhood in New England and eastern Canada, but his father was often away, and in 1888 the Lewis family crossed the Atlantic and settled first in Eastbourne and then on the Isle of Wight, funded by a stipend from Charles's brother. In 1893 however, his father left his wife and son; the marriage had been somewhat distant for a while, but Charles's affair with his sister's housemaid during a visit to New York in 1892 was the final straw, and Anne took their son to live permanently with her mother in Upper Norwood, within sight of the Crystal Palace, where they had been staying for several months already.

Wyndham's education began at Castle Hill School in south London, and his academic performance there was solid if not exemplary.[43] In 1897, aged 14, Wyndham arrived at Stallard's, the house on Horton Crescent that had been built in 1893 and, at his arrival, retained its original housemaster. His six terms at Rugby were undistinguished, and he himself described them as 'two years of kicking balls and being beaten for neglect of work.'[44] In this, though it may be an example of Wyndham's characteristic exaggeration, we see his general attitude to school, which was one of general apathy, and possibly even provocation.

---

39 O'KEEFE, 2015, p5.
40 O'Keefe undertakes a fascinating examination of the likelihood of these circumstances and, while unlikely, there is no conclusive evidence to condemn the tale told by Lewis.
41 EDWARDS and WALLACE, 1992, p13.
42 St Stephen's, Camberwell, 23rd February 1876.
43 O'KEEFE, p21.
44 O'KEEFE, p23.

Indeed, one of the stories he told in later life was of continually hitting a tennis ball against a Sixth's study door in order to reach a record sixth beating in one day, though his childhood letters show that this may have happened to another boy. Throughout his life Wyndham was to have a propensity for causing trouble, whether he intended to or not. The one subject at which he excelled was art, and after examining his drawings and paintings Mr Stallard arranged for Wyndham to have private lessons with the school's drawing master, the Glaswegian Thomas Mitchener Lindsay. Such talent was not necessarily something universally admired by Edwardian schoolboys, one of whom exclaimed, 'You frightful artist', after finding Wyndham, paints in hand, in his study.[45]

After a particularly condemnatory report from the Head Master, Dr James, Mr Stallard suggested to Wyndham's mother that he might best be placed somewhere where he could concentrate on art, as his particular strength, and so at the age of 16 he arrived at the Slade School of Drawing in King's Cross, London, arriving for the first time on the morning of Monday, 9th January 1899, to be confronted by the great canvas of Augustus John's, *Moses and the Brazen Serpent*, which had triumphantly won the Summer Prize the previous year. In spite of the inspiration at every turn, Wyndham remained essentially a schoolboy, ten years junior than many of his Slade contemporaries; he was expected to attend the school six days a week, but after two months of regular and conscientious work, the Beadle's book, recording the signatures of those at the Slade each day, contains only one more signature for the rest of the first term of 1899. It is most likely, however, that this is a record of Wyndham's lateness, rather than absence, as in due course he was allowed to progress from drawing the 'antiques' (sculptures), to the life models in the next room. It was here that he first came across Augustus John in person, but it was when he was sent to draw in the British Museum that he came under the influence of a loose group of older artists such as the poet Lawrence Binyon, serving at the time as Keeper of Prints and Drawings. The prompt for Wyndham to return to his earlier working habits, however, was the possibility of a scholarship, provided by the terms of Felix Slade's will, and after suitable diligence he was elected as such in June 1900,[46] working terrifically hard thereafter. Characteristically, this industry was

45 O'KEEFE.
46 O'KEEFE, p35.

not to last, and Wyndham's work and attendance both declined over the course of the 1900-1 academic year, even though he was conscious of the scholarship's clause which stipulated that it could be removed in the event of inadequate attendance. He preferred to smoke and chat in the drying room. The inevitable happened, and on the 10th June 1900 he entered the doors of the Slade for the last time. Frederick Brown, Slade Professor of Art, was watching him from the bottom of the stairs, already angered at Wyndham's continued acceptance of the scholarship without fulfilling its terms, and as the young student casually lit a cigarette, in contravention of the school's rules, he could contain his anger no longer. He marched across the hall, seized Wyndham by the collar and forcibly ejected him from the building, instructing Campion, the Beadle, to deny him entry henceforth.

With little money and no particular direction in life, Wyndham set out for the continent, heading first to Madrid with Spencer Gore[47], and once she heard of their departure his worrying mother sent him a cheque for £6 each week, allowing them to continue to survive. After that he visited the Netherlands and then, for longer, Paris, where he proposed to a German girl, Ida Vendel, though the relationship was not to last and he abandoned her in November 1905. He continued to see Ida on occasion for another two years.

The next decade of Wyndham's life was characterised by sporadic commissions but more frequent feuds, the most calamitous of which was with Roger Fry over the direction and style of his 'Omega Workshop' in Fitzroy Square. Wyndham was increasingly frustrated with what he saw as the polite, stifled nature of the workshop's product, and the discord erupted in the spring of 1914 over the Omega contribution to that year's Daily Mail Ideal Home Exhibition. After publishing an extraordinarily spiteful public letter, detailing what he saw as Fry's and Omega's failings, he left for good, establishing his own establishment, the so-called 'Rebel Art Centre' at 38 Great Ormond Street. Though the centre only formally operated for four months, it was here in 1914 and 1915 that Wyndham developed his distinctive style, in which he attempted to blend the structures of Cubism with the fluidity and energy of Futurism, incorporating many influences from his decade of travels across Europe. His intentions were made clear by the publication of *Blast*, of which two editions appeared on the 20th July 1914, which Ezra Pound described in a letter to James Joyce as '…a new Futurist, Cubist, Imagiste Quarterly... I can't tell, it is mostly

---

47 1878-1914, the first President of the Camden Town Group of artists.

a painters' magazine with me to do the poems'[48]; indeed it was Pound who proposed the name 'Vorticism'. After one exhibition however, in 1915 at the Doré Gallery[49] in London, the movement began to lose momentum, not least because of the distraction of the increasing horrors of the war.

Wyndham Lewis himself had volunteered for military service in April 1915, and having initially intended to apply for a commission, was persuaded to join the Royal Garrison Artillery as a Gunner by Maurice Bonham-Carter, private secretary and son-in-law of the Prime Minister. When Bonham-Carter's wife, Violet Asquith, heard of what had happened she exclaimed 'What! GARRISON artillery!! My dear, safe as a church!'[50], and indeed it seemed that might well be the case. Wyndham's military career began at Dover, quickly followed by promotion to bombardier and a posting as an instructor to Westham Camp, near Weymouth in Dorset. Here he was initially happy, and recorded a close escape from the police in the company of his sergeant major while frequenting the town[51], but he felt pangs of guilt at seeing the batteries he had trained heading to the front, and still intended to apply for a commission. He had his doubts when he heard of their experiences in France, and in August 1916 wrote to his mother:

> I have come to no decision about my commission. The R.G.A. is not quite so "safe as church" as Miss Asquith (or Mrs Bonham-Carter, rather) would have it, it seems. A man just back with shell-shock tells me that over a space of 6 months his battery (a "heavy") lost 5 officers killed, and the sixth wounded, arm amputated. The loss amongst officers in the Artillery seems higher than in the ranks, as in other arms. And I don't want to get killed for Mr Lloyd George, or Mr Asquith, or for any community except that elusive but excellent one to which I belong.[52]

Westham was also, increasingly, used to hold convalescing Australian soldiers injured at Gallipoli, and Wyndham's fear was increasingly not

---

48 BROOKER & THACKER, 2009, p293.
49 Open 1874-1913.
50 O'KEEFE, p177.
51 LEWIS, 1967, p30.
52 ROSE, 1963, p81.

that he should be killed, but seriously injured and thus disabled. It was while at Westham that Wyndham recorded an amusing incident in which the camp's adjutant, 'a placid little peace-time Major, with South Africa ribbons', questioned the meaning of Vorticism and its art, asking,

> They say – these newspaper-wallahs that is write – er – one has to look at these things you do as if one was inside them instead of outside them… Am I mad, Bombardier, or are these fellahs mad, that's what I want to know. It must be one or the other.[53]

Wyndham reassured the adjutant that it was them.

In July of 1916 Wyndham was posted to 183 Siege Battery, remaining in Weymouth, but in September he got his wish and was sent to No.2 Field Artillery Cadet School in Exeter, followed by No.1 RGA Officer School in Trowbridge, Wiltshire. After only four months' training, Wyndham Lewis was commissioned as a second lieutenant in the Royal Garrison Artillery on Christmas Day 1916; from this point it was quite clear that he would be heading for the Western Front. It was May 1917 before that happened, when he sailed from Southampton in the SS *Viper* with 330 Siege Battery, bound for Le Havre, then on to Rouen. When he reported to the RGA headquarters at La Clytte, south-west of Ypres, he was instead sent to 224 Siege Battery, arriving in the middle of the bombardment that preceded the Battle of Messines, and wrote to Pound that he seemed to have arrived 'in the midst of an unusually noisy battle'. It must have seemed something of a vorticist experience, with the noise of the shelling and the flash of the guns growing closer as he drew near to the batteries in the dark, until he saw them in action for the first time:

> Out of their throats had sprung a dramatic flame, they had roared, they had moved back… they hurled into the air their great projectile, and sank back as they did it.[54]

The experience of war was a jarring one, yet one that Wyndham seemed keen to play down in his letters, concentrating instead on the amount of time that he was able to spend smoking and reading Stendhal.

---

53 LEWIS, p22.
54 Ibid, p113.

On the 24th June 1917 he was removed from his battery, suffering from trench fever, and sent to the 46th Stationery Hospital at Étaples, but after convalescence at Dieppe rejoined his old battery, 330, at Dunkirk. From there they moved inland, to the Menin road, ready to support the opening of the Battle of Passchendaele, one of the costliest military engagements in history. As the battle began, Wyndham had fallen out with his commanding officer and so was sent to a forward observation point, which in the shell-shattered landscape of 1917 Flanders took two hours to reach. En-route he and his men came across a group of highlanders who had been killed shortly before, one of whom had been decapitated:

> As we approached them my party left the duckboards and passed round the flank of this almost sardonically complete tableau of violent death. Averting their heads, the men circled round. Their attitude was that of dogs when they are offered some food which they don't much like the look of.[55]

The experience of Messines and Passchendaele had changed Wyndham's attitude to war significantly; no longer did he explain the 'romance' of war in his letters, and his writing of all kinds concentrated more and more on the dismembered corpses with which he was confronted daily. It was an unnecessary slaughter, but one which he felt was fed by the clash of the national characters of the combatants:

> The appetite of the Teuton for this odd game called war—in which a dum-dum bullet is a foul, but a gas-bomb is O.K.—and British "doggedness" in the gentle art of "muddling through", when other nations misunderstand British kindliness and get tough, made a perfect combination.[56]

It was a timely illness of his mother's then that resulted in compassionate leave to England in November 1917, and it was during this trip that he had a brief interview with Sir Max Aitken[57], then in charge of Canadian war records and on the lookout for artists. Consequently both Wyndham Lewis and Augustus John were engaged for an initial three months

---

55 Ibid, p155.
56 Ibid, p151.
57 Later Lord Beaverbrook, 1879-1964.

secondment to the Canadian forces, and the permission for John to keep his beard apparently resulted in him being regularly mistaken for the King when in the trenches. Officers and men would leap to their feet as he passed; 'Augustus John—every inch a King George—would solemnly touch his hat and pass on.'[58] Wyndham's first task was to paint a twelve-foot-wide canvas, to be entitled *Canadian Gun Pit*, for a fee of £250, though the size of the painting meant that his three month attachment was extended to seven months, allowing him to also take on a smaller commission, for more money (£300), for the Ministry of Information. He very much preferred his own smaller war works, and indeed wrote in the catalogue for the first display of *Canadian Gun Pit* in an exhibition, 'It is an experiment of the painter's in a kind of painting not his own.'[59]

Wyndham Lewis was discharged from the Royal Garrison Artillery at the Officer Dispersal Unit, just off Sloane Street in London, on the 4th June 1919. He returned to painting and, though a major exhibition was held at the Leicester Galleries[60] in 1921, Vorticism as a movement was dead. From the late 1920s he began to concentrate more on his written works, though a decade later had to retract certain writings in praise of Hitler, and he again returned to painting, and the rejection of his portrait of T.S. Eliot by the Royal Academy in 1938 caused outrage on the front pages, with Augustus John resigning as a consequence. Also around this time his eyesight began to fail, as the result of a pituitary gland tumour pressing on the optic nerve, and by 1951 he was almost entirely blind. This was, of course, a great blow to an artist, but he continued to write. Eventually, in 1957 he died as a result of renal failure, caused by years of hypertension, aged 74. Wyndham Lewis had spent much of his adult life in controversy, often of his own making, and yet he had given birth to a movement, and a movement which might have grown significantly larger had its development not been strangled by war. He was probably correct, in that case, when he wrote in the catalogue for the last Vorticism exhibition before his death, at the Tate Gallery in 1956, 'Vorticism, in fact, was what I, personally, did and said at a certain period.'

---

58 LEWIS, p200.

59 O'KEEFE, p209.

60 Open 1902-77.

Lieutenant Donald Hankey (Kilbracken)

Donald William Alers Hankey was born in Brighton on the 27th October 1884, the fourth son and youngest child of William and Helen Hankey. His father had left Rugby School in 1853, and met his wife while working as a sheep farmer in South Australia, before returning to England when he had made a good deal of money. Donald entered Mr Collins's house at Rugby in 1898, a month before his fourteenth birthday and early in the headmastership of the legendary Dr Herbert James, who had already led Rossall and Cheltenham College before arriving. His three brothers, Hugh, Clement and Maurice, had all been members of the same house, and so 'Jackie' Collins had a kindly attitude to Donald. His performance in all elements of school life was successful, if not outstanding, and his letters home to his mother are largely happy; his attitude is perhaps illustrated by a letter in which he describes the unveiling of the statue of Thomas Hughes (author of *Tom Brown's Schooldays*) which still stands outside the Temple Reading Room, in June 1899:

> The Bodger (Dr James) made a very long speech during which he stammered very much; and a lot of the VI form read Latin essays and Greek poems, and got prizes from the Archbishop of Canterbury. Then a new statue of Tom Hughes was unveiled, only the effectiveness was rather spoilt by the "veil" coming off before the time. And then the Archbishop, and Mr Goschen, and Lord Somethingorother and Dr Jex Blake, and the Bishop of Hereford, and a lot of other chaps made long and tedious speeches, supposed to be about Tom Hughes but really all about Arnold: and a lot of chaps fainted from the heat and were laid out in rows like clothes hung out to dry: and then we went home and had dinner.[61]

Donald was already considering a military career, encouraged by Hugh, with whom he stayed in the officers' mess of the 2nd Battalion, The Royal Warwickshire Regiment, in Colchester, and by Maurice who had joined the Royal Marines, and so he decided to work for admission to the Army Class in the Upper School. His form master was Edward Kitchener,

---

61 DAVIES, 2016, p22.

cousin of the hero of Omdurman, and as well as encouragement towards the military, Donald was also introduced by Kitchener to another element of his life which was to become perhaps more significant than any other. That was the Rugby boys' clubs in Birmingham and London, the latter of which was such an influence on Ronnie Poulton Palmer a few short years later. This contact, first made when the London club came to give a display at the school, was the precursor of Donald's life-long concern for social justice, and was his first real contact with the inequalities of late Victorian life, and the idea that he could do something to address the concerns that he felt. It was also at this time, however, that the Hankey family suffered two tragedies. The first was that Hugh, who had become such a role model to Donald, was killed during the British victory at the Battle of Paardeberg on the 18th February 1900, having only been in South Africa for two months. Hugh's loss was a heavy blow to Donald, who was recovering from an eye infection in the school sanatorium when he received the news, but worse was to come. Their mother, Helen, became increasingly distracted, distant and forgetful, forgetting Donald's brother Robert's birthday altogether, and the children worried about their mother while she spent the summer staying with relatives in Herefordshire. When she returned home to Brighton at the end of the summer she was swiftly confined to bed, and died on the 9th September, shortly before Donald was due to return to school.

Helen's death prompted Donald's father, Robert, to be much more active in his children's lives than hitherto, and he positively encouraged Donald's military ambitions, despite Hugh's death. Donald's renewed ambition proved successful: he joined the Army Class under Mr Kitchener, and the Sixth in School House, before passing the entrance examination for the Royal Military Academy, Woolwich, at his first attempt, aged only 16. 'The Shop', as Woolwich was known, trained officers for the Royal Engineers and the Royal Horse, Field and Garrison Artilleries, so was more academically competitive than the infantry and cavalry, though it didn't require the same level of private income. Donald therefore entered the Shop in 1901, a few months before his seventeenth birthday. Such an achievement was admirable, but in later life Donald came to believe that he had been pushed into adult life too early, before he had fully taken hold of the opportunities that Rugby offered, and before he had developed emotionally to a point where he was ready for military life:

I got into the sixth my last term, but hadn't the force of
character to enjoy the prefectural powers which that fact
conferred upon me. The fact is that I left when I was 16, and
it is between 16 and 18 that the full enjoyment of school
life comes and boys reap the harvest they have sown. Had
I stayed another year I should have belonged to the leading
generation, strengthened my friendships, and developed
what was latent in my character. As it was, I left at an
unfortunate age. I was pushed into the sixth a year before
my contemporaries. My friendships were only half formed,
and I had only just begun to feel the strength of body and
mind developing in me.[62]

Donald later wrote that he was miserable for most his two years at
Woolwich, and that has come to be accepted, yet his peers remembered
only a happy and laughing young man, including his friend Ernest
Fleming[63], who had arrived with him from Rugby and so would have
been well placed to have noticed any change. It may be that he had
begun to feel the effects of the depression that was not unknown in the
men of the family, but whatever the cause, he entered Woolwich 41st out
of 71 in his entry, but passed out 73rd out of 79, having had to repeat
his last term. Another possible cause is the resurgent draw of life in the
church, and his conflicting thoughts over how to reconcile that with a
military career. In particular he recoiled from the 'blasphemy and filth'
with which he came into contact by living amongst the officer cadets of
Woolwich, and as he left the academy for the Royal Garrison Artillery
his letters to his father contained more and more of the intimation that
he felt his future lay in ordination. Robert's response was that his son's
'morbidity' made him unsuitable for the church, but that he would
withdraw his objection if Donald was to be posted to any of the more
unhealthy outposts of the empire. He was somewhat surprised, therefore,
to hear that Donald had accepted a posting to Mauritius, for which he
sailed on the 3rd November 1904.

Donald arrived in Port Louis, the capital of Mauritius, at the height of
the fever season, around Christmas, and joined 57 Company RGA, already

---

62 Ibid, p27.
63 Capt Ernest Fleming MC was killed near Ypres on the 18th July 1917.

much depleted by the malaria, dysentery and typhoid with which the town was rife, particularly since the conflict between Russia and Japan meant that the garrison were not allowed to withdraw to the hills to escape the disease, as they usually would. It wasn't long before Donald, aged only 20 and still a second lieutenant, found himself in command, but he was gradually weakened by overwork, recurring dysentery and, eventually malaria. His physical health reflected that of his faith, which was struggling because of the constant theological arguments with his only real friend on the island, Second Lieutenant Orde Browne[64], and somewhat but not entirely strengthened by his free access to the library of the Anglican bishop, Francis Gregory. What was to be the resolution of Donald's struggles of faith was not, however, to be a convincing of the strengths of one opinion or the other, but a changing of his own position. Until that moment he had been content to accept the infallibility of scripture, and fought feebly against Orde Browne's arguments through a lack of real theological education, but in a moment of revelation he was to revise his own position in a way which made the intellectual challenges that he faced infinitely more bearable. He was sitting one night in Port Louis, looking up at the starry night sky, and suddenly came to the conclusion that the emotion, consciousness and sense of purpose with which humanity is endowed made it, to his mind, exceptionally unlikely that we could be anything so unimportant as science might suggest, and that '…the difficulties of unbelief were greater even than those of belief'. Consequently:

> From that time unbelief was ruled out of court; but I began
> to try and remodel my religious ideas, seeking to find out
> what was well-founded and what ill-founded. I know longer
> defended the whole Bible, or the whole prayer book.

His revelation continued, and developed into the phrase 'If you would know the master, lo, he is working in his vineyard,' and to Donald this was a clear indication that he should work with the poor of England. This conviction was further encouraged in 1905 when he read with great relish Arthur Winnington Ingram's *Work in Great Cities* which had been published in 1896. By the time Donald came across the book Winnington Ingram was

---

64 Later Sir Granville Orde-Browne KCMG, pioneer of the improvement of conditions for native workers in British colonies in Africa.

Bishop of London, and his enthusiastic brand of honest evangelism was increasingly finding converts among the Oxford-trained ordinands of the Church of England. On the 30th September 1905 Donald, weakened by almost perpetual illness, wrote, 'I couldn't do it, I haven't got it in me, but by Jove its worth trying at all costs.' In a very similar vein he wrote to his father from the Royal Artillery Mess in Port Louis, beginning his letter,

> Do you think it is worth reconsidering the old question of Holy Orders? We are always being told that "the harvest is plenteous, but the labourers few", and I feel that a young fellow like myself who is not bound by ties of permanent importance should try and find out if he is not destined to take that most direct way of serving his Master.[65]

Before much more time had elapsed he was to have the opportunity to do so, as recurrent dysentery developed into a liver abscess, and after two operations to remove that and his appendix, Donald sailed for England, via the Cape, in November 1906. He arrived home just in time, as in December his father died, and Donald's newfound independence, both financial and moral, encouraged him to resign his commission early in the new year, before he made use of the money he had inherited by embarking on a four month tour of Italy. He then spent another four months at Rugby House, Rugby School's mission house in Notting Dale[66], where his nascent theology began to be shaped. In October 1907 he arrived at Corpus Christi College, Oxford, to read Theology.

Donald's theological studies served to retrospectively underpin the conviction he had first found on the starry hill-top in Mauritius, and in April 1908 he wrote to a friend who appears to have had similar rational problems with the claims of Christianity as he saw it:

> ...take it [Christianity], for instance, in its aspect as an explanation of things in general. It is not at all concerned with natural science. It says God is the creative and sustaining mind at the back of the universe, but it has no teaching as

---

65 MILLER E., 1920, p43.

66 Founded by Arthur Walrond in 1884, this club still exists as part of the Rugby Portobello Trust.

to the method of the creation nor of the preservation of the world. Those questions are quite apart from it. They do not really affect it at all.[67]

In building upon this acceptance of the ultimate mystery of God, Donald's faith in Jesus as God was strengthened, and that helped to construct an idea of atonement in his mind that was to fuel his social conscience for the rest of his life:

> ...for nothing could appeal more to our sense of goodness than that God should condescend to live with men, and without abating his perfect purity, to exemplify the possibilities of human good, to identify himself with man's struggle, to show him the way, to reveal to him his destiny, to give him a pledge of the victory of right over wrong.[68]

It was this realisation of the equality of mankind in the face of the atonement which reinforced Donald's frustration with the restrictions of the British class system and the way in which individuals felt bound to follow social conventions in their interactions with others when neither party benefitted from the situation. He had seen it amongst the military wives of Mauritius and now he saw it in the way that undergraduates carefully chose who to be seen with when walking through the city or attending dinners. He himself felt rather liberated from these constrictions, as the status afforded to him by virtue of his Rugby education and military career meant that he was less tied to the perpetual struggle for acceptance and advancement, but the petty privileges of class were an annoyance to him. As he wrote, 'Like the Princes of the Blood, I am above criticism in social matters, so long as I am here!'[69] To Donald the Crucifixion clearly demonstrated the illogical nature of this, as the paradigm of the perfect human submitting unhesitatingly to the will of God, even to the point of death, casting aside all worldly honours in the process. All happiness, then, was to be found in the conforming of God's will to that of God, and Donald found many examples of his acquaintance to justify that conclusion, asking,

---

67 Ibid, p96.
68 Ibid, p102.
69 Ibid, p134.

> Why is it that the people who spend their time bearing other people's burdens should be so happy – so much happier than many people who are free from care and anxiety? That is another fact which wants explaining. If the thing which the Christian calls "The peace of God, which passeth understanding" is not that, what is it?[70]

With such conviction, Donald completed his degree and was persuaded to return for a short time to Mauritius, via Kenya and Madagascar, though this time as a civilian. The visit helped to suppress the ghosts of the past, and provided for several happy reunions, allowing Donald to return to England content in his position, and certain that he had made the right decision to leave the army. His return, in January 1911, was to what he believed would be the next stage of his life, finally on the road to ordination at the Leeds Clergy School,[71] but it was not to be. Donald found the atmosphere of the school dry and uninspiring, and the nature of the teaching ultimately convinced him that ordained ministry was not the way in which he could break free of the restrictive expectations of society to truly help the poorest in society, in his own reflection of the equality of the atonement. For that, he felt, he must return to the work which had been most satisfying to him as an undergraduate, at the Oxford Mission in Bermondsey ('O.M.B.'). Here he felt that he could overcome the strictures which had driven him out of Leeds. But it wasn't the social expectations of the middle and upper classes which held him back from his work, but that of those whom he was there to help. His own class, with his private income and leisure time, was a barrier which meant that the boys of the club could never entirely accept the Oxford educated Donald. He tried living as a tramp, wearing worker's clothes and sleeping in doss-houses across Sussex and Surrey, but eventually felt that something more drastic was required, and so in August 1912 he decided to sail steerage to Australia, where the alien nature of life would mean that he could gain a genuine experience of life as an outsider, with physical labour an equalising force. By those means he would be leading by example when he wrote to his old friend Bernard Hartley, 'What is

---

70 Ibid, p139.
71 Closed in 1925.

wanted in the Christian… is not "a greater interest in social reform", but a greater humility, a greater love of human beings…'[72]

Even in the outback towns inland of Perth Donald found that his class and his past as an officer meant that often it was presumed that he wouldn't take well to manual labour, but after a year, during which he traversed the country, he had found some measure of acceptance and, more importantly, happiness in the knowledge that he had to a greater degree escaped the class system of Edwardian England. On the 1st September 1913 he sailed for England, via Sri Lanka, still considering the completion of his studies for ordination, but intending to return to Australia in a year's time. He never returned to Leeds, but after arriving at Southampton in January 1914 he spent six months at the O.M.B., writing by day and working in the club by night, and by the time the new academic year was approaching it was clear that war was on the horizon. On the day that war was declared he was staying with friends in the country north of Portsmouth, but he was determined to enlist as soon as possible, regardless of his commissioned past, and so on the 7th August he joined the Rifle Brigade at Winchester, becoming a member of the 7th Battalion when it was raised two weeks later. As much as he tried, Donald could not escape his past in the RGA; he was promoted to corporal the day after he enlisted and to sergeant a week later. In November the battalion moved to Elstead in Surrey to continue training, and Donald spent several happy months living with the elderly Mrs Coppin of Fir Tree Cottage, with whom he struck a friendship so close that his subsequent letters were addressed to 'Grandmamma'.

In May 1915 the battalion finally sailed for France, landing at Boulogne on the 19th. Before sailing Donald wrote to his sister Hilda, and his sentiment reflects his satisfaction at having devoted his time to his fellow man before facing the prospect of death:

> If I do survive the war I shall have gained immensely in every way by having been in the ranks; and if I do not, I feel that this is a good time to finish, when one is extraordinarily happy in many friendships, and when the world lies before one as an attractive place, full of promise and interest. I would not like to finish my life feeling disappointed and cynical. So either eventuality will find me philosophical.[73]

---

72 MILLER, p192.

73 Ibid, p290.

Donald's initial letters home talk of being a 'rather amateur rabbit', but the battalion had not yet faced much action. Their real induction to modern warfare was to take place on the 19th July 1915 at the Chateau of Hooge where the Menin Road crossed the front at the eastern edge of the Ypres Salient. The chateau itself had been heavily shelled by German artillery two weeks before and casualties had been mounting, but it was on the 18th and 19th that the battalion received upwards of three hundred casualties.[74] The enemy action was intense and a great shock to such a comparatively inexperienced battalion, but the struggle was not yet over. On the 30th July they took part in a counter-attack on Zouave Wood, south of Hooge, and again suffered heavy casualties. It was in this action that British troops faced flamethrowers for the first time in history; Donald received a bullet to his right thigh and lay in the open for the rest of the day, only being able to drag himself back to the British line after dark. He was returned to England to recuperate, first of all at Woolwich and then at Abbey Wood in north Kent, and it was at the end of August that he heard that he was to be commissioned again in the RGA. Though Donald did not want this, he spent his convalescence revising much of the gunnery that he had forgotten in the intervening years since he left Mauritius. It was then that he wrote to 'Grandmamma', Mrs Coppin, to explain a series of essays that he was writing for *The Spectator* in which he was able to use Lord Kitchener's New Army as an example of a 'union of the classes', in which circumstances had forced the abandonment of traditional class roles to the greater success of the whole endeavour. The five planned essays laid this idea out in five separate steps:

I. 'All classes were as one', in which he highlighted the way in which men of all classes had joined the ranks together in the first flush of national fervour after the declaration of war.

II. 'The Equality of the Classes' explained how those men had served together with success, and that those of character had come to the fore, regardless of their class.

III. 'The Super Class' was perhaps the most contentious, in which Donald examined the traditional officer class and how such standard roles had not always succeeded in the new force.

---

74 WO95/1896/1.

IV. 'Men Wanted' describes how the actions of those men of great character, both officers and NCOs, led others to see them as God does, by the greatness of their hearts, 'quite irrespective of their accents and manners'.

V. 'What of the Future?' asked whether society could, or should, fall back into its old ways once the conflict had ended, and highlighted the role that women must play in the subsequent reconstruction of society.[75]

It was partially through his sense of guilt at having left his fellow riflemen in the trenches of Flanders, and partially his lack of recent experience with artillery that Donald applied to transfer from the RGA to the Royal Warwickshire Regiment and, after a delay of some two months, this request was granted. In was when he had joined his new battalion, the 3rd, in barracks on the Isle of Wight that he heard that the *Spectator* had decided to publish his essays anonymously under the title *A Student in Arms*, a title which pleased him very much. In May 1916 Donald returned to France, a year after his original departure with the Rifle Brigade, but this time as a platoon commander, and joined the 1st Battalion at Gapennes, north-east of Abbeville, on the 22nd. A month later the battalion had just returned from the trenches at Auchonvillers and were preparing for the most famous day of the war – the 1st of July 1916. The battalion, serving with the 4th Division west of Beaumont Hamel, were in reserve during the initial attack, but halted at 9.15am and reformed in Tenderloin Trench; apart from a later patrol which was pinned down by enemy fire at 2pm, the battalion took no further part in the action, but stayed in the trenches until the 7th as the line was consolidated.[76]

On the 9th October the battalion again moved into the line, this time near the village of Les Boeufs on the main Bapaume to Peronne road, and several days of artillery bombardment from both sides began. It was in this action that Donald was killed, in a short-notice battalion attack on German lines east of the village. He was 31 years old. One of his fellow officers wrote to his sister Hilda:

---

75 MILLER, p310.
76 ASHBY, 2000, p140.

On the afternoon of the 12th this Regiment, among others, made an advance in four lines. Your brother was with the third, and I was just behind him with the fourth. By the time all our men were clear of our front line trenches the enemy's rifle and machine-gun fire had become serious, and the men wavered; and the last time I saw Lieutenant Hankey he was rallying the waverers and taking them on with him. Afterwards, when the advance had finally stopped, we found him where he had been killed by a machine-gun, along with his Platoon Sergeant and a few of his men, close to the trench the winning of which had cost him his life.

A second series of his essays was published, under the same title, after his death. Donald Hankey was a distinctly enigmatic character, partially because he was never entirely sure what his path in life should be. He was quite certain that the will of God was fundamentally inscrutable, and yet was always seeking a more explicit sign of his own vocation. What was clear was his indubitable love for all of those with whom he lived and served, at Rugby, in Bermondsey, Oxford, Australia and in the trenches, a love which crossed all contemporary conventions of class propriety and which was borne out of his ultimate conviction that the principal message of the Crucifixion was one of the equality of humanity in the face of God. His consequent submission to the will of God as he saw it is summed up by his last words to his platoon before his final attack began:

If wounded, Blighty; if killed, the Resurrection.

THE MILITARY

Major General Sir Ernest Swinton (Kilbracken)

Ernest Swinton had something of a nomadic childhood. He was born in Bangalore on the 21st October 1868, where his father, Robert Blair Swinton, was serving in the Madras civil service. Robert spent a good deal of time as a judge in Cuddalore, on the coast of Tamil Nadu, and consequently Ernest's early childhood was an extremely happy one, playing in the ruins of Fort St David and on the beach, but avoiding the surf that he and his brothers were told was filled with sharks. Their house, tied to his father's employment, was a large two-storied building with a colonnaded verandah all round, and as a young boy Ernest was fond of their Indian servants, particularly the boys' 'bearer' Brumyah. His first brush with death was one which stuck in his memory for many years: when the local butcher's dog killed his mother's Pekingese, the man slit his own dog's throat, and hung it by the head from a rope to make amends for what it had done. The gory sight, with blood running down the animal's body and dripping onto the floor, made a terrible impression on the young Swinton children.[77] Summers were spent in the hill stations of Nilgiri, escaping the heat in the very paradigm of a happy colonial childhood, but upon Robert's retirement the family returned to England, and the 5-year-old Ernest's last memory of his earliest home was of Brumyah, with tears in his eyes, bowing in farewell as the family's train pulled slowly out of Arkonum Junction railway station[78]. It was August 1874 and the Swintons made their way by train to Bombay, where they sailed for Southampton in the venerable three-masted steamer *Australia*, though the voyage was marred by the death of Ernest's infant brother Hugh shortly before they disembarked. Adjusting to a British summer, the family settled in Randolph Crescent, Maida Vale, and Ernest learned that English governesses were very different to Indian ones, and not in a positive way.

Ernest's education began at University College School, then still occupying a wing of the university in Gower Street. Each morning at 9am several satchel-laden boys poured out of Gower Street station and into school, including Ernest Swinton and one of his earliest school

---

77 SWINTON, 1951, p17.
78 Ibid, p13.

friends, Rufus Isaacs[79], but after only a year Ernest was sent to a dame school, run by two elderly spinster sisters near Portman Square specifically to prepare boys for entry to the major public schools. This was always intended to be a temporary stop on Ernest's educational journey, and in September 1881 he arrived at Mr Elsee's House (now Kilbracken) in Rugby a few weeks before his thirteenth birthday. Elsee was a mild and benevolent clergyman, though in the 1880s boys saw little of their housemasters except at lunch, where they presided with their Sixth from the high table at the head of the room. The Head Master, Thomas Jex-Blake, was an even more distant figure:

> His influence was not noticeable, at all events on the small
> boys of other houses, and we knew him only by sight. He had
> a large family, and was reputed to have lost the sight in one
> eye, put out by a falling rocket-stick. As the school doggerel
> ran: One eye, one lung, ten daughters and one son.[80]

Ernest's experience of Rugby life was typical of its time; in his first year he was fag to George Forestier-Walker, later Major General Sir George Forestier-Walker KCB[81], cleaning his boots and making his toast, though Ernest was 'duly and rightly castigated' when George found him using his rifle corps bayonet as a toasting fork.[82] Almost all of his memories of Rugby were happy ones, even those that were less than peaceful. At that time the school had a peculiar form of fighting not dissimilar to the Cotswold tradition of shin-kicking, with the combatants holding each other by the shoulders and kicking as hard as they could. Ernest fought a boy in this way for calling him by his nickname, which was only to be used in one's own house and, drawing blood first, was declared to be the winner.[83] He was certainly happy at Rugby, though he later believed that if he had stayed there he may well not have joined the army. The school

---

79 Rufus Daniel Isaacs, First Marquess of Reading GCB GCSI GCIE GCVO PC KC, Lord Chief Justice of England 1913-21, Viceroy of India 1921-26, Foreign Secretary Aug-Nov 1931.
80 SWINTON, p24.
81 Commander of the 27th Division 1916-19.
82 SWINTON, p24.
83 Ibid, p27.

had yet to begin its 'Army Class', particularly preparing boys for such a career, and with his elder brother already serving Ernest's family did not expect him to follow the same course. After a year in Mr Elsee's house he was very settled, and entirely used to the routines of the school, which was his third but his first at which he was a boarder. It was a great disappointment, therefore, when his father told him a year later that he must move again, as the Rugby fees were proving too much of a stretch for a retired colonial judge with a large family. Leaving was a sad task, but not one that could be avoided; he was to return as a day boy to University College School:

> And so, after a comparatively spacious and privileged life at Rugby, with its Close and immemorial Elms... the cawing of rooks and click of bat and ball, I again found myself every morning in a third class compartment of the murky Metropolitan en route for Gower Street.[84]

Further change was to follow, this time to Cheltenham College, which was cheaper than Rugby. Throughout the subsequent years of his education Ernest missed his little study at Rugby, even describing the school at the end his life as his 'first love'[85].

After such a changeable education the prospect of a career was principally one of stability, and Ernest's father was keen that he should follow him into the Indian civil service, but two cousins recently commissioned into the Royal Engineers persuaded him otherwise. He was aware of his academic weaknesses, but determined to follow his cousins, and so two crammers followed, after which he was admitted to the Royal Military Academy, Woolwich. Out of an entry of sixty, only fifteen commissions were to be offered by the Royal Engineers, in order of merit, so Ernest was delighted when he finished a truncated course of three terms in fourth place and was duly commissioned as a second lieutenant on the 17th February 1888, with orders to report to one of the historic homes of the corps, Brompton Barracks in Chatham. The country of his birth was a great draw, and Ernest applied for a posting to India, the 'shiny east', as he called it, so it was an excited young officer

---

84 Ibid, p26.
85 Ibid.

who boarded the troopship HMS *Euphrates*, crammed four to a cabin below the waterline for the long and hot voyage to Bombay via Valetta, Port Said and Aden. After a two-day train journey he was soon ensconced with two other subalterns in a thatched billet which they named 'the Pig and Whistle' in Lucknow. Life in Lucknow was one of some work, with a lot of polo and tennis, occasionally interrupted by snakes and scorpions, and Ernest easily settled back into the colonial life he had known as a young boy twenty years earlier. In September 1890 however, he suffered a great blow when his eldest brother was killed in action at Shillong, in Assam, serving with the 44th Gurkha Light Infantry.

Ernest spent five happy years in India, returning to Chatham in 1895, and he was serving as an assistant instructor there when the war began in South African four years later. Keen to serve, he found himself on a train from Waterloo, bound for the Union Castle steamer *Scot*, sailing for Capetown. In South Africa some elements of colonial life reminded him of India, but there was plenty more work to be done, bridging the Orange River all day and night, in eight hour shifts, to keep men and supplies moving forwards. Here the by-now Captain Swinton was promoted to temporary major, received the DSO in November 1900, and gained much experience of both military action and the engineering challenges of modern warfare.

A variety of operational and staff appointments followed, and by the outbreak of war in 1914 Ernest Swinton was a highly experienced major, and in the same month that war was declared he was personally chosen by Lord Kitchener to be a principal correspondent for the newly established War Office Press Bureau, under F. E. Smith[86]. Such work was novel, not least because he was given only twenty-four hours' notice of his tasking, and he was required to visit many different areas of conflict, sending in reports to be censored by Kitchener himself before they were released to the press. It was this experience in France as a war correspondent, with the nom de plume 'Eyewitness', which was to give him the idea for which he has become best known to history. In July 1914 he had received a letter from a friend telling him about a new caterpillar-tracked tractor, built by the Holt Manufacturing Company in California. It was petrol-driven and had a maximum speed of fifteen miles an hour. Could it, his correspondent wondered, be useful to military transport? Ernest

---

86 1872-1930. Lord Chancellor 1919-22, Secretary of State for India 1924-8.

considered it, and indeed similar vehicles were tested at Aldershot, but up to that moment they had only been considered suitable for towing heavy artillery. With Captain Lord Percy[87] of the Grenadier Guards as his assistant, he struggled across the Aisne, increasingly fearful of accidentally giving information to the enemy in his articles. On the morning of the 19th October 1914 he was driving from GHQ in St Omer to Calais, considering what to write in his next report. His mind was very much occupied with the effects of machine guns and barbed wire on infantry that he had witnessed in the preceding days. Again and again the British advance had been held up by these simple methods, and his thoughts returned to the importance of machine gun tactics that he had championed ever since he was in South Africa. As the light of the Calais lighthouse flashed across the car's windscreen he remembered the caterpillar tractors in California, and a sudden solution appeared:

> …within the last two weeks my vague idea of an armoured vehicle had definitely crystalised in the form of a power-driven, bullet-proof, armed engine, capable of destroying machine guns, of crossing country and trenches, of breaking through entanglements and of climbing earthworks.[88]

Boarding a ship for Folkestone, he felt instinctively that he had an idea of great national importance to propose. The only question was, to whom?

Upon his arrival in London Ernest's first intention was to take his idea straight to Kitchener himself, as the man who had personally chosen him for his present duties, but the Secretary of State for War's workload was such that impromptu meetings were out of the question. Instead, Ernest took his idea to fellow Old Rugbeian Maurice Hankey[89], Secretary to the War Council in Whitehall, and a man with regular access to the most senior figures of the allied hierarchy. Hankey was sympathetic to Ernest's idea of acquiring and modifying Holt tractors for immediate service in France, based on his experiences in the Aisne, and encouraged him to make his proposal to Kitchener, if he saw him, but certainly to Sir John

---

87 Duke of Northumberland 1918-30.
88 SWINTON, 1933, p57.
89 1877-1963, 1st Baron Hankey GCB GCMG GCVO PC FRS, Cabinet Secretary 1916-38.

French when he returned to GHQ in St Omer. It seemed, perhaps, that the idea might gain official support very quickly indeed. An extraordinary opportunity presented itself to him the next day, the 21st October 1914, when the Prime Minister asked to see him at Downing Street, but in the end Ernest faced an agonising half-hour private meeting in the Cabinet Room in which he felt he couldn't raise the issue until he had taken it to Kitchener. He returned to France, awash with excitement at the prospect of gaining Sir John French's support. If anyone should take to the idea then surely it would be the Commander in Chief who was losing so many men to the machine guns and wire that Ernest himself had seen? Upon his arrival at GHQ he reported to the Engineer in Chief, who reluctantly agreed to write to the War Office about it, and for a time nothing more was said. The months came and went, and at the turn of the New Year Ernest went home for a few days' leave. The first person he spoke to was Hankey, keen to hear what Kitchener had thought of his idea for 'machine-gun destroyers'. It was not good news. Under the increasing pressure of an ever-expanding theatre of war, the Secretary of State had briefly considered and then dismissed the idea, and Kitchener was not a man to submit to repeated requests of a similar nature. It seemed that the idea was dead, but Hankey was not to be deterred, and found a new avenue of approach.

As Secretary of the War Council it was Hankey's duty to report to the Prime Minister any issues which he considered to be of sufficient importance, and that he duly did at Christmas 1914, after Kitchener's rebuff. Hankey suggested to the Prime Minister that there was a serious risk of deadlock on the western front, and that innovation was required to prevent such a state of affairs from developing. As such, taking Ernest's idea almost verbatim, and neglecting to mention that it had already been rejected by Kitchener, he proposed,

> Numbers of large heavy rollers, themselves bullet-proof, propelled from behind by motor-engines, geared very low, the driving wheels fitted to 'caterpillar' driving gear to grip the ground, the driver's seat armoured, and with a Maxim gun fitted. The object of this device would be to roll down barbed wire by sheer weight, to give some cover to men creeping up behind, and to support the advance with machine-gun fire.[90]

---

90 SWINTON, 1933, p76.

Ernest returned to St Omer on the 9th January 1915 full of hope, but he had no idea of the direction from which help would come. In fact, when Hankey had made his proposal to the War Council the Prime Minister had little interest, and the Director of Fortifications and Works reminded Ernest that it was for GHQ to suggest ideas for development to the War Office, not the other way round, and though he had come from the front, he was not GHQ. Another member of the War Council had sat in silence however, listening intently to every element of Hankey's paper and eager to develop the concept further. That individual was the First Lord of the Admiralty, Winston Churchill; one section of his responsibility was the Royal Naval Air Service, which had recently begun to operate squadrons of armoured cars to protect their airfields in Belgium, and so Ernest's idea was a logical next step, regardless of whether it would be used by the RNAS or the army. This was particularly pertinent since the German army had begun to cut holes in roads specifically to limit the operation of wheeled armoured cars, and by November 1914 Churchill had already ordered the construction of experimental vehicles designed to assist heavy guns across trenches in open ground.[91] Suddenly the idea had momentum, and on the 5th January, the very same day that Ernest had unsuccessfully appealed to the Director of Fortifications and Works, Churchill wrote to the Prime Minister in a characteristically bullish tone:

> It is extraordinary that the Army in the Field and the War Office should have allowed nearly three months of trench warfare to progress without addressing their mind to its special problem... An obvious measure of prudence would have been to have started something like this two months ago. It should certainly be done now.[92]

Even with such support there was no movement after a further six months, nor did a chance meeting on Pall Mall with Admiral Ottley, a director of Armstrong-Whitworth, come to any fruition. On the 9th May however, Ernest's determination was redoubled, after he and Lord Percy watched for three hours from the church tower of Beuvry as British troops tried again and again to attack through wire that had not been

---

91 Ibid, p80.
92 Ibid, p81.

cut by an inadequate artillery bombardment. That inadequacy, and the enemy's greater number of machine-guns, meant that however great the weight of men thrown towards the German defences, it would simply result in more casualties rather than any convincing resolution. He could wait no longer, and on the 1st June 1915, coincidentally the day he was to discover that he was no longer to write the 'Eyewitness' despatches, Ernest handed a formal proposal to the office of the Commander in Chief, entitled 'The Necessity of Machine Gun Destroyers'[93], laying out clearly and succinctly the dreadful circumstances in which the infantry found itself and a brief outline of the specifications and employment of his proposed machines. Suddenly there was movement; on the very next day Ernest came across a convoy of Holt Tractors pulling howitzers to the front – finally he had seen the machines about which he had been dreaming for months. The next day after that there was news to confirm a reassuring rumour: Churchill had established a technical committee to examine the possibility of 'landships' to replace the increasingly obsolete armoured cars of the RNAS. Ernest was delighted, though baffled, by Churchill's involvement.

Meanwhile, the newly-appointed 'Inventions Committee' at GHQ had finally come to a similar conclusion as the Admiralty, and on the 22nd June Sir John French submitted further details of Ernest's idea to the War Office, asking whether such machines were available or could be constructed. Enquiries were made, but within a fortnight Ernest, now a lieutenant colonel, had been recalled to London and appointed as Secretary to the Cabinet Committee investigating the Dardanelles. Such an appointment was ideal, and allowed him to closely monitor and to encourage the development of his idea at every opportunity. Consequently he was introduced to Lieutenant Albert Stern of the RNAS, an enthusiastic young man brimming over with ideas. Finally a joint committee was established, combining the expertise of the Admiralty with that of the War Office and the Ministry of Munitions, and on the 28th August 1915 the members sat down as equals rather than rivals for the first time. In brief, it was agreed that the Admiralty should continue its experiments, before handing over to the Ministry of Munitions when a viable project had been identified.[94] It didn't take long, and on the

---

93 Ibid, p106.
94 Ibid, p145.

19th September Ernest drove to Lincoln to see the testing of a new machine, nicknamed Little Willie. While the machine was entertaining, Ernest was disappointed that it didn't fulfil the requirements he had laid out in his proposal to the commander in chief. But he was about to see a machine which was to become an iconic symbol of the Great War for the very first time:

> I was then conducted with some solemnity to a building nearby. Here, behind tightly-closed doors I saw a nearly complete, full size 'mock-up' or model of a very much larger track machine expressly designed to meet these conditions... Its most striking features were its curious rhomboidal, or lozenge, shape, its upturned nose, and the fact that its caterpillar tracks were led right round the hull instead of being entirely below it.[95]

The project gathered speed, and as Christmas 1915 approached Ernest proposed that a new force of 75 officers and 750 other ranks would be needed when the machines were ready. On Christmas Eve the next great step was taken; it was considered that the titles 'machine-gun destroyer' and 'land cruiser' were too cumbersome, as well as likely to give away their purpose before their introduction. It was Ernest Swinton who therefore, on that very evening, proposed the word 'tank', as a suitably vague name, while also being easy to remember and reminiscent of the prototype's box-like appearance.[96] This prototype, *Centipede*[97], moved under its own power for the first time on the 13th January 1916, and was soon delivered to Hatfield Park where it was to be tested on a variety of simulated battlefield obstructions. After a successful trial in the presence of Kitchener (who remained sceptical), the Prime Minister, the Home Secretary and others, the King indicated that he wished to comment on the new machine, so Ernest drove him from Buckingham Palace to see it for himself. Movement was swift, and Ernest was offered the appointment of raising and training the new 'Tank Detachment', which would then be commanded by more experienced combat officers at

---

95 Ibid, p147.
96 Ibid, p161.
97 Also known as 'Mother', and later as the Mark 1 Tank.

the front. It was a great honour, and an open acknowledgement of his pivotal role in the conception and development of the machines. Here, therefore, was the foundation of all tank warfare worldwide, at Siberia Camp, Bisley, and with a hand-picked core of officers the new unit had six months to master an entirely new form of combat, with an initial production of 100 machines.

From this point the history of the tanks is well documented, and they saw action for the first time, still under the title of 'Heavy Section, Machine Gun Corps' at 0620 on the 15th September 1916 when thirty-two tanks of C and D Companies rumbled into action and into history: tank warfare was born. Ernest continued to be involved with the development and training of what, in 1917, was renamed the 'Tank Corps', before retiring with the rank of major general in 1919. One of the final but most surprising honours of Ernest's life, at least to him, was his election as Chichele Professor of the History of War, at All Souls College, Oxford, in 1934. He was astonished to find himself, the career soldier who had never been to university, in such surroundings, but eventually settled very much into college life and remained at All Souls until his death on the 15th January 1951, aged 82. The Great War is, of course, well-known for its advancement of technology and the terrible consequences of the mechanisation of human conflict, but it may be argued that no single individual had a greater influence on the technology of war then and since than Ernest Swinton.

Lieutenant Colonel Jasper Richardson
(School Field)

Jasper Myers Richardson has a particular, if unfortunate, distinction in the history of the war, that of being the oldest British casualty of the conflict, killed a few days before his 69th birthday. He was born in 1849 in Newcastle to Jasper and Caroline Richardson, and entered Mr Arnold's house at Rugby in 1864[98] at the age of 15. After leaving Rugby he matriculated at Trinity Hall, Cambridge, where he read Law, graduating in 1871 and being called to the Bar at Inner Temple in 1874. He subsequently practiced law on the north-eastern Circuit, which also allowed him to receive a reserve commission with the Northumberland Militia Artillery, whose headquarters were in Berwick-upon-Tweed, and he served with the regiment for five years before returning to London having recently married Anne Longstreth, an American from Philadelphia, though they had no children. Jasper then pursued a successful career in law for a further thirty-four years, residing at 49 Campden Hill Square in London, but at the outbreak of war in 1914 he felt instinctively that he must do his duty by returning to the military service of his youth. Consequently he served as Assistant Deputy Censor in London for several months and on the 1st March 1915 was gazetted as a major (honorary lieutenant colonel) in the Royal Garrison Artillery at the extraordinarily unusual age of 65. At such an age he could not normally have expected to receive a commission, and certainly not to be engaged in foreign service, but in September 1916 he was appointed to the 38th (Welsh) Heavy Battery RGA. His knowledge of artillery was not quite up to date, however, and his talents lay elsewhere, and he became Agricultural Officer to V Corps, by then part of the Third Army.

The role of Agricultural Officer was an unusual but vital appointment, ensuring that farming equipment was gathered from areas of conflict and that any suitable land behind the lines was suitably utilised to produce food for the British Army. He was based in the V Corps headquarters at Villers au Flos, nineteen miles south of Arras, but in March 1918 that was directly in the path of the intended German Spring Offensive, which began on the 21st. The shelling on that day

---

98 Memorials of Rugbeians who Fell in the Great War.

began at 5am, and had continued for five hours when Jasper returned to HQ with one of his men. At just the moment that they arrived an enemy shell struck their location, killing the soldier outright and seriously injuring Jasper, who was taken to the nearby field ambulance. It was quickly ascertained that he had sustained a large number of shrapnel wounds, and one fragment was embedded deep in his chest close to his heart and no treatment was possible. Even so, with the German advance beginning, he was quickly evacuated to the Duchess of Westminster's (No. 1 British Red Cross) Hospital operating in the casino at Le Touquet, where he died on the 30th March 1918. Jasper was buried in Étaples Military Cemetery, across the Canche River from where he died.

For almost a century it was not known that Jasper was the oldest British casualty of conflict in the Great War. The Commonwealth War Graves Commission had accorded that title to Henry Webber[99], an old boy of Tonbridge School killed at Mametz Wood on the 21st July 1916, but when the *Daily Telegraph* featured an article about him in 2014[100] it was noticed by Rugby School, who notified the newspaper that Jasper was a year older when he died in 1918. It is certainly not a title to covet, but it is a great testament to Jasper's sense of duty and selflessness that, by whatever means, he managed to gain a commission to serve his country in the war in which he lost his life when he was already twenty-four years above the maximum age for conscription.

---

99 Lt Henry Webber, 7th Battalion South Lancashire Regiment.
100 *Daily Telegraph*, 26th January 2014.

Captain Frederick C. Selous DSO (Cotton) and Captain Frederick H.B. Selous MC (School House)

It is perhaps to be expected that Freddie Selous would never live a mundane life, considering his family background, but he can never have expected that it was to have been so short.

Frederick Hatherley Bruce Selous was born in his grandmother's house on the banks of the Thames in Wargrave, Berkshire, on the 21st April 1898. His father had hardly been in the UK at all for the preceding twenty years; Frederick Courtney Selous (OR 1868), friend of Theodore Roosevelt and Cecil Rhodes, had built a great reputation as an explorer and big game hunter. His own father had been chairman of the London Stock Exchange, but from a young age Selous had harboured a desire to explore Africa, and since 1871 had been living in the bush between South Africa and the Congo, so it's hardly a surprise that his son was born in his grandmother's house.

At the age of 8 Freddie was sent away to prep school, to Bilton Grange just outside Rugby, and in January 1912 he arrived in School House under the guidance of Head Master Dr Albert David. Freddie quickly made friends with another new boy, Louis Stokes, whose letters are preserved (and who died serving with the Royal Marine Light Infantry at Beaumont Hamel in November 1916), and so we have many records of their joint escapades, continually taunting the members of the Sixth, and decorating their shared study with hunting prints and a portrait of Napoleon. In another, rather poignant, letter Louis describes a wonderful lunch party held by a young master, Mr John Bruce Lockhart, for three of his tutees from School House: Stokes, Selous, and Ronald Glover. All three boys were killed in the war, whereas Lockhart survived and went on to become headmaster of Sedbergh School.

Freddie soon proved to be an able athlete across the board. He successfully represented School House in the 'Cock House' competitions for both Rugby Football and cricket, and so it's no surprise that in 1915 he captained the XV, the team which wear the white shirts that inspired the colours of the England Rugby team, having already been playing for them for two years. He also ran for the school VIII, and so was well-suited to the military career which, perhaps inevitably, awaited him. Freddie duly arrived at the

Royal Military Academy, Sandhurst, in September 1915, and was an immediate success, winning the seven mile steeplechase and being appointed under-officer of his company. He had quite a reputation to live up to, but had very much begun to do so, impressing the academy staff across the board.

His father had no intention of being left behind. In November 1914, with the prospect of his son's military service looming, he attempted to persuade the War Office to waive their usual upper age limit, but received a reply from H.P. Tennant MP informing him, 'I spoke to Lord Kitchener to-day about you and he thought that your age was prohibitive against your employment here or at the seat of war in Europe.' Eventually his persistence paid off and he was commissioned as a second lieutenant in the 25th (Frontiersmen) Battalion of the Royal Fusiliers. He travelled with his new unit by train from Waterloo, sailing for Mombasa from Southampton on the SS *Neuralia* and landing with them on the 4th May 1915. This rather extraordinary unit was specifically intended for service in East Africa and contained an unusual assortment of 'men from the French Foreign Legion, ex-Metropolitan Policemen, a General of the Honduras Army, lighthouse keepers, keepers from the zoo, Park Lane plutocrats, music hall acrobats, but none the less excellent stuff and devoted to their officers'. Selous fitted well into such an eclectic group and, with his unparalleled knowledge of southern Africa and of stalking and tracking, he became an important member of the battalion.

After a promotion to captain, F.C. Selous was awarded the DSO on the 26th of September 1916, the citation reading,

> For conspicuous gallantry, resource and endurance. He has set a magnificent example to all ranks, and the value of his services with his battalion cannot be over-estimated.[101]

It was on the 4th January 1917 that F.C. Selous, the hero of the 25th Royal Fusiliers, met his death after thirty-six years in Africa. The battalion marched from the Tchogowali River at 0530 under their commanding officer and founder, Lieutenant Colonel Daniel Driscoll[102], and engaged

---

101 *No. 29765. The London Gazette (Supplement).* 26th September 1916.
102 WO 95/5332/15.

the enemy at 1030. The action of that morning was described by General Smuts, commanding British forces in German East Africa:

> Our force moved out from Kissaki early on the morning of January 4th, 1917, with the object of attacking and surrounding a considerable number of German troops which was encamped along the low hills east of Beho-Beho (Sugar Mountain) N.E. of the road that led from Kissaki S.E. to the Rufigi river, distant some 13 miles from the enemy's position. The low hills occupied by the Germans were densely covered with thorn-bush and the visibility to the west was not good. Nevertheless, they soon realized the danger of their position when they detected a circling movement on the part of the 25th Royal Fusiliers, which had been detailed to stop them on the road leading S.E., the only road, in fact, by which they could retreat. They must have retired early, for their forces came to this point at the exact moment when the leading company of Fusiliers, under Captain Selous, reached the same point. Heavy firing on both sides then commenced, and Selous at once deployed his company, attacked the Germans, which greatly outnumbered him, and drove them back into the bush. It was at this moment that Selous was struck dead by a shot in the head. The Germans retreated in the dense bush again, and the Fusiliers failed to come to close quarters, for the enemy then made a circuit through the bush and reached the road lower down, eventually crossing the Rufigi.

The action that day was ultimately successful, and F.C. Selous was buried under a tamarind tree close to where he died, in what is now the Selous Game Reserve, Tanzania. His death was a great blow, understandably, to his many friends across the world, and President Theodore Roosevelt wrote,

> There was never a more welcome guest at the White House than Selous. He spent several days there. One afternoon we went walking and rock climbing alongside the Potomac; I think we swam the Potomac, but I am not sure....

Later I spent a night with him at his house in Surrey, going through his museum of hunting-trophies. What interested me almost as much was being shown the various birds' nests in his garden. He also went to the British Museum with me to look into various matters, including the question of protective coloration. I greatly valued his friendship; I mourn his loss; and yet I feel that in death as in life he was to be envied.

It is well for any country to produce men of such a type; and if there are enough of them the nation need fear no decadence. He led a singularly adventurous and fascinating life, with just the right alternations between the wilderness and civilization. He helped spread the borders of his people's land. He added much to the sum of human knowledge and interest. He closed his life exactly as such a life ought to be closed, by dying in battle for his country while rendering her valiant and effective service. Who could wish a better life or a better death, or desire to leave a more honourable heritage to his family and his nation?

In April 1916, while his father fought in German East Africa, F.H.B. Selous had passed out of Sandhurst and been commissioned into the Queen's (Royal West Surrey) Regiment, being almost immediately attached to the Royal Flying Corps. The excited young second lieutenant found himself learning to fly at Catterick, four months after fellow Rugbeian Arthur Keen had attended the same training course, and on the 3rd May he received his Royal Aero Club Aviator's certificate, proving to be an exceptionally able pilot. Unlike Arthur, Freddie was to have no advanced training, and by July he found himself in France, on active service with the Royal Flying Corps. He was quickly awarded both the Military Cross and the Italian Silver Medal for Military Valour, clearly demonstrating his outstanding ability as a military aviator. As such, it is no surprise that ten months later, in April 1917, he was recalled to serve as an instructor at the Central Flying School at Upavon in Wiltshire. Another move, and promotion to captain, followed five months later as Freddie returned to the front as a flight commander in 60 Squadron, flying the formidable new fighter aircraft the SE5a, and by the end of the year he had destroyed two Rumpler C Type reconnaissance aircraft, at Klein-Zillebecke on the 8th November and Roulers on the 28th December.

Over the new year the squadron moved again, this time back to Ste-Marie-Cappel, where they had been filmed in August 1917[103], and on the morning of the 4th January Freddie's mind must very much have been on the death of his father exactly one year before, but he could hardly have known of the further tragedy that was to occur on that day. Flying SE5a No. 5334 Freddie led his flight on patrol along the Menin Road, again near Roulers, and soon encountered enemy aircraft. It's not entirely clear what happened – either a structural failure or a mid-air collision, but the effect was that the wings of Freddie's aircraft collapsed in a steep dive and the SE5a plummeted to the ground. His body was never recovered, and still lies somewhere in the mud of western Belgium; his name appears on the Flying Services Memorial at Arras.

The effect on 60 Squadron was one of profound grief. Freddie's commanding officer wrote to his mother:

> It is a severe blow to the squadron to lose him, for he was beloved by officers and men alike. In fact, his popularity extended to a much greater area than his own aerodrome. In the short time that I have known him I have been struck with the courage and keenness of your son—always ready for his jobs, and always going about his work with the cheeriest and happiest of smiles. He was the life and soul of the mess.[104]

Group Captain Alan Scott, in his book *Sixty Squadron RAF 1916-1919* wrote of Freddie Selous:

> As good a flight commander as we ever had, he was a great loss to the squadron. Without, perhaps, the brilliance of Ball or Bishop he like Caldwell, Summers, Armstrong, Hammersley, Chidlaw-Roberts, Belgrave and Scholte, to name a few only of the best, played always for the squadron, and not for his own hand. He took endless pains to enter young pilots to the game, watching them on their first patrols as a good and patient huntsman watches his young hounds... The character of Selous, like those whom

---

103 IWM Film 141.
104 Memorials of Rugbeians who fell in the Great War.

I have mentioned, not to speak of many others whom their comrades will remember, attained very nearly to the ideal of a gentleman's character as described by Burke, Newman and Cavendish.[105]

F.C. and F.H.B. Selous, father and son, both lived quite undeniably exhilarating lives, which both ended violently as a result of the war, exactly one year apart. Their lives and, indeed, their deaths illustrate yet further the extraordinary devotion to duty exhibited by Rugbeians throughout the war.

---

105 SCOTT, 1990, p73.

Brigadier General Sir Percy Sykes (School Field)

Percy Sykes was one of the last Victorian gentleman adventurers, whose military career served in part to accommodate his wide-ranging interests, as well as to further the interests of empire. He was born on the 28th February 1867, the only son of the Reverend and Mrs William Sykes, in Brompton, Chatham, where his father was serving as a military chaplain. His uncle was the well-known Richard Sykes, Captain of Football at Rugby School in 1857, who arranged the famous 'Rugby vs The World' match which resulted in the foundation of Liverpool Rugby Club in the same year. In January 1882 the 14-year-old Percy arrived at Rugby, joining Mr Scott's house under the benevolent but energetic headmastership of Thomas Jex-Blake[106]. His name remains inscribed upon the walls of the racquets courts, as he represented the school in the Public Schools Championships of 1885 and 1886, before passing on to the Royal Military Academy, Sandhurst, the following year and commissioning into the 16th Lancers in 1888. His first choice of regiment didn't last however, and in the same year he transferred to the 2nd Dragoon Guards (Queen's Bays) in Rawalpindi. The adventurous Percy was soon to travel, and made several expeditions through Persia and Baluchistan, but it was in November 1892 that his tenacity and ingenuity were put to use, as he was sent to Samarkand (in modern day Uzbekistan) to secretly survey the Trans-Caspian Railway recently completed by Russia. The success of this trip effectively put an end to his active military career for several years, as his diplomatic skills proved a greater claim on his time. In 1893 and 1894 he travelled widely in northern Persia, cultivating relationships with local tribal leaders in order to guard against Russian expansion from the Caucasus towards India. In 1894 he was appointed as the first British Consul to Baluchistan, a post which he held for nearly ten years, and during this period he was promoted to lieutenant in 1895 and captain in 1897.

In 1899 the 32-year-old Captain Sykes was appointed second in command of the Montgomeryshire Imperial Yeomanry in the Second Boer War, but his diplomatic strengths meant that in September 1901 he was transferred to intelligence duties, during which he was wounded in the leg.[107] As the war drew to an end Percy's reputation had grown

---

106 Dean of Wells 1891-1915.
107 LEACH & FARRINGTON, 2003, p185.

further and he was appointed a Companion of the Order of St Michael and St George in the Coronation Honours List of 1902, before transferring to the Indian Army at the end of that year to take up an appointment as Consul in Kerman, in Persia. In 1905 he moved again, to be Consul-General for Khorasan, based in the town of Mashhad. All of these appointments were intended to make use of Percy's diplomatic and linguistic skills, in what may be seen as the final stages of the 'Great Game' of the nineteenth century, and in which he was largely successful. When war was declared in 1914 he initially served as interpreter for the Lahore Division in France, and then Consul-General in Chinese Turkestan, but it was perhaps inevitable that he would find himself a position in which to return to Persia.

Percy's work in northern Persia had successfully ensured the loyalty of the tribes there to British influence over that of Russia, but the south of the country was a different question entirely. In 1915 German agents provoked anti-British actions which threatened to divert troops which were desperately needed in operations against the Ottoman Empire in Palestine and Mesopotamia and at Gallipoli. This situation was particularly acute in the provinces of Fars and Kerman, where it was feared the Swedish-officered armed police could cause serious trouble. Major Sykes was knighted in that year, before being promoted to the temporary rank of brigadier general for his most delicate task yet. He again sailed for Persia, with the Shah's consent to raise a force of up to eleven thousand men, and arrived in Bandar Abbas in March 1916 with a small group of British officers, a company of Indian soldiers, and an ample supply of weapons and ammunition. Though his arrival was sanctioned by the Foreign Office in London, no formal agreement had been made with the government of the Shah, and it wasn't until August that an accord was signed with the Persian Prime Minister and the Russian Minister in Tehran. Russia was thereby allowed to increase its Cossack force in the north of the country to eleven thousand also, maintaining the balance of influence across the country as a whole. Recruitment began at once, with training mirroring that of the Indian Army wherever possible, and by December the South Persia Rifles had brigades in Bandar Abbas and Kerman, with a third located with Percy's headquarters in Shiraz. The first regiment of three hundred men from the Kamsa tribe had been raised within a month, but now with 3,300 infantrymen and 450 cavalry troopers, as well as a small number of artillery pieces, the SPR successfully suppressed the previously regular raids of the Qashqai tribe, who eventually came to an agreement with the British officers of the regiment in early 1917. This allowed them to concentrate on the many smaller tribes who were still open to German influence and whose loyalty to the Shah was shaky at best. The principal tactic of the SPR was to attack the tribes in their own villages, thereby destroying their crops and means of transport rather than necessarily killing large numbers of tribesmen; this allowed them to achieve their aim without provoking hostility from wider Persian society. They also restored property and livestock to the owners from which they had been taken, further cementing the loyalty of the local population.

This success was not to last unhindered however. In June 1917 the pro-British government of Hassan Vosugh Al-Dowleh fell, and the new Prime Minister, Mohammad-Ali Ala Al-Saltaneh refused to recognise the legitimacy of the SPR. This permitted the southern tribes, including the Qashqai, to legitimately renew their raiding campaigns. Though the government changed again in December, the policy did not, and morale amongst the SPR, now numbering seven thousand, continued to drop. The Qashqai became bolder, attacking SPR posts themselves as well as rival villages, and the encouragement of Shia mullahs further increased the rate of desertion, with the Fars Brigade falling to a third of its former size. The crisis came to a head in May 1918 when the Qashqai declared war on the British, and raids further intensified in both size and regularity, though the conflict was sparked by something as innocent as the arrest of some Qashqai tribesmen for the theft of two donkeys belonging to the SPR. Violent anti-British protests erupted in Shiraz, and religious leaders continued to encourage the local dissent. Early clashes resulted in SPR victories, but on the 25th May news arrived of a mutiny at Kana Zenyan that had resulted in the deaths of two British officers, and it was clear that the conflict was far from over. The next development was more serious, as the SPR garrison in Shiraz was essentially besieged for several months. The Indian soldiers suffered greatly from scarcity of food, and cholera broke out, but gradually the siege fell away, as British influence in the area and in Tehran itself broke down the loyalty of the tribes to their leader Sawlat al-Dawla. His troops, too, had suffered from the cholera which plagued Fars province that summer, and news of British victories in Europe served to convince the tribesmen that the British war machine was too big an enemy to convincingly engage and defeat. A further siege of the SPR forces at Abada began in early July, but was relieved by a column from Shiraz only ten days later.

This near-chaos had the inevitable result that many in the Foreign Office called for Percy Sykes' removal as GOC South Persia and Inspector General of the SPR, but as long as he had the support of Lord Curzon as Leader of the House of Lords (and former Viceroy of India), his position was safe. That could not last forever in the face of ever-mounting opposition however, and in spite of Curzon's influence in the Foreign Office, Percy was recalled to London before the armistice with Germany in November.[108] Though the SPR continued until 1921, when their disbandment was demanded by Reza Khan (the Minister for War who later became Reza Shah Pahlavi), Percy Sykes' involvement was at an end. He continued to serve in the army until retirement in 1924, when he was permitted to retain his rank of brigadier general, and from 1932 until his death he served as Honorary Secretary of the Royal Central Asian Society, which continues today as the Royal Society for Asian Affairs. He died in Charing Cross Hospital on the 11th of June 1945, having just lived to see the end of the second great war of his lifetime, and was survived by his wife Evelyn and six children. In his time Brigadier General Sir Percy Molesworth Sykes was a scholar, a soldier and a diplomat; he served his country in two of its the three greatest ever troop deployments, he published seventeen books on Persia and Central Asia, and skilfully represented the United Kingdom in the closing stages of one of the greatest diplomatic struggles of history.

---

108 GALBRAITH & HUTTENBACK, 2013, pp117-9.

SPORT

Captain Adrian Stoop MC (Stanley)

Adrian Dura Stoop was perhaps an unusual Rugby hero, as the son of a Dutch businessman born almost fifty years before the formation of a Netherlands national team. His father Frederick had been living in England for six years when Adrian was born, running the London offices of Stoop & Co, the Java-based oil exploration company founded by his brother Adriaan. It was in London that he met and married Agnes Clark, and they married on the 1st June 1882. Adrian was their first child, named in accordance with family tradition, and he was born at the family home of 5 Collingham Gardens, near Cromwell Road in London. The rapid expansion of both their family and Frederick's income prompted him to decide that a larger house was needed, preferably in the country, and after a considerable search the Stoops settled on West Hall, just outside Byfleet in Surrey; within easy reach of Frederick's offices in London, yet with considerable grounds of its own in which the seven Stoop children could play. After an initial education at Locker's Park School in Hemel Hempstead, Adrian passed on to Dover College for a short time, where his talents began to be focussed on Rugby Football, rather than cricket as at prep school, though in his first year there he played a great part in his house winning the junior cups in both sports. Frederick Stoop, however, was ever mindful of his son's education, and had been reading about the restoration of Rugby School's fortunes over the previous ten years under the strict moral guidance of Head Master Dr John Percival, formerly President of Trinity College, Oxford. So it was that in September 1897 Adrian left Dover for Rugby, settling in to Mr Steele's house (now Stanley, on Barby Road).

In many ways Adrian was a classic Victorian public school all-rounder, joining the Rifle Corps, debating and playing chess, but it was sport that became an almost all-consuming call on his time. In the Steele's team Adrian found himself at half-back, whose duties at the time were chiefly concerned with dribbling the ball, and to be fast from a standing start in order to reach and fall on the ball before the opposition. In the late nineteenth century there were few 'foreign' games (against other schools), but at the end of the Advent term in December 1899 Adrian had the perfect opportunity to demonstrate his rapidly increasing ability when one of the half-backs dropped out of the XV at short notice immediately before the annual match against Cheltenham College. He grabbed the opportunity with both hands, and further cemented his reputation in the subsequent set of house matches, most noticeably in a surprise 18-11 victory over Collins's house. Adrian was never a great academic, though in the summer of 1900 he passed his school certificates in English, French, German, Greek, elementary mathematics, and scripture knowledge, and on the 1st November that year he achieved his primary goal in being awarded his football colours, cementing his place in the XV for the rest of the season. For perhaps the first time in the sport's history, both captains and masters had begun to offer a little training and to insist upon practice between matches. The 1900-01 leadership of Vincent 'Lump' Cartwright[109] proved to be a great example to Adrian, and the two were later to represent England together on several occasions; the season was a resounding success, beginning with a 19-8 win over the University of Oxford and including convincing wins over the two oldest sporting rivals of Rugby, Uppingham (58-0) and Cheltenham (29-8). The *Cheltenham Echo* reported on the latter, particularly noting Adrian's compelling performance:

> Individually the Rugby halves stood out most prominently. They were simply irresistible behind a good pack of forwards, and besides making many fine runs themselves, they fed their three-quarters in the best style, making their play almost perfect… it is many a long day since a more balanced team was seen on the College enclosure.[110]

It was one match that season, Adrian's last at school, which was to influence his life more than perhaps any other in his career. Harlequins Football Club had been founded in 1866, but were only now beginning to find the fame which would follow them for decades, and indeed still does, though finances were tight. Adrian was invited to join the club by his old friend 'Lump' as he left school and matriculated at University College, Oxford, and chose to do so over an invitation from the much more prominent Blackheath FC; that decision was to change his life

---

109 H.V. Cartwright (1882-1965) captained England in 1905-6 and later served with the Royal Marines on the Western Front, receiving a DSO, Croix de Guerre and being twice mentioned in despatches, reaching the rank of temporary major in 1917.

110 COOPER, 2004, p37.

irrevocably. His first match, ironically, was against the university that he had just joined, on the 16th October 1901, and he scored the club's only try against the university. Perhaps that, alongside his increasingly regular calls to radically reform midfield play, was a reason for which Adrian was not selected for the 1901 Varsity match, which Oxford won, but nevertheless Harlequins were settling in to a new home at Wandsworth Common and the future was beginning to brighten. Adrian was also elected to the club's committee, alongside Cartwright and luminaries such as W.A. Smith, the 'Father of the Club', who had been involved since its foundation thirty-five years earlier.

1902 was even more promising, and on the 11th December Adrian wrote to his parents to tell them that he had finally been selected for the Varsity match; Oxford began as firm favourites, yet the match ended in an unexpected draw; but it gained Adrian a trial for England, even if that particular avenue did not extend very far that time. The 1903 match was a nail-biting affair[111], with Oxford snatching victory with a fourth try in the last minute of play, but it was in 1904 that the great accolade of captaincy was bestowed upon Adrian, as the university club finally admitted that his unconventional methods had contributed much to their recent victories. After a great victory over London Scottish in early December, a record crowd flocked to the Varsity match at the Queen's Club, then considered to be the finest ground in the country. Oxford lost, but an extraordinary try by Adrian, between the Cambridge posts after covering the length of half the pitch, again brought him to the notice of the England selectors. Still he was not chosen after a trial match, but the England side was in despair, losing the first two matches of the 1905 Home Nations Championship, each one by an embarrassingly large margin, and letters to the press made it clear that something radical had to be done. The name A.D. Stoop began to appear in the newspapers as the likely man for the job, and before the championship finished he finally received an invitation to join the national side for the first time, in the 1905 Calcutta Cup. England suffered another loss, but Adrian's promise was clear for all to see.

He now became a regular face on the England team, receiving fifteen caps between the Calcutta Cup matches of 1905 and 1912. Twice he served as captain, but it was perhaps his first winter on the team which had one

---

111 Ibid, p37.

of the greatest influences on Adrian's style of play and of captaincy, and not only from matches in which he himself played. It was in 1905 that New Zealand toured the UK for the first time, in their new 'all black' kit, and trounced all opposition except in a controversial 3-0 loss to Wales, scoring a total of 730 points across their matches, for a loss of only 47. It was clear to the entire England hierarchy that the nature of the game had changed, and was continuing to do so at a rapid pace. Adrian knew that both New Zealand and Wales were taking the sport much more seriously than England, where its origins as a school pastime and its history of a lack of coaching and practice between matches still coloured the play on the pitch. The All Blacks were noticeably more versatile in their abilities, changing positions between matches, particularly the backs. Until now English half-backs had played either left or right, but the tourists brought with them the new concepts of Scrum Half and Fly Half, and it was these innovations that Adrian gently introduced to both Harlequins and England. His influence at club level had continued to grow as the success of his unconventional tactics had been proven time and time again; as club secretary at Harlequins from 1905, as well as captain from 1906, he very much led from the front, in the committee room as well as on the pitch, right up to 1914. It was also that time that he had the great privilege to be the first captain to lead England onto the pitch at their new Twickenham home in 1910.

Nine days after the declaration of war in August 1914, the RFU sent out an open letter encouraging all players to join up, and across the country, except in schools, all matches for the forthcoming season were cancelled. Adrian's life at West Hall, playing regularly for club and country, was bound to change suddenly and considerably. Already feeling the call of duty, he had been commissioned as a second lieutenant in the 1/5th Battalion The Queen's (Royal West Surrey) Regiment, and on the day after the war began the battalion was ordered to proceed from its drill hall in Guildford to barracks in Strood, Kent. Moving east, they must have assumed that they were beginning their journey to France, but in fact they were bound for India, and by September were in Southampton, ready to sail on the SS *Alaunia*.[112] They stopped briefly to store ship in Suez, but though their progress was otherwise slowed by the threat of German cruisers, soon enough they arrived in Bombay and joined the

---

112 WO95/5145/3.

12th Indian Division at Lucknow. This was a shock to the inexperienced reserves of the 1/5th Queens, more used to the North Downs than the plains of northern India. The temperature took its toll and the men's feet suffered because the dryness of the climate made their boots stiff. Still, it was a gentle introduction to war compared to many, though they couldn't ignore the events unfolding in Europe; by May 1915 Adrian had already lost several friends from Rugby, Harlequins and England, not least Ronnie Poulton Palmer and Kenneth Powell. Later that month he wrote to Ronnie's sister:

> So many of the best men have gone under that one feels that the most satisfactory thing would be to follow their example. The gap among one's friends will be too awful when the war is over. The Harlequins also have Tom Allen and Kenneth Powell to avenge, and I do not think we shall forget when the time comes.

On the 27th October the battalion was still in Lucknow and received orders to mobilise. This threw them into confusion, with stores unavailable, officers' chargers and tents to be purchased, and the commanding officer protesting that their baggage was to be left behind for transport with another battalion. The confusion was compounded on the 5th November by a telegram from HQ at Allahabad which stated, 'Chief General Staff wires that the mobilization of the first fifth Queens is only a precautionary measure and unit should be informed accordingly.'[113] No one in the battalion knew exactly what this meant, nor how it should affect the process, but when they were instructed to return certain vital items of stores it was assumed that there would be no movement for a while.

Finally, at lunchtime on the 25th November another telegram was received, directing that they should '…be prepared to move first fifth West Surreys Lucknow to Bombay at few hours' notice'. Finally they were on the move, and made their way slowly by train across India, arriving in Bombay on the 1st of December, where the battalion's officers enjoyed a night in the Taj Mahal Hotel before boarding HMT *Elephanta* the next morning. They were bound for Mesopotamia, and after an uneventful journey they arrived at Basra on the 7th, where they transferred to barges

---

113 Ibid.

towed by tugs for the long journey up the Euphrates. The final stretch of the journey was by steamers and barges to Nasiriyah, where they heard that much was happening across Mesopotamia, with the Turkish forces constructing strong defensive positions amongst the marshes. The 1/5th Queens however were set to work on more mundane tasks, building a road to Ur, well-known to them all as the biblical home of Abraham, and guarding Turkish visitors in a local camp. Christmas Day arrived and with it the first post since they had left Lucknow, as well as a Christmas dinner of cold beef, hot chicken and plum duff. 1916 was a slow, hot, unhealthy year for Adrian and his battalion; cholera and dysentery raged nearby, but there was still very little engagement with the enemy. When it finally came, as a rearguard action against a force of 7,000 Arabs, it was short but successful. Another Christmas came and went quietly without any leave for Adrian, but on the 27th March 1917 the battalion entrained for Basra, then boarded steamers up the Tigris, en-route to Baghdad. The quietness which followed allowed Adrian to take his first leave since December 1915, and he undertook the long journey back to India, proposing to Audrey, whom he had met a year before and to whom he had continued to write from Mesopotamia. The leave was not to last long however, and on the 17th June he was back with the battalion in Baghdad, but the confusion which had accompanied their departure from England nearly three years earlier seemed to have returned, with many hints that a large-scale attack was in preparation, but with no official notification from Divisional HQ. Finally the order came, and on the 14th September they departed for a renewed effort to take Ramadi, the scene of a defeated British attempt fourteen months earlier.[114]

For two weeks the 1/5th Queens continually marched and dug in as they and the Turks vied for the most favourable position from which to attack, but the final order came and they attacked the ridges south of Ramadi at 5am on the 29th September. As company commander of D Company, Adrian led his Lewis Gun sections in the capture of Faraja Ridge, and the capture of Ramadi was a resounding success, taking large numbers of prisoners in the process, but in the thick of the battle he received a bullet wound to the groin. Losing lots of blood he was lucky to be alive, and the end of the campaign season was upon them and he had the winter to recuperate. It must have been with a great sense of

---

114 Ibid.

relief that he returned to his company on the 25th November, spending the winter testing new Lewis Gun mounts and organising boxing and football tournaments, but another setback was just around the corner. Adrian had been lucky to avoid the waves of disease which had swept Mesopotamia since their arrival, but now he succumbed to a serious bout of malaria, and coming so soon after his battle injury a longer period of recovery was required. It eventually passed, and on the 30th April 1918 Adrian proceeded on leave to Bangalore; he hadn't forgotten Audrey, indeed her letters had been a great comfort during his injury and illness, and they married in St Mark's Church[115] on the 8th May. From gun battles in the desert plains of Mesopotamia to honeymoon in the hills of India, Adrian's life had taken another sudden turn, thankfully this time for the best. On the 16th June more good news arrived: Adrian had been awarded the Military Cross for his actions at Ramadi, with the *London Gazette* recording the citation:

> For conspicuous gallantry and devotion to duty in action. He commanded the Lewis Guns of his battalion with great skill and daring under heavy fire, rendering invaluable assistance, and only desisted on being seriously wounded. He has previously done good work as Lewis gun officer.[116]

From this point the battalion's life returned to the comparative quietness of the time before Ramadi, and it was only five months until the armistice was signed with the Ottoman Empire on the 1st November. Even so, it was another whole year before Adrian and Audrey, accompanied by their first child, born in India, returned home to Surrey.

The country to which the Stoops returned was far removed from that which Adrian had left behind five years earlier, and English rugby had to be rebuilt almost from scratch. So many of the great names of the pre-war years had been killed in action: Poulton, Powell, Lambert, Mobbs and others. Indeed on the 21st February 1921 King George V laid a tablet at Twickenham after England's match against Ireland which read, 'In proud and grateful memory of rugby football players who gave their

---

115 The garrison church of Bangalore. It suffered a serious fire in 1923 but was rebuilt and remains open.
116 COOPER, p128.

lives in the Great War.' Adrian returned to his beloved club and continued to play in Harlequins colours until the extraordinary age of 56 in 1939, by which time he had represented the club 182 times, 143 as captain. In 1950 he finally stood down after thirty years as president, having also been president of the RFU in 1932, and was revered as the grand old man of Twickenham, indeed the Harlequins ground was later renamed in his honour. Adrian Dura Stoop died at home at the age of 74 on the 27th November 1957 and was buried in his home village of Hartley in Hampshire. English rugby mourned the loss of one of its greatest and most distinctive players, but through his service as school, university, club and national captain, as well as his service to his country in wartime Mesopotamia, he had given so much of his life to and for others, to their greater good.

Private Kenneth Powell (Michell)

Kenneth Lawrence Powell, one of six children, was born in Hampstead on the 8th April 1885 to James and Mary Powell, and grew up in the family home at Reigate. The Powells were a keen sporting family, with their own tennis courts, cricket pitch and pavilion at their house, Ivanhoe, so it is perhaps unsurprising that the young Kenneth had a good grounding in many different disciplines. After prep school Kenneth arrived at Michell House in 1899; the house was at that time still run by Mr Michell[117] himself, who had built the place in 1884, and was, with Robert Whitelaw further down Hillmorton Road, one of the last of the somewhat regal housemasters of the late nineteenth century, legendary men who often lasted for decades in charge. Kenneth may best be known for his prowess at tennis, but at school he was a genuine all-rounder who triumphed in almost every element of sporting life at Rugby. He played for the XV in 1902 and 1903, taking the captaincy in 1904, along with several other sporting responsibilities, for example he represented the school in the racquets pair in 1903 and 1904, and was a prominent and regular member of the gymnastics VIII.[118]

In 1904 Kenneth, by now a near-legend in the sporting life of the school, left Rugby and went up to King's College, Cambridge, to read History. There too, however, it was his sporting prowess for which he was to be known, not academic work: he represented the university at hurdles for four years in a row against Oxford, being elected President of Cambridge University Athletics Club in 1907, and setting a new hurdles record in the university competition of 1908. It was in the same year that Kenneth's international sporting career began. The Olympic Games of that year had been scheduled to take place in Rome, but an eruption of Mount Vesuvius in 1906 meant that funds for building the Olympic stadium were diverted to the rebuilding of parts of Naples, and that prompted the International Olympic Committee to move the games to White City in Shepherd's Bush. At that time the president of the IOC was still Baron Pierre de Coubertin, who had been instrumental in re-establishing of the games in 1896, and indeed it was from Rugby School and Thomas Arnold that he took much of his inspiration. To de Coubertin it was the

---

117 Walter Michell built the house in 1884 and died in 1925.
118 Memorials of Rugbeians who Fell in the Great War.

prominent role (as he saw it) of sport in Arnold's system of education that had underpinned to the expansion of the British Empire, via the spread of his system of education throughout public schools in the latter half of the nineteenth century. It was appropriate therefore that at least one Rugbeian should compete in the first games to take place in the country that inspired their re-emergence in the modern world.

Kenneth's particular athletic strength at the time was the hurdles, and he was chosen to represent the United Kingdom in the 110 yard race. He took to the track for heat five and started strongly, keeping level with the USA's William Rand, but as they neared the end of the race Kenneth hit the ninth hurdle and that fraction of a second difference allowed Rand to take the lead, leaving Kenneth in second place. The event continued to an all-American final, with Forrest Smithson winning the gold medal with a world record time of 15.0 seconds on the very last day of the games.[119] In 1912 Kenneth was again selected to represent the UK in the 110 yard hurdles, this time in Stockholm, which de Coubertin was determined would be an altogether more dignified affair than those which had gone before. Kenneth's performance was an improvement on that of 1908 and he won heat eleven with a respectable time of 15.6 seconds. In semi-final one he achieved exactly the same time, earning himself a place in the final on the 12th July 1912. Again the USA had dominated the event, and Kenneth was the only non-American athlete to reach the final, where he reached fifth place, gold going to the distinctive hurdling style of Fred Kelly.

Kenneth's childhood tennis matches had introduced him to what was to become the other principal sport of his adult life. The Wimbledon tennis championship was first established in 1877, and by the turn of the century it was an established part of the summer's social and sporting circuit. Kenneth competed in eight out of the nine championships between 1905 and 1913, for both singles and men's doubles. In 1913 he reached the quarter-final of the men's singles, losing to Oskar Kreuzer of Germany, but his highest achievement in the men's doubles had been in 1910 when he and Robert Powell of Canada lost to Major Ritchie of the UK and Anthony Wilding of New Zealand.

In all of his sporting endeavours he was, as was expected at the time, an amateur, and in his private life he worked as a leather merchant[120],

---

119 MALLON & BUCHANAN, 2009.
120 *The Leather World Journal*, Vol. 7, 1915, p271.

having followed his father into the family business, while still living at home, now at Bodleian House on Doods Park Road in Reigate[121].

With the declaration of war in 1914 Kenneth volunteered, and did not seek a commission like most of his Rugbeian contemporaries. He enlisted as 1832 Private K Powell in the 1st Battalion of the Honourable Artillery Company, and they were inspected by the King in London shortly before they moved to Belhus Park in Essex for further training. They sailed for France on the 18th September that year in the SS *Westmeath*, landing two days later at St Nazaire, and joined the 8th Infantry Brigade. By February 1915 the 1st HAC were at Locre in West Flanders and Kenneth was acting as one of the battalion's snipers, but at 10pm on the 17th he was hit by a stray bullet while returning from the front line with a working party. Confusion added to the delay in his removal from the trenches, but he was eventually evacuated to No. 7 Field Ambulance near the village, and at 8.45am an emergency operation was conducted to remove the bullet. Despite the best efforts of the medical officer he died at 0920 on the 18th February 1915, aged 29. He is buried in the village churchyard at Locre.

Kenneth's death was a great shock to the Rugby School community, as he was one of the first famous figures from the school's recent past to be killed. The grief was exacerbated by the death of Rupert Brooke, his contemporary, only a few weeks later. The school magazine, *The Meteor*, wrote of him on the 19th March:

> No man ever changed so little in the fifteen years from his arrival at a Public School. From first to last he was the same entirely simple, straight and unassuming fellow, whom all respected, most liked, and many loved. To anyone who knew him, the idea of Kenneth Powell showing arrogance or swagger is simply an absurdity. Yet no one could follow more unswervingly his own straight path, all unconscious of what others might think, and quite unsuspecting the influence he exercised. It is not very uncommon to see a nature that instinctively attracts to itself others of a like fashion. But he had the rarer and far more subtle magnetism that drew to itself what was good in natures of little excellence; so that

---

121 1911 Census, Ref: RG14PN3215 RG78PN121 RD37 SD2 ED8 SN95.

many of us, wholly below his calibre, honestly called him friend and were unreservedly admitted to his friendship. To refrain from ill-temper, or ill-language, or coarseness in word or act—these are common and negative virtues; a very few men carry that gentle power which unconsciously curbs the tongues and, what is more, the thoughts of others. Of these few he was one... in the hearts of a few closer friends there is something like despair that one so gifted and so lovable is gone, yet a great joy and encouragement to know that gentleness and simplicity and mere goodness can effect what cannot be achieved by natures more powerful or intellects keener and more ambitious than his.'[122]

---

122 Memorials of Rugbeians who Fell in the Great War.

Lieutenant Ronald Poulton Palmer (School House)

'Ronnie' Poulton (usually Poulton-Palmer after 1913, in honour of the Rt Hon G.W. Palmer MP, the uncle to whom he was heir) was perhaps the greatest English Rugby player of the early twentieth century, and it can only be wondered how his sporting career might have continued had it not been cut short by the conflict that engulfed Europe in 1914.

Ronnie was born at Wykeham House, Oxford, on the 12th September 1889, to Sir Edward Bagnall Poulton (1856-1943), Fellow of Jesus College and shortly afterwards the Hope Professor of Zoology, and his wife Emily. A happy childhood followed in the leafy environs of Banbury Road and the very active Ronnie attended the Oxford Preparatory School, now the Dragon School, from 1897. It was quite clear to those who knew him that Ronnie was to be a boy whom others would admire, and who had a natural affinity for both friendship and leadership. In his school report of April 1903 the Head Master wrote that 'His presence is like a gleam of sunshine'[123]. His sporting prowess was not immediately apparent however, and it was not until the age of 12 that a certain degree of ability became apparent; the same school report described his sporting performance as, 'Very good indeed. Takes his success with a most becoming modesty'[124], but it was in September 1903 that he arrived at Rugby and really took to the sport for which he was to become famous.

The copious letters sent by Ronnie to all of his family ('five to seven each Sunday', he boasted in one sent during his first term at Rugby) tell of a happy boy whose reputation had preceded him but whose increasing reputation was tempered by humility. It wasn't long before his name began to appear in the sporting columns of *The Meteor*, but it was in the spring of 1904 that Ronnie's ability was made clear to the whole school. In the Junior Sports of that term he won almost every event that he entered, setting new records in several of them, and *The Meteor* recorded,

> In the under events Poulton stood out pre-eminent. He won the 100yds. both under 14 ½ and under 16, the 150 yds. under 16, the 300 under 14½, the Broad Jump under 16, the half mile under 14½, was second in the High Jump and

---

123 POULTON, 1919, p45.
124 Ibid, p51.

Steeplechases under 16, and third in the Hurdles under 16. A wonderful all round performance. His times in the 300 yds. and half-mile under 14½ were excellent, and his winning two 100 yd. races one after the other in 12 secs. was a very fine performance.

In December 1904 Ronnie was awarded his 'Bags' for football – the first rung on the ladder of sporting awards, but one which was only awarded to approximately thirty boys in the school at any one time, and so to do so only a year after arriving was a significant achievement. Even so, Ronnie objected to the fact that as such he was required to leap-frog over his juniors in the dormitory passage, as much out of concern for his injured toes as for the welfare of the younger boys. One of his 'fags', however, later wrote anonymously to Ronnie's father to praise his gentleness with his juniors, much different to the approach of his peers, and said, 'A word of praise from him on these occasions was more valued by us than the highest commendation from anyone else.'[125]

In the 1907-8 season Ronnie served as joint-captain of the XV with C.C. Watson[126], and it proved to be one of the great seasons of the XV's history. They won every match but one, easily beating both Uppingham and Cheltenham (then the two principal 'foreign' matches of the year), and scored 250 points for only 59 against them. It was clear to all that if he chose to pursue his sporting career Ronnie had a great future ahead of him, and *The Meteor* described his form thus:

> R. W. Poulton (S. H.), '05, '06, '07. – A brilliant centre three-quarter. Holding the ball in both hands, at arms length, he relies on his great pace and a most deceptive swerve to get through, and seldom without success. He gathers the ball beautifully, and has always combined excellently with his neighbours in the line. If his tackling improves, he will become a great player.[127]

---

125   Ibid, p89.
126   Charles Challinor Watson (Michell House), killed near Lens on the 1st June 1917, aged 28, while serving with the Royal Field Artillery.
127   *The Meteor*, Vol xli, p175.

Ronnie Poulton was a truly exceptional schoolboy sportsman, yet his talents also extended into the academic sphere, and in 1907 he successfully sat for and was awarded the Williams Exhibition in Natural Sciences to Balliol College, Oxford[128]. The day on which he heard was one which stuck in his memory; not only did he receive news of his Exhibition, but Rugby beat Cheltenham in the last 'foreign' match of Ronnie's school career, and he also received an invitation from Adrian Stoop asking him to play for Harlequins. Ronnie was undecided and wrote to his father that 'It only means half a day away. I should be back to dinner,' but eventually declined, acting on the advice of his friend and teacher C.P. Evers that he was too young for such adventures.[129] At the end of the season, Ronnie received an unexpected gift: a silver cigarette case, engraved with his initial, from an anonymous admirer who wrote in the accompanying letter of the great pleasure that Ronnie's playing had brought the school. And so it was that, in the summer of 1908, Ronnie Poulton left the school that had done so much to shape his sporting and academic skills, and yet which he himself had shaped perhaps in equal measure. He was aware of the significance of the moment, and wrote in his account of the year,

> I feel sure that no one enjoyed every moment at school more than I did. I felt a pang at leaving, and the feeling was increased very much when the school went back in October. I made a large number of friends at school, among whom were several masters, and it is pleasant to think that one is at least welcome there at any time.[130]

Ronnie spent part of that summer working at the Rugby Boy's Camp, which was run annually on Romney Marsh for the members of Rugby's missions in Notting Hill. It was the third annual camp that he had assisted with, and it was a great pleasure to Ronnie to spend his time so usefully, alongside two of his former tutors (H.H. Hardy and C.W. Hawkesworth) and 'Billy Temple' – later Archbishop of Canterbury. These camps were

---

128 The Exhibition was awarded by Harold Hartley, who during the Great War reached the rank of brigadier general, responsible for the British Army's chemical warfare capabilities.

129 POULTON, p101.

130 Ibid, p107.

becoming a regular feature of Ronnie's summers and are an indication of the charitable element which was an integral part of his character; he later went on to help with similar camps for the boys' clubs of Balliol and St John's Church, Reading.

Oxford was Ronnie's home, and in arriving at Balliol he was following in the footsteps of his brother Teddy, so it was a confident young man who matriculated in the Sheldonian Theatre to read Engineering in October 1908. Harold Hartley was responsible for his academic progress, but he began his studies under Professor Jenkin[131], Oxford's first Professor of Engineering Science. In his first term he was elected to the Brackenbury and Shaftesbury Societies (the former of which still exists), and spent a good deal of time playing tennis and working very hard in the university laboratories, but it was perhaps inevitable that Rugby Football should soon emerge as a great part of his university life. Within a year he had not only succumbed to Adrian Stoop's invitation to play for Harlequins, but had also been selected to play for England. The unorthodox nature of his play actually meant that he was left out of the University XV for the 1908 varsity match, but only weeks later he made his national debut, playing at Leicester's Welford Road ground against France on the 30th January 1909. England won 22-0, but it was in their next match, against Ireland on the 13th February, that he scored his first points for the team, scoring two tries to take England to an 11-5 victory. In the following month Ronnie played for both Harlequins against Leicester, and England against Scotland within the same week. At Richmond, England lost 8-18 in what was their last match of that year's Home Nations Championship, but Ronnie scored again, converting their only try, and confirming his place in the national side. After the Harlequins match, which they won 39-12, *The Sportsman* reported,

> The hero of the afternoon was R. W. Poulton, who played right centre. Poulton is taking up to Oxford from Rugby School one of the greatest of schoolboy reputations; and as good as the Oxford three-quarters are, they will have to look to their laurels to withstand this competitor in genius.

---

131 Professor Charles Frewen Jenkin CBE FRS, served as a lieutenant commander in the Royal Naval Air Service during the Great War before returning to his academic career in Oxford.

After such a season and with three international caps to his name, the University XV selectors could not ignore Ronnie's ability any longer, and so it was that he took to the field for the 1909 varsity match against Cambridge. Perhaps he felt the need to justify his place, but whatever the reason, Ronnie played an extraordinary match, and set a record that is still to be beaten by scoring five tries to contribute 15 points to Oxford's 35-3 victory.

Of course at the time (and for a long time afterwards) all Rugby Football players were amateurs, and so even with such an obvious sporting skill Ronnie was required to find a profession. Many of his friends, familiar with his approachability and leadership at Rugby and Oxford, tried to push him towards a career in teaching, but he was personally set on following the subject of his career. So in January 1910 he was offered employment by his uncle. G.W. Palmer had twice been MP for Reading and was joint proprietor of Huntley and Palmer, which was fast becoming the world's largest producer of biscuits, so Ronnie would be joining a burgeoning business after he left Balliol. Consequently he worked very hard for his finals in Trinity term of 1911 and was awarded a second class degree, about which both he and the college were content. Ronnie wrote to his father,

> The mathematical papers were too much for me, but I found I knew a good deal about the other subjects. The Second I obtained was really what I expected.

Professor Jenkin also wrote to Professor Poulton:

> None of my men this year get Firsts. Ronald is at the top of the list of the Second Class. He has done his final papers very well. He only worked for me for two terms really hard, and has done extraordinarily well in that time… I have never met a young man I would more gladly recommend for any post of responsibility. It has been a great pleasure having him in my class.

It was early in 1913 that G.W. Palmer died and, upon receiving his inheritance, Ronnie changed his name to Palmer in honour of his late uncle. Despite the draw of an increasingly demanding business career,

Ronnie continued to play for his university and his country, captaining both in due course. It was for the 1914 international campaign that he was appointed to lead the national team, and he did so with his characteristic calmness, individuality and entirely unpredictable body-swerve. That year's Home Nations Championship was consequently very much Ronnie's competition: England won only their second ever Grand Slam, with the Calcutta Cup being added to the haul on the 21st March. The last match of the tournament, against France in Paris on the 13th April, was to be Ronnie's last international appearance, sealed with a 13-39 win at the Parc des Princes. Ronnie scored four tries and was hailed as the world's greatest Rugby player by the French press. At the time no one could have known that he would be dead only thirteen months later.

Ronnie's military career had started years before; he was one of the first members of the University of Oxford Officer Training Corps upon its foundation as part of the Haldane Reforms of 1908, and when he moved to Reading in 1912 he was commissioned into the 1/4th Battalion, Princess Charlotte of Wales' (Royal Berkshire Regiment), being promoted to lieutenant in July 1913. It was at the declaration of war in 1914, however, that he volunteered for overseas service, and joined the battalion for several months' training in Chelmsford. Yet again Ronnie's extraordinary sense of duty was apparent, as he immediately left his business and sporting careers behind for what he saw as the greater good of his country. Finally, on the 30th March 1915, the battalion entrained for Folkestone, and boarded the South Eastern Railway's packet ship *Onward* for Boulogne[132]. Less than a year before Ronnie had boarded the same ship for his last international match[133]; now he was heading again to France under very different circumstances. They were attached to the 10th Brigade of the 4th Division, and on the 13th April Ronnie played his last ever rugby match, describing it in his journal:

> After breakfast drove into Nieppe in a motor lorry to see an exhibition of bomb-throwing. After that we drove in a motor ambulance to Armentieres to have lunch and to shop. This town seems none the worse and there is plenty of business, though everything is expensive. After lunch we moved to

---

132 CRUTTWELL, 1922, p3.
133 POULTON, p336.

Nieppe, and I played Rugger for the South Midland Division [48ᵗʰ] against the 4ᵗʰ Division. It was an amusing game; we had opposite us players like W. J. Tyrrell [Ireland: Captain], H. J. S. Morton [Cambridge and England], J. G. Keppell [Ireland: Trials], W. P. Hinton [Ireland: Full Back], and we were refereed by Basil Maclear[134] [Ireland]. I had a goodish side, chiefly 5ᵗʰ Gloucesters and we won 14-0, but they stuck it well considering their condition.

Two days later the battalion moved into the front line, east of Ploegsteert Wood. In that first occupation of the sector Ronnie's battalion had a comparatively easy time, with very few casualties in trenches festooned with flowers and overhung by trees not yet destroyed by shell-fire.[135] Within a week, however, everything was to change with the opening of the second battle of Ypres. After five weeks' service at the front, Ronnie was still a newcomer to the horrors of trench warfare, and life at 'Plugstreet' had become much less pleasant than before. Even so, his last letter, written on the 4th May 1915 but not posted until after his death, was still full of optimism, thanking his mother for some socks and a cap that she had sent, and speaking excitedly of the oven, removed from a local farmhouse, which they had installed in their mess dugout. That night was to be Ronnie's last, and it is perhaps best to leave it to his father to describe what happened in his own words, with information gleaned from the letters of condolence which poured in:

Ronald was as usual in charge of the working party from D Company on the night of May 4-5 – the last night of the four, and he would have gone into rest on the following day. It was exceptionally dark, for the moon had not yet risen, and there was a slight fog. One other Company with its own Works Manager was working simultaneously in the firing line. Sergeant Perrin, since killed, told me that Ronald had just spoken to him and had then moved on to look at another group of workers near the new officers' mess dugout in Trench 40,

---

134 Captain Basil Maclear of the Royal Dublin Fusiliers was the first Ireland international to be killed in the war.

135 Ibid, p7.

a prominent structure covered with corrugated iron, but never shelled. It was here, while standing on Capt. Thorne's dugout and superintending the completion of a dugout immediately in front of the mess, that Ronald was shot, at twenty minutes past midnight. The bullet entered at about the level of the third rib on the right side; Ronald said 'Oh! Oh!' and fell into the arms of Sergeant Brant. His friends Capt. Thorne and Lieut. Challoner who were with him almost at once, as well as the doctor who arrived soon after, were sure that death was instantaneous and that he suffered no pain. His expression in death was peaceful and happy.[136]

He both died and was buried wearing the cap that his mother had sent him. The battalion's war diary is somewhat sparse for that month, with the day in question baldly stating, 'Lt R. W. Poulton Palmer killed,'[137] but the next day a telegram arrived at his parents' house in Oxford which said, 'Regret your son killed last night. Death instantaneous. Colonel Serocold.' When light came Ronnie's body was carried through the lines of the 1/7 Warwicks to the Field Ambulance set up in the former convent of the Sisters of Charity, on the Le Bizet road just south of Ploegsteert village, a mile behind the front line. News of his death spread quickly throughout the battalion and beyond, and so by the time he was buried in Hyde Park Cemetery at 1830 on the following day a great gloom had descended on the 4th Division. The funeral was conducted by Michael Furse, the Bishop of Pretoria and, by chance, a friend of the Palmer family. He consecrated the ground before the service, and the battalion's officers sang 'Jesu, Lover of my Soul' and 'Abide with me' as Ronnie was buried. Bishop Furse wrote the next day to Professor Poulton, saying,

> ...we buried him yesterday evening in a wood where everything told us of the Resurrection and New Life in the glorious outburst of a new spring. It was a beautiful service because so simple and so real: just his Company and his brother Officers and a few others who could get away.

---

136 POULTON, p365.
137 WO 95/2762/1.

Many of the letters of condolence which arrived in Oxford over the subsequent weeks and months spoke of the absolute desolation felt by those in Ronnie's battalion; the universal tears when they stood to without him the next morning, and the wave of grief which followed his body as it was carried from the front line. Captain Thorne wrote, 'It was a very nasty blow for us, and I personally feel intensely about it. He was idolised by the men and their grief is very severe,'[138] and Lieutenant Challoner wrote to his aunt, 'The whole world has lost a friend and an upright man… It has upset me as you can well guess. I must end now. I feel so miserable.'[139]

Ronnie was a man who made a universal impression of friendliness, dependability and sincerity on all those who met him in his comparatively short life. He had a great skill of endearing himself to anyone with whom he found himself in company, and in that sense he was the ideal that Rugby sought to engender; appropriately, then, the new Head Master Dr Albert David praised him as such in a sermon preached in the school chapel four days after his death, on the 9th May 1915:

> We have indeed given of our best. If we were asked to describe what highest kind of manhood Rugby helps to make I think we should have him in mind as we spoke of it. God had endowed him with a rare combination of graces, and given him an influence among men such as very few in one generation can possess. What had we hoped would come of it! There are those here and in Notting Dale, in Oxford, in Reading and in his Battalion, who will be better men all their lives and do better work because he was their friend – is their friend. Strong and tender and true, he lived for others and for others died.

---

138 POULTON, p371.
139 Ibid, p372.

Lieutenant Duncan Mackinnon (Tudor)

Rowing is a sport to which Rugby School has never taken, due to the lack of any suitable stretches of water nearby, but it has certainly produced successful athletes who have taken to the sport after leaving. The greatest of these in the early twentieth century was Duncan Mackinnon. Born in Paddington, London, on the 29th September 1887, his father was for many years the chairman of the British India Steam Navigation Company, founded by his own grandfather in 1856. Duncan spent his childhood between the family's houses at Balinakill in Argyll, and in Hyde Park Square in London, but in 1895 he began boarding at Grove House School near Guildford, and in September 1902 he arrived at Rugby, joining Stallard's House[140], now Tudor, on Horton Crescent. The house had been built and opened by George Stallard in 1893, and he remained housemaster for the duration of Duncan's time there, as well as that of his brother William. Duncan was a popular boy, but never particularly excelled in sport, as he had yet to find his greatest strength, which was to become apparent after he left school in 1905. The following year Duncan went up to Magdalen College, Oxford, matriculating on the 16th October 1906, and like many undergraduates tried rowing on the Isis. Soon the college barge was to be his second home. The prowess of the 6'1", 13 stone undergraduate at his newly-discovered passion became increasingly apparent to Southwell, Magdalen's Captain of Boats, who described his nascent style: 'He rowed at first with power but natural clumsiness, gaining his place in the 1st Torpid.' In the summer of 1907, less than a year after beginning his rowing career, Duncan won the Visitors' and Wyfold Cups at Henley (resulting in his election to membership of the Leander Club), followed by the Visitors' and Stewards' Cups the next year, both in record time. To finish 1908 on an increasingly positive note, he was elected President of Magdalen College Junior Common Room for the new academic year in the Michaelmas term.

It was also in 1908 that his greatest sporting achievement occurred; the Olympic Games were being held in London, and so the rowing regatta was held on the historic course at Henley. Magdalen College Boat Club was entering a hugely successful period in its history; they dominated the GB selection, and Duncan won Gold rowing at number three in the coxless fours, despite still being relatively new to the sport. They beat Canada convincingly in the heats, and in the final took off flyingly from

---

140 Memorials of Rugbeians who Fell in the Great War.

the start to beat Leander in an all-British final. Further successes followed, with wins for Oxford in the Boat Races of 1909, 1910 and 1911, setting a new record of 18 minutes 29 seconds in the latter, as well as further wins at Henley, including the Grand Challenge Cup in 1910 and 1911. In 1910 Duncan was appointed president of Oxford University Boat Club (OUBC), and served with distinction in his role as senior oarsman of the university. Duncan was a prominent individual in several different spheres of university life, as president of OUBC, JCR president of his college and an officer of Apollo University Lodge, the masonic lodge of the university.

With his formal education complete, Duncan followed his father into the world of Indian shipping, becoming a partner in Messrs Macneill and Co, and Messrs Mackinnon Mackenzie of Calcutta, operating across the Far East and Indian Ocean, as well as fortnightly services from Calcutta to London. Duncan's first taste of military life had been as a private in the Oxford University OTC, and to this interest he returned, serving as a lance corporal in the Calcutta Light Horse under the legendary Lieutenant Colonel Archie Pugh. In February 1915 Duncan returned home to England and to full-time military service. It was natural that he should join a regiment roughly analogous to his own in India, and so he was commissioned into the Royal North Devon Hussars the following month, sailing with them for Gallipoli in September, after a summer's training in dismounted roles and a long period guarding the east coast of England. The Royal North Devons had the distinction of sailing to war from Liverpool in the RMS *Olympic*, sister-ship of the *Titanic*, arriving at Moudros in the northern Aegean on the 1st October. They arrived at Suvla Bay during terrible rainstorms on the late evening of the 8th, but the weather prevented any landings until the next morning, when they were met by constant shell-fire from the Turkish artillery further inland. On the first Sunday ashore Major Greig, commanding C Squadron, was killed by a shell, providing an early shock to a regiment that had never originally been intended for foreign service at all. The next two and a half months were a trying time of dysentery, flies and intermittent shelling by the Turks. On the 3rd November they relieved the 8th Battalion Northumberland Fusiliers in the trenches of Karakol Dagh, one of the few areas of high ground in British hands, but the casualties continued regardless. Duncan was not injured, but he fell foul of the illness that plagued the regiment, and on the 31st October 1915 he was one of four men admitted to hospital with dysentery. He was treated with magnesium sulphate and opium but his admission to hospital at least meant that he missed the worst of the winter weather, which reduced the regiment to less than half its full strength.

On the 19th December 1915 the Royal North Devons were evacuated from the hellish environs of Gallipoli and spent Christmas Day on board the SS *Novian*. After a three-day voyage they landed at Alexandria. Here they were engaged in the more sedate duties of guarding the Suez Canal and the western frontier, as something of an extended recovery period for the first half of 1916, but Duncan decided that a change was required. The Royal North Devon Hussars, though a reflection of his service in Calcutta, had been an interesting choice for the London-born and Scottish-raised Duncan, and so it was perhaps of little surprise when he transferred to the Scots Guards on the 1st June 1916. He was promoted to acting lieutenant on the 19th July, though he didn't move to join the 3rd (Reserve) Battalion of his new regiment until the 6th March 1917. The 1st Bn was already in Belgium, so Duncan did not join them until the 1st August, having been confirmed in his new rank in June. He arrived in heavy rain on the second day of the Battle of Pilckem Ridge, and with no time to settle in, the battalion proceeded to the firing line the next day with Duncan commanding a platoon of the Right Flank Company. They relieved the 1st Battalion Irish Guards along the line of the Steenbeck River, but the whole process was slowed by heavy enemy bombardment. After a few days in the line Duncan's time was split between a variety of camps and dugouts, though a period of four days' leave in Paris in early September was certainly well-received. Upon his return Duncan went straight into leading a series of patrols through no-man's land and along the Ypres–Staden railway line, with several casualties on each occasion.

On the 7th October the battalion collected extra equipment and rations and again went into the line ready for an attack[141], this time at the Broenbeek stream near Langemarck, for what became known as the Battle of Poelcapelle. On the three nights before the action the Royal Engineers and 4th Battalion Coldstream Guards (as divisional pioneers) had laid 355 mats and 180 infantry bridges across the water. The Scots Guards were in position by 0100 on the 9th and crossed the stream at 0520 with little opposition due to the heavy British bombardment; the first and second objectives were both quickly achieved and the advancing troops pushed on towards the Houthulst Forest. At 1500 B Company and the right flank company had dug

---

141 WO95 1219/3/2.

in, with French troops and the 1st Battalion Coldstream Guards on either flank, both of which repulsed an enemy counter-attack at 1730. At 1915 another counter-attack was attempted and was quickly put down by the Scots Guards, but it was in this action that Lieutenant Duncan Mackinnon, Rugbeian and Olympic gold medallist, was killed by shellfire. He was acting company commander at the time and had reached his objective of Louvois Farm, next to the forest, but the heat of the battle meant that his body could not be recovered, and he remains buried somewhere in the fields outside Langemarck, with his name inscribed on the Tyne Cot Memorial nearby.

Duncan's death was deeply felt by the battalion, many of whom wrote to offer their sympathy to his family. It came only five months after the death of his brother, Captain William Mackinnon of the London Scottish (also an old boy of Stallard's and of Magdalen), who was killed at Guimappe, east of Arras in May 1917. President Warren of Magdalen described his death as 'one of those very special losses of a young man, the depth of which only his own generation and friends fully realise', and in his notebook wrote 'Unde pares invenias?' (whence shall we find their like). Duncan was only 30 years old and unmarried at the time of his death, but he had already amassed a substantial estate. He left £54,143 in personal property, plus other significant assets, half of which was left to Magdalen College, after a life interest in favour of his sister, and after her death in 1937 it was used to found the Duncan Mackinnon fund, which formed the largest single benefaction to the college since its founder, and which still continues to provide scholarships for junior members of the college. Under the care of the college it is set to continue to remind college members of Duncan's influence and generosity for many years to come. It was as a rower, however, that he is and was best known; Lieutenant Colonel Harcourt Gold RFC, himself the president of OUBC in 1898/9, wrote,

> Duncan Mackinnon was without doubt one of the finest oars that ever rowed for Oxford. His strength, stamina, and will-power were unsurpassed. It is probably no exaggeration to say that his strength of character and determination had an effect on the crews in which he rowed almost without parallel in the history of modern rowing.

No doubt it was this strength of character which also inspired such devotion from those whom he led into battle on that day in October 1917.

ACADEMIA

Sergeant Richard Tawney (Whitelaw)

Richard Henry Tawney, usually known as Harry, was born in Calcutta on the 30th November 1880, the son of noted Sanskrit scholar Charles Tawney[142], also an Old Rugbeian, and his wife Constance[143]. They had married in India in 1867, as Charles was teaching there at the time, for the Bengal Education Department, and by the time of Harry's birth he was Professor of English and Principal of Presidency College in the University of Calcutta. Richard was one of eight children, and when he was 5 years old their mother brought them all to live in England, and their father joined them in 1892. He had retired from teaching and took an enjoyable job as librarian to the India Office in London. The family lived in several places in Kent and Surrey, but when Harry was 13 he was sent to Rugby, following a family tradition of many generations. Harry's Head Master was Dr Percival, of whom he was initially terrified[144], but there are clear influences on his later thought from his earliest days at Rugby. Percival was a great exponent of the higher education of women, and later served as chairman of the committee which founded Somerville College, Oxford, as well as a patron and keen supporter of the Workers' Educational Association (WEA), which still exists to offer adult education across the UK. Another master in Harry's time was J.L. Paton, who taught Classics to the Lower Bench of the Sixth Form; noted for his austerity of living and informal dress, he organised and taught classes to local working men in his spare time, and this undoubtedly made a significant impression on the young Harry Tawney. The two were to remain friends for many years afterwards, as Paton was successively headmaster of University College School in London and then high master of Manchester Grammar School. He was also instrumental in helping Harry to find employment with the *Manchester Guardian* in later years.

As a schoolboy Harry featured little in that important element of Edwardian school life, games, playing a small amount of football and cricket. This is probably best explained by his small stature, though he continued to grow after he left school, but his academic life was a strong

---

142 1837-1922.
143 1841-1920.
144 GOLDMAN, 2013, p16.

one, particularly in Classics. He won four prizes in Latin and Greek in four years, across the range of different prose and poetical disciplines, and in the academic year of 1898/9 he served as head of house in Whitelaw. It wasn't just the masters whom he met, such as Paton, but the other pupils who were to prove important in Harry's life. One of his greatest friends was William Temple, son of the former head master and Archbishop of Canterbury, who was to be enthroned as archbishop himself in 1942, and it is often said that they met at school having arrived on the same day, but that is incorrect. Harry arrived a year ahead of 'Billy' Temple, and as boys in different years and different houses they would have had very little contact in the Rugby of the 1890s. It was in the summer holiday of 1896 that they met, when by coincidence their parents both hired houses at Ambleside in the Lake District for the duration of the holiday. Here their friendship was both established and cemented, and Harry later wrote,

> I took some long walks with him and his brother, and spent afternoons with him on a boat on Windemere, him reading Kant's Critique of Pure Reason, while I dabbled in the water or fished.[145]

Whatever the difference in their hobbies, the friendship begun then in the Lakes was to last for many years, until Temple's somewhat early death in 1944. It is curious that the two should have become and remained such close friends, when Temple represented the very heart of the social and political institutions that Harry came to distrust. In a similarly Cumbrian theme, in Harry's last term at Rugby, in 1899, his fag was Arthur Ransome, later known as the author of *Swallows and Amazons*, who had joined Whitelaw that year. Many years later they exchanged correspondence on the occasion of Harry's eightieth birthday, in which Ransome praised Harry as 'a very good employer of labour', and in response he wrote that he was sure that he felt more scared of the fags than they were of him, as many sixth form boys must have done when confronted with their new-found powers.

It was in Michaelmas 1899 that Harry, with a classical scholarship, went up to Balliol College, then at the height of its powers of

---

145 Ibid, p18.

scholarship, and the intellectual influences on him there built upon the foundations laid down by Dr Percival and his staff. Edward Caird[146], Master of Balliol, was an inspiration, and A.L. Smith[147], a history tutor, was to be a particular ally of Harry's in establishing projects to promote adult education in subsequent years, but life was exceedingly social too for Harry Tawney, and he soon developed a good-natured reputation for parties and dancing. His Old Carthusian friend William Beveridge[148] wrote,

> ...that gay wretch Harry went off and danced the whole night knowing multitudinous maidens, and has been talking about his dancing and flirtations ever since, saying how many girls he was introduced to with whom he did not in the least desire to dance and how any more whom he knew he cut altogether; and all the time he never once thought of introducing me to a single person, not even to any of those whom he discarded himself as not up to his own high standard in girls.[149]

Harry took to the sports that he had neglected at Rugby, becoming secretary to the Balliol hockey and tennis clubs and even playing for the college XV. Throughout his social, academic and sporting endeavours there was a particular strain of social responsibility; in the Hilary term of 1902 he and Beveridge resolved to found a new society at Balliol, one which would discuss the social issues of the day from a predominantly practical attitude, considering what might best be done to resolve them, though membership remained small, and only one meeting is recorded, at which Harry delivered a paper on the thrilling topic of the 'Taxation of Site Values'[150]. It was also at about this time that Harry made the

---

146 Master of Balliol 1893-1907.
147 Master of Balliol 1916-24.
148 Author of the 1942 'Beveridge Report', which laid the foundations of the welfare state. Master of University College, Oxford, 1937-45 and MP for Berwick Upon Tweed 1944-5.
149 GOLDMAN, p19.
150 Ibid, p21.

acquaintance of the Reverend Charles Gore[151], who was to remain something of a theological mentor for many years, and so assisted Harry in considering how his ideas about the necessity of universal education might have a Christian theological underpinning, long after he left Oxford upon his consecration as Bishop of Worcester in 1902.

At the end of his second year Harry had received a first in 'Classical Moderations'[152] and was a strong enough candidate to be declared *proxime accessit* (second place) for the distinguished Craven Scholarship of that year, and so it was entirely expected that he should reach similar levels in his examinations for Greats, the university's degree in Classics, at the end of his fourth year. However, it may be that the universal acclaim of his abilities tempted him to cut corners in his work as his talents and time were drawn in ever more directions. When he achieved a second in Greats he was given a viva (oral examination), and those who examined him felt that he was

> ...a 'fraud': who wrote long essays on what in viva he was proved not to have read at all. This getting up of a common notebook a vice of Balliol men this year.[153]

Harry tried to shrug off the disappointment, but he cannot have failed to feel downcast at the result, not least because of the horror of his father's reaction, and because it debarred him from his hoped-for college fellowship. Eventually Canon Samuel Barnett, Warden of Toynbee Hall in London, suggested that he might be a suitable candidate for the appointment of secretary to the Children's Country Holiday Fund (CCHF), which provided trips away to private houses in the countryside for approximately 40,000 children of inner-city London each year[154]. Harry jumped at the opportunity and took up the post at the end of 1903, after a trip to Germany to improve his German. He moved into Toynbee Hall with Beveridge, who had been appointed sub-warden alongside an

---

151 Bishop of Worcester 1902-05, Bishop of Birmingham 1905-11, Bishop of Oxford 1911-19. Also co-founder of the Christian Social Union in 1889.

152 The second year exams for those reading *Literae Humaniores* (Classics) at Oxford.

153 GOLDMAN, p22.

154 Ibid, p25.

Oxford fellowship, and the two young graduates set about work in their environs of Whitechapel, then still one of the most notorious Victorian slums. In 1904 he was elected to a Jenkyns Exhibition, which provided him with a small income from Balliol, but a fellowship still eluded him. Harry remained at the CCHF for three years, a period which was to make a distinct impression upon him as he worked with and amongst the children of the East End, and they were to feature many times in his future campaigns. It was this same period, however, which provided him with his first opportunity to speak regularly on topics of social reform to adult audiences, to the 'Toynbee Hall Enquirers' Club', which met regularly and which Harry lectured on subjects such as 'British Political Institutions' and 'Social Aspects of Industry'[155]. It was experiences such as these which led him to believe that the teaching of economics was a valuable way in which he could contribute to the furthering of the working classes, and so in 1906 he took up the appointment of assistant to Professor William Smart. In 1909 he married Jeanette, William Beveridge's sister, and his old friend William Temple officiated at the marriage.

In the five years leading up to the outbreak of war it became ever more evident to Harry that there was an obvious problem with certain elements of British social reform, which did not in fact seek to reform society at all but only to resolve acute problems as they arose. Through his work since leaving Oxford he had become convinced that there existed differences between the working class in London and other places, such as Lancashire, where co-operatives, trade unions, friendly societies and educational institutions existed for the long-term good of their members. This was made most clear in his lecture 'Poverty is an Industrial Problem', given as his inaugural lecture as Director of the Ratan Tata Foundation[156], founded by an Indian businessman to analyse the causes of poverty and propose possible solutions.[157] It was for this appointment that he had left Glasgow, and from which he was to resign in favour of military service in November 1914.

---

155 Ibid, p27.
156 Founded by Sir Ratan Tata in 1912, with a donation to the University of London of £1,400 per year for three years.
157 ARMSTRONG & GRAY, 2016, Ch.3.2.

At the outbreak of war, therefore, Harry found himself as an established member of the University of London, and was torn between a variety of different priorities. At the same time he criticised both the forms of patriotism which can never last long in battle and the pacifism which does not consider the social and political conditions under which mankind is compelled to live. A war against the militaristic and oligarchic Germany that he saw and, he believed, had experienced on his visits there was an elemental part of the establishing of true social democracy in England. His balanced opinion was that if the country must fight, then so must he, and so he enlisted in the 22nd Battalion of the Manchester Regiment, raised by the lord mayor of the city, eschewing the conventions that expected the Rugby and Oxford educated Tawney to join up as an officer. Even so, he was quickly promoted to sergeant and after nine months in billets at Morecambe and Grantham the battalion moved to Larkhill Camp on Salisbury Plain to continue training. Finally the move to the front began and, having travelled by train from Amesbury to Folkestone that afternoon, the 22nd Manchesters landed at Boulogne at 1930 on the 11th November 1915, joining the 91st Brigade, 7th Division. As yet they remained untested in action, and received their first experience of trench life under the guidance of the Royal Irish Fusiliers, with companies rotating through the lines to shadow the more experienced Irish soldiers. It wasn't until the 1st February 1916 that they took over a section of the front line on their own, occupying Subsector C1, south of Mametz on the Somme, and the next day they received their first two casualties when two men were wounded and subsequently died. This life continued for a further six months, with regular casualties and patrols towards the enemy line. As a platoon sergeant Harry took a full part in this routine, but as the spring and summer of 1916 wore on it was clear that they were building towards a large-scale assault, preceded by a huge artillery bombardment of the enemy, and Harry wrote an account of the course of events for the *Westminster Gazette*. On the night before the attack Harry received communion from the chaplain, reciting the words by memory over the laughing and joking of the other soldiers and the rattling of rifle butts on a concrete floor. It was a beautiful evening, and almost possible to forget their destination as they lined up by companies at the edge of the wood, before moving off at 2130 for the front line. It took a good deal of time to get there, stopping every few yards as the machine gun section readjusted their heavy load, but in due course the battalion was lined up in the firing line in two rows, sleeping where they were, leaning against the revetments and each other. Harry found a shallow dugout and settled down to rest, happy that his new platoon commander, who had joined them only a week before, was sensible enough to leave the men to themselves.

On the morning of the 1st July 1916 the 22nd Manchesters were in their usual sector on the Somme, south of Mametz, but it was not a usual day. The sun rose on a glorious summer's morning, but the Manchesters had had little sleep as the artillery bombardment had grown little by little to its terrible crescendo. Harry was mesmerised by the experience, unlike any other:

> The sound was different, not only in magnitude, but in quality, from anything known to me. It was not a succession of explosions or a continuous roar; I, at least, never heard a gun or a bursting shell. It was not a noise; it was a symphony. It did not move; it hung over us. It was as though the air were full of a vast and agonised passion, bursting now into groans and sighs, now into shrill screams and pitiful whimpers, shuddering beneath terrible blows, torn by unearthly whips, vibrating with the solemn pulse of enormous wings. And the supernatural tumult did not pass in this direction or that. It did not begin, intensify, build and end. It was poised in the air, a stationary panorama of sound, a condition of the atmosphere, not the creation of man. It seemed that one had only to lift one's eyes to be appalled by the writhing of the tormented element above one, that a hand raised ever so little above the level of the trench would be sucked away into a whirlpool revolving with cruel and incredible velocity over infinite depths.[158]

The message came down the line – five minutes to go. Harry's company commander, a man for whom he had great respect, came to borrow a spare watch from him, and that was the last time that Harry ever saw him. At last the moment had come; 0730 on the 1st July 1916. Whistles blew and the Manchesters climbed the ladders into no-man's land.

---

158 TAWNEY R.H., 'The Attack' in *The Westminster Gazette*, August 1916.

XV platoon, B Company, of which Harry was platoon sergeant, was at the front, so they doubled through the gaps in the wire and threw themselves down in the mud until the line had formed on either side. At this stage the German troops were still sheltering from the British shelling, so there was an eerie calm, just for a few moments. The battalion had a long way to go – nine hundred yards past the right-hand edge of the village to the German line known as Danzig Alley – and so as they rose together they walked, rather than ran, towards their objective. It was now, after twenty-four hours of fear, of a dreadful sense that when under fire he might run away, or freeze, that Harry found that, on the contrary, he felt no fear at all, and instead strode confidently towards the enemy:

> Now I knew it was all right. I shouldn't be frightened and I shouldn't lose my head. Imagine the joy of that discovery! I felt quite happy and self-possessed. It wasn't courage. That, I imagine, is the quality of facing danger which one knows to be danger, of making one's spirit triumph over the bestial desire to live in this body. But I knew that I was in no danger. I knew I shouldn't be hurt; knew it positively, much more positively than I know most things I'm paid for knowing. I understood in a small way what Saint-Just meant when he told the soldiers who protested at his rashness that no bullet could touch the emissary of the Republic. And all the time, in spite of one's inner happiness, one was shouting the sort of thing that NCOs do shout and no one attends to: "Keep your extension"; "Don't bunch"; "Keep up on the left"[159]

Harry and the front line crossed the first three German lines, shelled almost beyond recognition, and tumbled into Danzig Alley. Injured men lay on the parapet but they hurriedly dug a firing step to return fire, while on their left flank the distant kilted figures of the 2nd Gordon Highlanders fought their way into the village of Mametz. It was here that Harry realised that they were late; three minutes had passed since the bombardment of the next line had ceased, and that delay had given the German soldiers a brief opportunity to emerge from their reinforced

---

159 Ibid.

dugouts and man their guns. With that at the forefront of his mind, Harry led the Manchesters on, and as they reached the top of a low ridge, 'The whole line dropped like one man, some dead and wounded, the rest taking instinctively to such cover as the ground offered.'[160] They Germans were emboldened by their success, and began to emerge from the trench, rifles raised, but the sight of the enemy raised an instinct in Harry of which, at any other time, he would have been thoroughly ashamed, yet at just that moment was all he could do; before the war he felt guilty at shooting birds, but now:

> Now it was a duty to shoot, and there was an easy target.
> For the Germans were brave men, as brave as lions. Some
> of them actually knelt -- one for a moment even stood -- on
> the top of their parapet, to shoot, within not much more
> than a hundred yards of us. It was insane. It seemed one
> couldn't miss them. Every man I fired at dropped, except
> one. Him, the boldest of the lost, I missed more than once.
> I was puzzled and angry. Three hundred years ago I should
> have tried a silver bullet. Not that I wanted to hurt him or
> anyone else. It was missing I hated. That's the beastliest
> thing in war, the damnable frivolity. One's like a merry,
> mischievous ape tearing up the image of God. When I read
> now the babble of journalists about the "sporting spirit of
> our soldiers", it makes me almost sick. God forgive us all!
> But then it was as I say.[161]

Men continued to fall around him; Harry looked down to see his former batman, whom he had sacked for laziness, looking almost asleep apart from the large hole of a bullet's exit wound in the back of his head. His best friend lay dead beside him. Their platoon commander, the young man who had left them to rest the night before, lay on his back in the mud, his face and hands marble-white as his chest heaved with the gasping breaths of his last moments. There was one officer left, a teenager really, in charge of the bloodied remnants of the battalion whom Harry gathered from among the corpses. As he crawled to their

---

160 Ibid.
161 Ibid.

left flank to check on their progress it seemed absurd to Harry that down in the mud everything felt almost calm, yet two feet above their heads the air was deadly. He returned towards the single officer, and noticing a group of soldiers further back, waved to them to come up. They didn't move. Not realising that they were dead Harry got up on his knees to wave again, and at that moment he was hit:

> I don't know what most men feel like when they're wounded. What I felt was that I had been hit by a tremendous iron hammer, swung by a giant of inconceivable strength, and then twisted with a sickening sort of wrench so that my head and back banged on the ground, and my feet struggled as though they didn't belong to me. For a second or two my breath wouldn't come. I thought – if that's the right word – "This is death", and hoped it wouldn't take long. By-and-by, as nothing happened, it seemed I couldn't be dying. When I felt the ground beside me, my fingers closed on the nose-cap of a shell. It was still hot, and I thought absurdly, in a muddled way, "this is what has got me". I tried to turn on my side, but the pain, when I moved, was like a knife, and stopped me dead. There was nothing to do but lie on my back.[162]

Unable to crawl, Harry lay waiting for death or the dark, whichever came first, as the German heavy artillery opened up from behind their lines. Having lost his watch, and emptied his water bottle, he lay in the hot sun and tried to guess the time, but as he had been hit at about 8am it was to be a long time before he might be found. He drifted in and out of consciousness, and, in the light of the July evening, realised that a man was standing beside him, and that it was an RAMC corporal. Harry grabbed his ankle, and his shouts brought a medical officer. He was found:

> He can't have been more than twenty-six or twenty-seven; but his face seemed to shine with love and comprehension, not of one's body only, but of one's soul, and with the joy of spending freely a wisdom and goodness drawn from

---

162 Ibid.

inexhaustible sources. He listened like an angel while I told him a confused, nonsensical yarn about being hit in the back by a nose-cap. Then he said I had been shot with a rifle-bullet through the chest and abdomen, put a stiff bandage round me, and gave me morphia.[163]

To Harry the young medical officer was the paradigm of divine compassion, and he felt nothing but adoration for what he did. It was only later that he realised that the way in which he was treated probably meant that they thought he had little hope of survival. The 22nd Manchesters lost more than fifty per cent of their strength that morning, with 18 officers and 472 men killed or wounded. They stayed in the occupied line until relieved on the 5th July, but by that time Harry was far from the front, in hospital. Harry Tawney's war was over.

As his injuries meant that he could not return to the front, Harry returned to his academic career, and was finally elected to a fellowship at Balliol in 1918, as well as continuing to lecture at LSE. That gave him an excellent foundation upon which to build his post-war academic career, which flourished for a further forty years; after resigning his fellowship in 1931 he served as Professor of Economic History at LSE until 1949, and during his career he received honorary doctorates from no less than eight different universities. He died aged 81 on the 16th January 1962 and is buried in Highgate Cemetery, but Harry Tawney's legacy lives on in many areas of modern British academia and government: 'In effective intellectual terms it is doubtful whether anyone else had remotely comparable influence in the evolution of British society in his generation.'[164]

---

163 Ibid.
164 HASTINGS, 1991, p184.

Captain Percy Hugh Lyon MC (Stanley)

Hugh Lyon was born in Darjeeling, where his father was serving in the Indian civil service, on the 14th October 1893. His father, also Percy, had a distinguished career before returning to England to take up the position of Bursar of Oriel College, Oxford, but Hugh's early childhood was one of colonial comfort, rudely interrupted at the age of 9. It was then that he was sent to England for his education, arriving at the Neo-Gothic Bilton Grange in Dunchurch just outside Rugby in 1902. His uncle Herbert was a member of staff, which can only have helped him to feel at home, and the young Hugh was soon thriving in all elements of school life; he won academic prizes in Classics, Mathematics, English, French and General Knowledge, and the acting skill which had first become apparent at his Darjeeling kindergarten was once more at the fore. A review in the school magazine of the French farce *L'Avocat Patelin*, in which Hugh played the title role, described his as 'by far the best performance, showing real thought and careful study in pronunciation, elocution and acting; in fact as good a piece of boy's acting as our stage has produced. Patelin was a Frenchman to his fingertips and never forgot it.'[165] Further successes followed, and by the time Hugh won a scholarship to Rugby in 1907 he was both head of school and captain of the cricket XI.

Hugh joined Steele's house (now Stanley), and again, as at prep school, it is the breadth of his talents which is most striking. By 1912 he was head of house, secretary to the debating society, a sergeant in the OTC, and represented the school at cricket and running. His oratory was well-known throughout the school, an example of which features in a letter sent by 14-year-old Louis Stokes[166] (School House) to his father on the 26th November 1911. It shows both the persuasiveness and humour evident in his conversation:

> The motion was that this house envies the state of a savage. It was lost by 68-37. I voted against it. There were some quite good speeches. Lyon, Head of Steele's, was best. He is

---

165 WRIGHT & LYON, 1993, p10.

166 Louis Stokes, as a second lieutenant in the Royal Marine Light Infantry, was killed at Beaumont Hamel on the 13th November 1916. His letters and other effects are preserved in the school archives.

awfully good. The point of the proposers was that a savage had no troubles such as getting up for the 1st lesson, could wander into the woods and pick peaches etc, had the fun of killing his dinner, or having his child when he couldn't kill ought else. The opposition replied that when the savage was picking peaches, an ichthysaurus might walk round the corner and pick him. Also, his children might be shot. Besides, a savage would not appreciate the fun of sitting outside a wigwam etc, and if he couldn't kill his dinner he went without.

Hugh's academic life at school was also exemplary, and passing both the School and Higher Certificates with distinction meant that he was offered a classical exhibition at Oriel College, Oxford. When two years later he achieved a second class in Mods he was very much disappointed and, though he had intended to continue on to Greats and a degree, when war was declared that summer he immediately left Oxford to join the army.

The 20-year-old Hugh Lyon was commissioned as a second lieutenant in the 6th Battalion of the Durham Light Infantry, joining his new unit at Gateshead, though they soon moved to billets in Bensham, which he described in his diary as 'a particularly unattractive suburb of Newcastle... an unsavoury district of dingy streets and drab houses.' The officers' billets came in for particularly scathing comment. Another unit training in the same area was the Green Howards, and Hugh bumped into his former fag from Steele's, Arthur 'Jock' Richardson, who was also serving as a second lieutenant. The happy reunion was to be short-lived however, as Jock died of meningitis in his Newcastle billet on the 4th January 1915[167], but it was still to have a great effect on Hugh's life. He decided to offer his sympathy by visiting the Richardson family at their Guisborough home, and it was there that he met Nan, Jock's younger sister who at the time was recuperating from appendicitis. She made an impression on Hugh, who returned shortly afterwards for a second visit, and though her parents were not particularly keen to encourage him at first, the couple were finally married in 1920.

At 0815 on the 16th April 1915, the 6th DLI finally left Newcastle by train and, crossing from Folkestone to Boulogne, arrived in France.

---

167 Memorials of Rugbeians who Fell in the Great War.

Six days later they reached the Ypres Salient, and on the 24th they had their first experience of enemy fire as the battalion marched into the centre of the town:

> It entered the town as night settled on it. At this date the town was not ruined and the results of shelling were hardly noticeable. As the Battalion was passing the Cloth Hall a shell came screaming faintly towards it, and passing over, burst with a dull roar in the city a quarter of a mile away. There had been no talking in the ranks nor any sound except the beat of ammunition boots on the pavé, but when this shell screamed overhead and burst, ejaculation in the good old Durham tongue could be heard passing cheerily up the length of the column. Two or three more shells passed over, but none burst near the Battalion.[168]

The battalion suffered much in its first experience of combat: in one week sixteen officers, including two company commanders, and approximately three hundred other ranks were killed, wounded, or were laid low by illness.[169]

Hugh served as a platoon commander in D Company, which suited him well, but it wasn't to last; in May he was sent on a bombing course at Vlamertinghe, and then took up the appointment of Brigade Bombing Officer. This kept him from the front line, and his diaries became more sporadic in such a 'busy but sheltered life'[170] but in November he moved again, this time back to the battalion at Mount Sorrel, as adjutant. Such an administrative task suited Hugh's strengths, and allowed him close contact with all ranks of the battalion, many of whom were Durham miners who had joined up in the first weeks of the war, whom he described in his diary as '…some of the finest fighters the country possesses… They possess a power of endurance and a courageous spirit, very admirable in adversity.'[171] After a few days' rest in billets and lots of inter-platoon and brigade league football

---

168 AINSWORTH, 1919, p10.
169 LYON P.H.B., Unpublished diary, Durham Record Office: D/DLI 7/424/2.
170 WRIGHT & LYON, p19.
171 Ibid, p15.

matches in Poperinghe[172], the battalion took over the front line at the Bluff sector, south-east of Ypres, where the numerous bodies requiring burial and heavily damaged trenches spoke of recent attention by the enemy. Again the moved was to be short lived, as in early December Hugh injured his knee playing football, and the battalion war diary for the 8th records, 'Lt P. H. B. Lyon granted sick leave to England. 2 Lieut C. E. Yaldwyn temporarily appointed Adjutant.'[173]

Hugh's return to England meant that he was away from the front line for twenty-one months, firstly in hospital, and then with a reserve battalion and officer cadet battalion. Also during this time he continued to write poetry, a long-standing habit; indeed a volume of his work, *Songs of Youth and War*[174], was published in 1918, and when he returned to Oxford after the war Hugh won the 1919 Newdigate Prize for his poem 'France'. Some of his work was a little more light-hearted, and in 1918 Boosey and Hawkes published a song he had written, *Company Sergeant Major,* set to music by Wilfrid Sanderson and sung in a popular recording by Harry Dearth. In 1917 he returned to Belgium and to the front, but by luck was on leave in England when the German Spring Offensive began in March 1918, and in the following month was both mildly wounded by a falling timber and was awarded the Military Cross, but soon his war was, in effect, to end. On the 27th May the battalion was stationed near the Chemin des Dames and was taken entirely by surprise by the German army's Operation Blücher, the beginning of the Third Battle of the Aisne, resulting in the capture of Hugh and several of his men, most of them wounded. They had found themselves cut off by the swift German advance and Hugh, though horrified at the prospect of being a prisoner of war, had no choice but to surrender. He wrote in his diary:

> The wounded men were shouting at me to surrender, and indeed I saw nothing else for it, so I just stood up and in a minute we were prisoners… The shame of that moment has proved ineffaceable. I suppose that every man taken in battle

---

172 The battalion war diaries give the impression that the DLI were particularly keen on football.

173 WO95/2840/2.

174 LYON, *Songs of Youth and War*, 1918.

must feel that smart of indignation and remorse, for every such man has deliberately chosen life before freedom. And such a choice, even in the most desperate conditions, is a falling off from the ideal (so often in men's mouths) of 'resistance to the last shot and the last man!' For myself, I only know that it seemed inevitable, and that in similar circumstances I should almost certainly do the same again. It may be a taint of cowardice or merely an unheroic common sense.[175]

The march east was long and dull, though tempered by the arrival of spring, and in due course they arrived at an officers' prisoner of war camp at Graudenz[176] in Poland. The camp was well-appointed, and in his diary Hugh speaks about the excellence of the beds and the well-stocked library. The only real challenge was the terrible quality of the food, but it was 1918 and the food with which they were met was nothing worse than that endured by German civilians at the time, since years of blockade had caused widespread malnutrition amongst the population. Before too long, however, parcels began to arrive from home, significantly alleviating that concern. Time was otherwise spent walking, reading, playing many games of bridge and organising concert parties, but in a few months rumours trickling in from the outside world began to encourage Hugh and his fellow prisoners, as the allied forces advanced towards and then beyond the Hindenburg Line. The rumours became more and more convincing, and on the 10th November it became known not only that a German delegation was meeting with Marshal Foch, but also that later that day the German soldiers in the town had replaced the imperial eagles in their caps with red cockades. When the Armistice was signed the following day, the prisoners heard, and Hugh wrote in his diary,

> ...the Armistice appears to have been at last signed, and all we really know about it is that it provides for the immediate return of Allied prisoners. The feeling here is absolutely indescribable. It is like a dream come true.[177]

---

175 WRIGHT & LYON, p22.

176 Now the Polish city of Grudziadz, Graudenz had been ruled by Prussia since the First Partition of Poland in 1772.

177 Ibid, p24.

It was, tragically, at that moment that Spanish 'flu arrived in the camp, and the death of four officers felt like a terrible blow when they were so close to returning home, but eventually trains were organised to take them to Danzig, where they boarded the Danish hospital ship *Mitau*[178], and after a somewhat circuitous journey they woke on the morning of the 18th December 1918 to see the Scottish coast on the horizon.

Hugh was home, and set out to re-establish his civilian life. He returned to Oriel where we gained a first class degree, and in August 1920 he fulfilled his long-held wish of marrying Nan at her home parish church of St Nicholas, Guisborough. With the war over he needed some form of employment, and with an excellent degree behind him he turned to teaching, and so wrote to his old tutor, and friend of many others mentioned in this book, H.H. Hardy, who had recently been appointed headmaster of Cheltenham College[179]. He was offered an appointment, but only remained at Cheltenham for five years before being appointed the youngest public school headmaster of the day, as Rector of Edinburgh Academy, where he again spent five years.

It was in 1931 that Hugh was approached by a group of governors from Rugby to ask if he might allow his name to be considered for the appointment of the new Head Master upon the retirement of William Vaughan that year. His first response was that he couldn't possibly run against H.H. Hardy, but was assured that he wasn't being considered, as at 50 he was considered too old! Hugh was not yet 40, and though he offered to remain at Edinburgh, the chairman of the governors, Lord Murray[180], felt that he couldn't deny Hugh the possibility of returning to his old school as head master, and Hugh was duly appointed and arrived at School House in time for the Advent term. His headmastership was one of distinction; the longest serving since Dr Arnold himself, Hugh could have been remembered as one of the great builders of the school's history, had his ambitions not been curtailed by the outbreak of another war. As it is, following the opening of Sheriff House in the year before his appointment, Hugh continued the trend for modernisation by building Kilbracken House on the site of Hillbrow Prep School (which had been attended by Rupert Brooke, as well as many other staff sons), and the

---

178 Formerly *Arundel Castle* (until 1905) and *Birma* (until 1914), the *Mitau* was again renamed, as *Josef Pildudski*, in 1921 and was scrapped in Italy in 1924.

179 Headmaster of Cheltenham College 1919-32.

180 Rt Hon Charles David Murray, Lord Murray CMG PC KC DL FRSE, 1866-1936.

new Sanatorium on Hillmorton Road, which was visited by HRH the Prince of Wales on 3rd July 1934. Other changes were afoot, with the traditional black uniform coats being changed to those made of tweed, worn with grey flannels, but the events of September 1939 put an end to any further innovation. Air-raid shelters were constructed in houses, with gas decontamination centres in the gymnasium and the James Pavilion. One-way systems of pedestrian traffic were adopted on Barby Road and around the Close to stop collisions between boys in the black-out, and fire-watching rotas were drawn up, manned by boys on the roof of the school and on top of the large water tower on Ashlawn Road, from where the Coventry Blitz could clearly be seen on the night of the 14th November 1940. Sir John Osborn, later MP for Hallam[181], was on duty that night on the roof of Sheriff House, and Hugh himself stayed on the roof of School House until the last bomber had departed, fixed in horror at the sight.

With the arrival of peace in 1945 Hugh was tired; still only in his early fifties he had achieved much as headmaster, but the strain of war and its consequent losses could not be avoided. In April 1944 he entirely forgot about his own daughter's wedding, which had happened only a week before, and an unknown Chinese man arrived for lunch one day in School House, apparently invited during the black-out in Stratford, though Hugh had no memory of the affair. In 1948 he was therefore ready to pass the reins of the school to another, and Sir Arthur fforde was appointed by the governing body. To leave School House, even under such circumstances, was a blow to the man who had led the school safely through some of the hardest years of its existence, but at first settled into a somewhat quiet early retirement. He had hoped to become Master of an Oxford college[182], but stayed on as head master until after he had been chairman of the Headmasters' Conference, and at that time no such positions were available. Two years later Hugh was appointed director of the Public Schools Appointments Bureau, work to which he was devoted during his retirement at Amberley, Gloucestershire. His life slowed significantly after Nan's death in 1970, but Hugh remarried in 1973, to Biddy, and died quietly at home on the 18th January 1986, aged 92. A great memorial service was held in the chapel at Rugby. Almost forty years after he retired as head master the school still had much to thank him for.

---

181 1959-87.
182 WRIGHT & LYON, p78.

Captain Charles Cruttwell (School House)

Charles Robert Mowbray Fraser Cruttwell was a historian, a soldier and a writer, but has the dubious fortune to be remembered primarily as the target of a long-standing vendetta by the novelist Evelyn Waugh. He was born in Denton, Norfolk, on the 23rd May 1887, the eldest son of the village's Rector, also Charles Cruttwell, and at the time of his death his grandfather, Sir John Mowbray, was one of two Members of Parliament to represent the University of Oxford.[183] Charles's father was also a Roman scholar of some note, and before his son's birth he had been a Fellow of Merton College, Oxford, and headmaster of both Bradfield and Malvern College. Though the elder Charles had been a scholar of the Merchant Taylor's School, London, he sent his three sons to Rugby, where Charles was a contemporary of Rupert Brooke, though Rupert was not particularly impressed with their acquaintance:

> Last week I dined with H.A.J. & sat next to Cruttwell. We conversed…amicably about A. Beardsley, whom Crutters disliked. I said that I adored Beardsley because he caricatured Humanity, & I was amused by caricatures of Humanity. As I spoke I beamed on him, but he did not grasp the insult: he was merely impressed, & bit his nails in wonder and perplexity.[184]

It was from here in 1906 that Charles won a scholarship to The Queen's College, Oxford, where he achieved a considerable amount of academic success, not least in receiving first class results in Classical Moderations, Greats and Modern History. It was quite clear that he was at the beginning of an impressive academic career, and in 1911 he received a prize fellowship to All Souls, a much coveted honour, followed in 1912 by a lectureship in History at Hertford College. At the declaration of war in August 1914, Charles was an established junior Fellow with a great deal of promise, but he was also an individual of the age and social background that would very much be expected to apply for a commission

---

183 These two constituencies were abolished in 1950, by the Representation of the People Act 1948.
184 KEYNES, 1967, p39.

in the armed forces. That he did, following his brother into the 1/4th Battalion of the Royal Berkshire Regiment, the same battalion as Ronald Poulton-Palmer, who had been two years his junior at Rugby, indeed as lieutenants they were both appointed to D Company. With Ronnie and the rest of the battalion he embarked, 'amidst many expressions of goodwill and regret from the townsfolk, who thronged the streets',[185] at Folkestone and sailed for Boulogne at 11.40pm on the 31st March 1915. Charles was present at Ploegsteert Wood when Ronnie was killed on the night of the 4th May; he had watched him play his last Rugby match at Pont de Nieppe three weeks week earlier. In general, however, Charles found life in the trenches at Ploegsteert much more tolerable than he had feared, perhaps prepared by a life up to that point entirely lived in conservative institutions. He wrote of the conditions after the war:

> The actual routine of life in the trenches was pleasant enough. The men knew exactly where they were. There was a time to eat, a time to sleep, a time for fatigues, and a time for sentry-go. There was little rain, and no bitter nights. The shelters, which held two or three men a-piece, though mere flimsy shell-traps, were comfortable, and either boarded or lined with straw, which was frequently renewed. When the Warwicks took over from us they exclaimed in admiring surprise, 'Why, they're all officers' dugouts.' Each section had its little oven made of a biscuit tin built round with clay. For the officers' mess in D Company we had the kitchen range from Anton's Farm, and a large zinc-covered erection in which six people could eat or play cards at once. The domestic element was supplied by two cats, who safely reared their offspring among us. Indeed, the calm of that placid series of days was such that it was difficult to realise that the second Battle of Ypres was raging with unbroken ferocity a few miles to the north, until we listened to the unwearied rumble of the guns and saw by night the great light in the sky where the doomed city blazed.[186]

---

185 CRUTTWELL, 1922, Ch.2.
186 Ibid, Ch.3.

The lack of sleep was of greater irritation to Charles, however, particularly since the quietness of the enemy meant that he found it entirely unnecessary, but the battalion war diaries of that summer, after the battalion moved south to relieve the French at Hébuterne, make it clear why he was feeling such fatigue. He is regularly named as the officer leading patrols into no man's land at night, often returning to their own line at 3 or 4am; for example, on the 1st September Charles led a patrol right up to the German front line at 3am, examining saps and trip-wires, and only returning at 4.10am when conversation in the trench made it clear that they had been noticed and the enemy were standing to.[187]

Hébuterne was a heavily fortified village, whose dozen or so remaining buildings were used for billets because a slight rise in the ground protected them from direct fire, and Charles was distinctly impressed by the quality of the trenches that he inherited from the departing soldiers. In particular, the clay and chalk soil meant that trenches and dugouts could be much deeper than at Ploegsteert, and consequently much more elaborate. The Berkshires used bricks from shelled houses in the village to provide solid floors, and even appropriated furniture; though not every element of life in a dugout was as comfortable as it could be:

> One of those which I inhabited contained a mattress, two chairs, a table, a large gilt-framed mirror, some artificial flowers, a portrait of the Czar and his wife, and an engraving called 'Le Repos du Marin,' which depicted an old sailor drinking peacefully under a tree. All would have been well but for the small game; lice, a legacy from the French, enormous red slugs, which ate any food which lay about, and left a viscous trail behind every movement, countless swarms of mice and gigantic rats, some of which were so bold as to gnaw through the men's haversacks, as they slept, in search of the food contained therein.[188]

Regardless of the comforts available, the patrols continued, and on the 14th October Charles led a patrol out from a sap, and proceeded four hundred yards towards the German defences of Gommecourt.

---

187 WO95/2762/1.
188 CRUTTWELL, 1922, Ch.5.

There they were challenged, and in thick fog attacked by two German patrols at a distance of only twenty yards; they returned fire and threw their bombs, but were extremely lucky to return without casualties, though a Private Knapp had to wait alone in a shell hole until 6am when the fog lifted and he could return to his own line.[189] Though Charles found trench life more comfortable than he had expected, it was having a deleterious effect on his health; his rheumatic myalgia, with which he had suffered in the past, was intensifying. In the new year of 1916 he returned home on leave, and at the end of the month he attended a medical board to decide his future in the battalion. Their conclusion was that he was not fit to return. Between that time and August 1917 he was regularly reassessed, and when it was finally concluded that his condition would not improve enough to allow him to return to front line service he was instead employed as an instructor with the 4th Officer Cadet Battalion, in Oxford. In April 1918, making good use of his intellectual abilities, Charles was sent to assist H.W.V. Temperley[190] in MIE2, an intelligence department of the War Office. Here he remained until he resigned his commission 'on account of ill health contracted on active service [on] 17th April 1919' [191], when he was finally able to return to Oxford and to his teaching duties at Hertford in time for the beginning of the new academic year, the first of a new peacetime era.

Charles was probably expecting, indeed hoping, to settle into a long period of research and teaching, uninterrupted by trouble and the worries of the preceding four years, but it wasn't too long until he was to meet the young man who was to devote a great deal of time and effort to making Charles's life unhappy, and whom many believe contributed to his early death. His resettlement began positively. In 1920 he was appointed Dean of Hertford, and two years later published a wartime history of his late battalion[192], but on the morning of the 15th December 1921 a young man on the south coast received two letters. One informed him that he had been

---

189 WO95/2762/1.
190 Professor Harold W.V. Temperley OBE FBA (1879-1939) was Professor of Modern History at Cambridge University from 1931 and Master of Peterhouse from July 1938 until his death almost exactly a year later. He also founded *The Cambridge Historical Journal* in 1923.
191 WO 374/17060.
192 CRUTTWELL, 1922, Ch.5.

awarded a £100 scholarship to Hertford College, and the other was a letter of congratulations from the Dean, Charles Cruttwell[193] – the young man was Evelyn Waugh, at that time a somewhat precocious sixth former at Lancing College in Sussex. As Waugh was to read History it was inevitable that Charles should tutor him, but the differences between the two men became apparent very soon after they first met. They only lived and worked in close proximity for three years (1922-24), but the immature Waugh was not able to contain his contempt for his tutor, who suffered from Waugh's attacks intermittently until his death fifteen years after the writer left Oxford. The principal difference between them was the war itself. Charles represented everything that Waugh rejected about the previous age and its survivors: his youthful optimism saw the war as an unnecessary folly that his own generation would surely have avoided, and Charles's earnestness, born as much out of the experience of Flanders and the Somme as of an Edwardian schooling, clashed inevitably with the aestheticism of Harold Acton[194] and Bryan Howard[195] which Waugh tried, if unsuccessfully, to emulate as an undergraduate. Throughout Waugh's first year at Hertford it also became increasingly clear that he saw his scholarship as a reward for his hard work at school, whereas the college saw it as a sign of promise to come. The feud between the two men had hardened by the end of the academic year[196] and the following term Waugh wrote a short story for *Cherwell*[197], called *Edward of Unique Achievement*, about a History undergraduate who murders his sexually deviant tutor, Mr Curtis.[198] Waugh made similar insinuations about his own tutor at every opportunity (including leaving a stuffed dog under his study window and barking in the quad at night). Charles made no public response to Waugh's provocation, beyond referring to him as 'a silly suburban sod with an inferiority complex'[199], but it was to be harder to brush off the published attacks of a popular author than the childish jokes of an uncertain undergraduate.

---

193 DAVIE, 1979, p152-3.
194 1904-94. Acton and Howard were the two principal models for the characters of Sebastian Flyte and Anthony Blanche in *Brideshead Revisited*.
195 1905-58.
196 WAUGH, *A Little Learning*, 1983, p175.
197 An undergraduate newspaper in Oxford.
198 CARPENTER, 1989, p124.
199 BYRNE, 2010, p50.

Waugh left Hertford without a degree, and with a note from Charles Cruttwell expressing his disappointment, but that wasn't to be the end of their relationship. Though they probably never met again, Waugh included a variety of unsavoury characters in many of his books by the name of Cruttwell. In his first novel, *Decline and Fall* (1928), Toby Cruttwell is a psychopathic burglar, in *Vile Bodies* (published in 1930, the same year that Charles was elected Principal of Hertford) he is a particularly unpleasant MP, in *Black Mischief* an irritating social climber and in *A Handful of Dust* (1934) he appears as a suspicious 'bone-setter'. It began to appear that Waugh couldn't publish a book without using it as an opportunity to denigrate his former tutor. *Mr Loveday's Little Outing* (1935), about the dark deeds of an accidentally released murderer, was originally entitled *Mr Cruttwell's Little Outing*. In his 1938 publication *Scoop*, the name is given to a tragic fake-tanned salesman in the Army and Navy Stores known as General Cruttwell, and finally, in the 1939 short story *An Englishman's Home*, he appears as an embezzling scout master. In 1935, to get in an extra attack between publications, Waugh told a survey which asked novelists to nominate their best work that his had yet to be written, but that it would be

> ...the memorial biography of C. R. M. F. Cruttwell, some time Dean of Hertford College, Oxford, and my old history tutor. It is a labour of love to one to whom, under God, I owe everything.[200]

It is significant that Waugh's attacks ended in 1939, as in that year Charles stood down as President of Hertford; his physical health had never entirely recovered from the war, and his mental health had begun to suffer too. Waugh, who had once said about the affair '...one must have someone to persecute'[201], may have considered that his task was complete. Shortly after Charles's resignation he was confined to a mental hospital near Bristol, where he died on the 14th March 1941, aged 53.

Charles Cruttwell was a historian of note, and an authoritative writer on the histories of the Rhineland and the Great War, so it is unfortunate that in recent decades Waugh's published works have achieved his aim

---

200 PATEY, 1998, p366.
201 HOLLIS, 1976, p86.

of ensuring that he is remembered as a comic figure. Indeed subsequent generations of the Waugh family have done their best to drive home the nails in the coffin lid of his reputation.[202] He was certainly, at times, a forceful, stubborn and indeed rebarbative figure, but one who was often goaded into such positions, upon his return from the war, by the new generation of undergraduates who saw such individuals as outdated examples of an old order whose time had passed. Perhaps more than anything else he was a nervous and uncertain man, who lived his life in the shadow of others, uncertain of how to respond except through the quality of his scholarship.

---

202 WAUGH A., *Fathers and Sons*, 2004, pp175-180.

Right: The Cap badge of Rugby School Officer Training Corps.

Below: The Rugby OTC summer camp of 1907.

Left: Rupert Brooke and Claude Evers as Rugby OTC officers. Evers was tutor to Ronald Poulton Palmer in School House.

Below: Rugby OTC Cyclist Company under the command of Lt Costley-White, 1908.

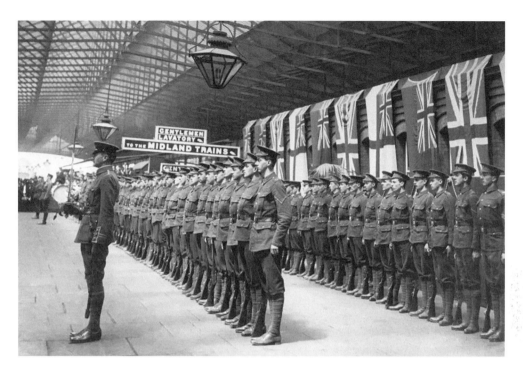

Above: Rugby OTC awaits the arrival of HM King Edward VII, 3rd July 1909.

Below: Kit Inspection, summer camp 1913.

Above: The victorious Rugby team at the 1913 Public Schools Snap Shooting Competition.

Below: Rugby cadets on exercise, 1914.

Above: The Rugby School shooting team in New Quad, 1914.

Below: The 'Special Class' of boys intending to join the army, 1914.

Above left: The grave crosses of Rupert Brooke and his brother Alfred, relocated to the Memorial Chapel at Rugby.

Above right: 2Lt Donald Hankey.

Left: Capt Frederick C. Selous DSO.

Capt Frederick H. B. Selous MC.

The memorial to F. H. B.
Selous in the Natural History
Museum.

Left: Maj Gen Sir Ernest Swinton KBE CB DSO.

Below: The Tank Mk.1, developed under the influence of Ernest Swinton.

Right: Lt Col Jasper Richardson, the oldest British serviceman to be killed in the war.

Below: The Rugby OTC Annual Inspection, 1917.

Above: Rugby OTC Band on parade in 1917.

Left: Revd Mr Rupert Inglis CF.

Above left: Ronald Poulton Palmer on the pitch.

Above right: Lt Ronald Poulton Palmer.

Right: The grave cross of Ronald Poulton Palmer, relocated to Holywell Cemetery in Oxford.

Above left: Pte Kenneth Powell of the HAC.

Above right: Duncan Mackinnon at Oxford.

Left: Adrian Stoop as a Cadet Serjeant at Rugby.

Above: Rugby OTC parading on the Close, 1917.

Below: The officers of Rugby School OTC, 1917.

Left: Charles Cruttwell, Dean of Hertford College Oxford.

Below: The officers of D Company, 1/4th Bn Royal Berkshire Regiment, including Ronald Poulton Palmer (back left) and Charles Cruttwell (front left). Ronald was killed less than a week after this photograph was taken. (Courtesy of R. van Emden)

Right: Lt Frank Lucas.

Below: Capt and Adjt
P. H. B. Lyon in the trenches.
(Durham Records Office)

Left: Harry Tawney serving as
a Corporal in the Manchester
Regiment.

Below: The Rugby OTC Annual
Inspection, 1918.

Above left: Capt the Hon Oswald Cawley MP.

Above right: Capt Harold Cawley MP.

Maurice Hankey, Cabinet Secretary.

Above left: Sir Austen Chamberlain KG.

Above right: Lt Col Christopher Bushell VC DSO.

Left: Lt Geoffrey Cather VC.

Right: The grave of Lt Frank De Pass VC, in Bethune Communal Cemetery.

Below left: Lt Frank De Pass VC.

Below right: Lt Robert Vaughan Gorle VC.

Capt John Norwood VC of
the 5th Dragoon Guards.

John Norwood as a 17 year old
cadet at Rugby.

The Battle of Jutland depicted in a Rugby window.

The Retreat from Mons depicted in a Rugby window.

The figure of Lt Wilfred Littleboy, 16th Bn Royal Warwickshire Regiment, atop the lectern given by his parents in his memory in Rugby School Memorial Chapel.

A depiction of 2Lt Henry Gair in the school window donated by his parents.

But as for me, I will behold thy presence in righteousness: and when I awake up after thy likeness, I shall be satisfied with it.

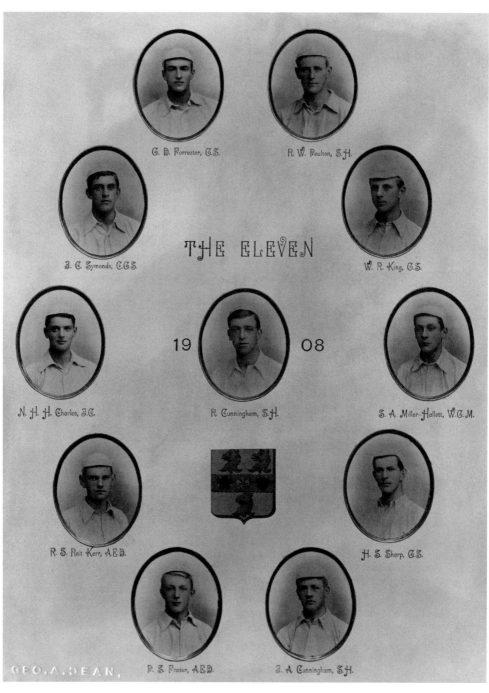

The Rugby School Cricket XI of 1908, including Ronald Poulton (later Poulton Palmer). (Rugby Public Library)

POLITICS &
RELIGION

Sir Austen Chamberlain (Cotton)

Today Joseph Austen Chamberlain is often forgotten in the shadow of his half-brother's declaration of war on Germany in 1939, but though both Neville and Austen attended Rugby, it was the latter who was of much greater influence on British politics during and immediately after the Great War.

Austen and Neville were both sons of the influential, if populist, Mayor of Birmingham Sir Joseph Chamberlain, who dominated many elements of British politics in the later nineteenth century. Austen's mother Harriet died in childbirth when he was born on the 16th October 1863, and the horror of her loss had a great impact on his father, who struggled to identify with his eldest son. It was many years later when Austen's father spoke to him about another man whose wife had died in similar circumstances, and he realised "…for the first time, what he had so carefully concealed from me, that in my earliest years I had been to him the living embodiment of the first tragedy of his life." [203] Sir Joseph sought solace with his late wife's family at their home in Edgbaston, where Austen spent the first five years of his life, and his father eventually married his first wife's cousin, but Austen himself was sent to a distant prep school in Brighton, where he was far from happy under the regime of the somewhat authoritarian Mr Hanbury. At the age of 14 however, he proceeded to Rugby, where he joined the house of Henry Lee-Warner (now Cotton), an Old Rugbeian himself who had been a classical scholar at St John's College, Cambridge, and soon became a great favourite of the house. In due course he became head of house, and continued to be a great friend of his former housemaster for many years, writing in 1923, "I owe him an immense debt, for he made the happiness and the interest of my Rugby days and did more for my education in the full sense of the word than any man except father." [204] It was with his son's housemaster that Joseph Chamberlain, now a Member of Parliament, intervened when the Head Master, Dr Jex-Blake, intended to beat the teenaged Austen for a minor infringement of the school's rules, but a threat to remove him from the school altogether successfully countered

---

203 PETRIE, 1938, p130.
204 CHAMBERLAIN, 1995, p220.

the usually benevolent Head Master[205]. Austen made an equally lasting impression on his masters, and Lee-Warner himself later said that he had never parted with a pupil as reluctantly as when Austen left to read History at Trinity College, Cambridge, in 1882.[206]

At Cambridge Austen's interest in politics began to more clearly emerge than it had at Rugby, and he served as vice-president of the Cambridge Union Society. His father noted this interest and from that moment supported Austen's nascent political career wherever possible; consequently, upon graduating from Trinity he was sent to the Paris Institute of Political Studies for nine months, where he developed a life-long admiration for the French people, and during which he dined with several future prime ministers of France, such as Georges Clemenceau and Alexandre Ribot. The third great political power to be grasped in Europe was Germany, and so after Paris Austen spent a year at the University of Berlin, where he dined with Bismarck, but his letters clearly show a preference for the life he had left behind in Paris. In addition to the social opportunities, Austen quickly developed a suspicion of the Prussian school of history which was developing in the German capital's universities, and which showed to him a somewhat sinister element of his host country, particularly in the lectures of Heinrich von Treitschke, who "…opened to me a new side of the German character – a narrow-minded, proud, intolerant Prussian chauvinism."[207] In 1888 he returned to England and was prepared for parliamentary service by his father; he was elected unopposed to the constituency of East Worcestershire[208] in March 1892, representing his father's Liberal Unionist party. Though he was escorted into the House of Commons for the first time by both his father and uncle, he was initially prevented from making his maiden speech by the general election of August that year, and was not able to do so until April 1893, when his efforts were lauded by the Prime Minister, Gladstone, even though he was speaking against Gladstone's own Second Home Rule Bill.

Swift promotion followed; Austen was appointed junior whip in the wake of the general election, before appointment as Civil Lord of the

---

205 DUTTON, 1985, p14.
206 ELLETSON, 1966, p96.
207 BURNS, 2006, p19.
208 Abolished in 1918.

Admiralty only two years later, as Financial Secretary to the Treasury in 1900, and Postmaster General and membership of the Privy Council in 1902. But it was in 1903 that Austen first reached one of the great offices of state, with his appointment as Chancellor of the Exchequer by Prime Minister Arthur Balfour on the 9th October, as a compromise candidate between the entrenched positions of his father Joseph and Balfour himself over the problem of tariff reform. Such glory was not to last, however, as Balfour took his party into opposition in December 1905 in the face of mounting Liberal pressure and growing tensions within his own party. The general election of 1906 left Austen as one of the few remaining Liberal Unionist MPs, but he continued to serve as his party grew closer once again to the Tories as the decade came to a close, and it was at this point, following Balfour's departure from the leadership in November 1911, that his chance at leadership came. It was a great reflection upon Austen's character, therefore, that he withdrew from the competition to replace Balfour as leader of the Tory Party, convincing his main rival to do the same in favour of compromise candidate Andrew Bonar Law, who was to serve as Prime Minister a decade later. At the outbreak of war in August 1914 Austen remained in opposition against the seemingly secure Liberal government of H.H. Asquith, though now representing West Birmingham, but the failure of the Gallipoli campaign and the 'Shell Crisis' of 1915 prompted the emergence of the coalition government, still led by Asquith, on the 25th May 1915. Austen was appointed Secretary of State for India and returned to the Cabinet, but Asquith's position of power was increasingly untenable, not least because of the undermining tactics of his Minister of War, David Lloyd George.

In December 1916 the perhaps inevitable happened, and the King invited Lloyd George to form a new coalition government in consequence of the great losses suffered under Asquith. Austen continued to serve in the India Office, and from this position in Whitehall was able to exert considerable influence on the affairs of government; in particular, with Lord Curzon he supported the British military presence in Mesopotamia, principally to maintain respect for British influence in the area, thereby discouraging a German-supported Muslim rebellion in north-western India.[209] The Mesopotamian Campaign was not successful,

---

209 WOODWARD, 1998, p113.

however, and the loss of the 6th (Poona) Division at the Siege of Kut, with many of its survivors dying in prison in Aleppo, combined with the embarrassment of the British government trying to buy back its confined soldiers, prompted a formal inquiry to be conducted on behalf of the General Staff, India, by Lieutenant General Sir Percy Lake[210]. As minister ultimately responsible for the Indian Army, Austen resigned as Secretary of State for India in July 1917, and was widely praised in the press for his principled decisiveness in doing so, but it was less than a year before high office beckoned once more, when he was appointed to Lloyd George's War Cabinet in April 1918, replacing Lord Milner as Minister without Portfolio.

With the coming of peace a new peacetime government was required to rebuild the country, and so the general election of December 1918 was to be a decisive moment, but the scale of the victory won by Lloyd George's coalition over Asquith's remaining loyal Liberals was still a surprise to many. Austen had been a strong supporter of Lloyd George throughout the war, and so it was inevitable that he would play a significant part in the new Cabinet, and in January 1919 he returned to the Treasury as Chancellor of the Exchequer for the second time in his career. Here he faced the gargantuan task of rebuilding a country that had spent four years focussed entirely on the efforts of war; his pre-war experiences, his self-confidence and his gift for administration meant that he was well-suited to the challenge, but it remained something of a poisoned chalice. Servicing the debts incurred during the war, combined with the recession of 1920-21, was a huge challenge for even the most talented of economists, and as unemployment rose to 23% and GDP fell by 13% the task loomed ever greater. In the end it was Austen's loyalty to Lloyd George which was to prove his downfall; with Bonar Law's resignation as leader of the Tory Party in 1921 it was seen as inevitable that Austen should succeed him, as he duly did. His character, however, was at odds with that of the ambitious new intake of Tory MPs from the 1918 election, who increasingly saw him as an ageing irrelevance who was unable to identify with his younger colleagues. His bad eyesight didn't help either; he had damaged his left eye while playing rackets at Rugby[211], and was short-sighted in his right, and even with his ubiquitous

---

210 British Library IOR/L/MIL/17/15/105.
211 DUTTON, p338.

monocle he often appeared to ignore fellow members in Parliament when in fact he simply hadn't recognised them. Discontent came to a head in the autumn of 1922, and on the 19th October Austen called the Carlton Club meeting in what proved to be a disastrous miscalculation. The Tory rebels, led primarily by Stanley Baldwin, passed a motion to fight the forthcoming election as an independent party, and though the primary aim of the move was to precipitate the end of Lloyd George's rule, Austen resigned the leadership of the party. He felt that it was his duty to support his friend and colleague of many years, and so became the first ever Tory leader never to lead his party into a general election and, until William Hague, the only one of the twentieth century not to serve as Prime Minister.

Bonar Law won the election as predicted, but no-one expected Austen to be appointed to his government, and it wasn't until his resignation due to ill health in May 1923 (he died of throat cancer within a few months) that a return to the Cabinet seemed at all likely. Even so, Law's successor, Stanley Baldwin, was not keen to include Austen, who could hardly hide his belief that the new Prime Minister was his inferior, and it wasn't until the election of October 1924 that the next and perhaps greatest stage of Austen's political career began. The next day Baldwin appointed him Foreign Secretary, a post which he filled to great effect for the next five years, not least because of the free hand which the Prime Minister allowed him, though this did occasionally irritate parliamentary colleagues. It was in this position that Austen achieved what was possibly the greatest single achievement of his career: the Locarno Treaties. Through a series of seven treaties agreed in Locarno, Switzerland, in October 1925, the principal powers of Europe settled an agreement, the Rhineland Pact, which aimed to reassure France of its security after the end of its occupation of the Ruhr. It did this by guaranteeing German respect for that frontier by allowing certain claims on the Sudetenland, the Polish Corridor and Danzig. Czech and Polish concessions on these points were secured by the fact that, as newly-independent nations, they had no great power to protect them. Though the minor partners in the arrangement were unhappy with its results, and indeed the Polish government fell shortly after, the longer-term effect was one of widespread, if fragile, peace for the second half of the 1920s. Indeed, it paved the way for the admission of Germany as a permanent member of the League of Nations a year later.[212] Austen Chamberlain was the principal architect of the treaties, which were conceived in a series of small-scale meetings over several days, and his role was one for which he received recognition. In 1925 he received the Nobel Peace Prize for the part he had played, and shortly afterwards was created a Knight of the Garter by His Majesty King George V. It was also in 1925 that he was elected Rector of the University of Glasgow, and at his installation dozens of undergraduates of the university arrived wearing monocles in imitation of their new head.

The Conservative defeat in the 1929 general election marked the end to Austen's Cabinet career, (though he briefly served outside it as First Lord of the Admiralty in 1931) but he continued to influence British policy as something of an elder statesman, particularly as an early and vociferous opponent of appeasement, alongside Winston Churchill and very much in opposition to his half-brother Neville. He was conscious of the possibility of appearing a bore in such circumstances, and wrote to Neville:

> The first lesson I shall have to learn is to keep my hands off the wheel when the navigation of the ship is the business of a junior.[213]

It was also in this period of partial retirement that he returned to Rugby as a member of the governing body, and it is in this capacity that his portrait now hangs in the Temple Speech Room. He also served as chairman of the General Committee of the School of Hygiene and Tropical Medicine, but he often said that such positions simply served to fill time, and it was clear to both family and friends that he missed the excitement and challenge of public office. Age and health were not on his side, but he wrote articles and planned a lecture tour of America to help secure a future income for his wife and daughters. However hard he worked, Austen's lack of involvement in the political life of the country was a continual source of anguish in his later years, not least because he fully understood the extent of his newfound irrelevance, which contrasted so

---

212 RICH, 2003, pp148–49.
213 CHAMBERLAIN, p400.

starkly with the perpetual involvement for which he had been trained since school. In September 1932 he wrote to his sister Hilda:

> Nor is there anything in public affairs to console me. If I felt older and less able to work, it would be easier to reconcile myself to the place on the shelf to which I have been relegated. As it is I am bitter at heart tho' not even Ivy knows that & still thinks me a marvel of charity & forgiveness, but I eat my heart out in idleness & uselessness & see my work undone & feel myself unwanted & unregretted. All this is very bitter – forgive me and destroy this screed. I shall recover my equanimity one of these days, but just now I am in despair.[214]

Austen retained his seat for West Birmingham, but backbench life suited him little, and he died at the age of 73 at home in Egerton Terrace, London, on the 16th March 1937, two and a half months before Neville's election as Prime Minister. Though his life and career had dominated British public life for forty years, it was his half-brother who was to be best remembered in the country's collective memory for events that Austen, perhaps more than most, could have foreseen.

---

214 Ibid, p416.

Maurice Hankey, 1st Baron Hankey (Kilbracken)

Maurice Pascal Alers Hankey (his middle name reflected his Easter birth) was the fifth child and third son of Robert Hankey, himself an Old Rugbeian who had joined the school in 1853. He was born during a family trip to Biarritz on the 1st April 1877 and grew up at home in Brighton. After six years in a local private day school, the 13-year-old Maurice yearned for a naval cadetship and a life at sea, describing the feeling as 'an itch – like being in love'[215], but his hopes were vetoed by his father and in May 1890 he joined Mr Collins's house (now Kilbracken) which his elder brothers Hugh and Clement had joined in 1887 and 1889. Hugh went on to join the 2nd Battalion of the Royal Warwickshire Regiment and was killed fighting the Boers at Paardeberg in 1900. Their youngest brother Donald joined the house three years after Maurice left and is described in detail elsewhere in this book.

Maurice's school career was one of academic success but sporting obscurity. Beginning in the form known then as Upper Middle 1, he was soon raised to the Lower Vth. His analytical powers and keen eye for detail were clear from an early age, but he determined to follow Hugh into a military career, and so in 1892 was moved to the Army Class. His letters home contain the peculiarly Victorian schoolboy combination of the shocking and the mundane, such as when he wrote to his mother not long after arriving at Rugby:

> The other day one of the boys who clean the boots drowned himself in the canal, he did not only clean the boots but is like a butler in the house. There are two of them who had been suspected of stealing money lately, of which £4 worth has been missed, so Jacky (Mr Collins) stuck 'the lout' in a study to watch them go into the bathroom, who saw them steal some money out of a fellow's trouser pocket, then Jacky said he'd bunk them and the younger one went and committed suicide while the other is in jail. I wonder if Pa would let me get a bat with my purse money… The confectioner has got some cakes in.[216]

---

215 WENTWORTH ROSKILL, 1972, p29.
216 Ibid, p31.

Upon leaving school in 1895 he joined the Royal Marine Artillery as a probationary second lieutenant at the Royal Naval College, Greenwich. It was here that he first became friends with Commander John Jellicoe, later Admiral of the Fleet and commander of the Grand Fleet at the Battle of Jutland in May 1916, as they both played cricket for the college XI. During his training there and at Eastney Barracks in Portsmouth, from September 1897 he came first in every single exam and was awarded the Sword of Honour. On completion of his training in late 1898 Maurice's report stated that he was 'An exceptionally zealous and promising young officer. Physically strong and athletic. Ability very good indeed,'[217] and with such a position in his class was able to choose his first appointment. Jellicoe pushed for him to choose *HMS Centurion*, where he was serving as flag captain, but Maurice chose *HMS Ramillies*, flagship of the Mediterranean Fleet soon to be under the command of Admiral Jackie Fisher. He came to believe the choice was providential, as the Royal Marine Artillery officer appointed to the *Centurion* in his place was killed in the Boxer Rebellion.

Ordered to join his new ship at Malta, Maurice just missed the ship which was sailing to Greece, and so had several weeks in which to get to know the island and its people, in contrast to many British officers who concentrated on the sporting possibilities of the place which remained the headquarters of Royal Navy polo right up to the 1960s. It was during his stay in the draughty accommodation hulk *Hibernia* that Maurice first met Captain Mackay, the intelligence officer of the Mediterranean Fleet, and soon began working for him in an unofficial capacity, eagerly writing home to ask for textbooks of Italian and modern Greek. He found the wardroom of the *Ramillies* a congenial place, though he objected to the exclusivity of the Executive branch and was delighted by the shake-up given to them when Admiral Fisher arrived and began to reform the old-fashioned and lethargic fleet. When Rear Admiral Beresford joined the fleet as Fisher's second in command he brought with him R.S. Lowry from naval intelligence as his flag captain, and Maurice was soon working for them both as intelligence and staff officer, confirming his suspicion that he would enjoy a career which lay in such a direction.

---

217 Ibid, p35.

In December 1901 Maurice was laid low by a fever, and the doctors of the naval hospital in Malta asked that he be sent home. During his three years in *HMS Ramillies* he had built a great reputation amongst the senior officers of the Mediterranean Fleet, including letters of recommendation from Admirals Fisher and Beresford, and support for his application for the position of assistant adjutant at Eastney, though he was unsuccessful. His intelligence work had been noticed in the Admiralty, and so on his recovery in April 1902 Captain Maurice Hankey RMA joined the Naval Intelligence Department in Whitehall, thereby embarking on a path that would colour the whole of his career. He was surprised to be tasked with the analysis of coastal defences across the British Empire but found the work far more congenial than life at sea. In 1905 he was appointed to the Owen Committee on imperial defence, and it was on Maurice's suggestion that the committee sailed for several months in *HMS Terrible* to inspect the sort of installations on which they were to report. His knowledge of military matters was astounding, and his recommendations, such as that against the withdrawal of the British garrison from St Helena, were much respected by the committee. Arriving in Simonstown, South Africa, he was greeted by many members of his wife Adeline's family, but the next stop was Mauritius, where he was greeted by the sad sight of his brother Donald bed-ridden by a liver abscess and the effects of major surgery. The *Terrible* returned Maurice to Portsmouth, and to his wife and baby son Robin, in the closing days of 1906, but it wasn't long before his services were required for a further, secret, committee, the Ballard Committee, which worked to produce the naval war plans to be used in future conflict. After a further six months' work he returned to his real love, as head of naval intelligence in the Mediterranean, and sailed to join *HMS Irresistible* in Valetta.

The summer cruise of the Mediterranean Fleet in 1907 provided Maurice with the ideal opportunity to survey the coastal defences of the tottering Ottoman Empire, and his recommendation that in time of war troop landings should not be attempted on the Dardanelles was to return to mind in 1915 when just such a disastrous move was made. He took every opportunity to increase his already encyclopaedic knowledge of military affairs and the cruise provided further evidence, if any were needed, that he was a hugely valuable asset to the Naval Intelligence Department. Adeline and Robin sailed to join him in Malta, and they hired a house just outside Sliema, but Maurice's talent for organisation and efficiency meant that he couldn't rest and he set about reforming the logistical organisation of Valetta Dockyard, much to the annoyance of its civilian hierarchy. It was at that moment, in January 1908, that a telegram arrived appointing Maurice to his greatest position yet, as Assistant Naval Secretary to the Committee of Imperial Defence in Whitehall. Robin fell seriously ill, however, and for a time it was uncertain whether the Hankey family would be able to return home, but return they did, and for the first time in Maurice's career his family were able to settle in England for a good period. They bought a house in Oxted, on the Kent and Surrey border, where their daughter Ursula was born.

For four years Maurice proved an extremely able assistant secretary, and his tact, diplomacy and intelligence made him a sought-after counsellor to the powers of the Admiralty. 1912, however, was a momentous year; firstly, Maurice's recommendation of the formation of a Naval War Staff was enthusiastically endorsed by Winston Churchill, appointed First Lord of the Admiralty a year earlier. Secondly, his extremely valuable work in service of the empire was rewarded by his appointment as a Companion of the Order of the Bath, and finally he was promoted to the position of Secretary, which he was to hold for the next twenty-six years. This appointment was undoubtedly due to the involvement of the recently retired Admiral Fisher, who bombarded Churchill and Asquith with letters of support. His promotion further widened his influence, as he regularly briefed the King on the work of the CID and attended several dinners at Downing Street. On the declaration of war in August 1914 the committee was placed in a state of suspended animation by the Prime Minister, and Maurice was instead appointed Secretary to the War Council, and it was in this position that he analysed and supported the idea of a 'Machine Gun Destroyer' proposed by fellow Rugbeian Ernest Swinton. Though Lord Kitchener remained sceptical, it was Maurice's intervention with Churchill on Swinton's behalf on Christmas Day 1914 which led to the establishing of the Landship Committee and the subsequent development of the first tanks in military history.

On the 13th January 1915 Maurice recorded Churchill's extraordinary proposal to the committee of a land attack on the Dardanelles in contravention of his advice of eight years earlier. The minutes record the horrifying conclusion that

...the Admiralty should also prepare for a naval expedition in February to bombard and take the Gallipoli Peninsula with Constantinople as its objective.[218]

In the absence of Lord Kitchener, Maurice was summoned at once to Downing Street, where the Prime Minister Herbert Asquith, Foreign Secretary Sir Edward Grey, and David Lloyd George questioned him closely on the military implications of such a plan. On the 24th he redistributed his earlier report on the fortifications of the area, and in a letter to the Prime Minister made it clear that he was not opposed to such an action but believed it foolish to do so as a naval action alone without the support of the army. Turkish responses to the initial bombardment in February 1915 would support him in this, and the first landings by the Royal Marine Light Infantry to destroy the guns of the shelled forts were unopposed, but the vacillation of the British commander in chief, Sir Sackville Carden, allowed massive reinforcement of the area by Turkish forces. It also allowed the laying of mines in the straits which, though small in number, were strategically placed to cause havoc amongst the battleships of the fleet the following month. If Carden had acted more decisively, and Kitchener had been able to offer a more cohesive land force, the outcome of the Gallipoli campaign may well have been as Maurice intended. He was clearly aware of the importance of his work for the War Council, and from the 5th of March began keeping a diary, on the opening page of which he wrote,

> Now as Secretary to the Prime Minister's War Council I find myself directly associated with the central policy of the great European war. Though regretting that I have not commenced this diary earlier I have decided that no further time should be lost, and that, so far as time permits, I will jot down from time to time any incidents of historical, political, military or personal interest with which I may be personally connected.[219]

Maurice's great prescience again came to the fore when on the 16th March he wrote a long secret letter to the Prime Minister warning of

---

218 Ibid, p153.
219 Ibid, p159.

the impending threat of disaster due to Carden's failures and Kitchener's delay in confirming the availability of the Mediterranean Expeditionary Force. His fears were clearly laid out:

> It is suggested that the War Council ought to cross-examine the naval and military authorities on the extent of the preparations, and particularly with regard to such points as the following:
>
> (a) The number of troops it is proposed to employ?
>
> (b) The arrangements made for the supply of boats and tugs?
>
> (c) The preparations made for the provision of landing piers, pontoons etc?
>
> (d) The arrangements made for the supply of water and provisions?
>
> (e) The hospital arrangements. Is it contemplated to use nothing but floating hospitals, or will there be field hospitals on shore?
>
> (f) Is it expected that the Dardanelles will be carried by a coup-de-main, or is the possibility of siege operations contemplated?
>
> (g) In the latter event, what siege guns will be available, and what arrangements have been made for landing them and their ammunition?
>
> (h) Possibly, it is proposed that the men-of-war should supply the necessary heavy artillery to overcome the enemy's movable heavy artillery. If so, are the military authorities satisfied that the projectiles available in men-of-war are suitable for this purpose?
>
> (i) What arrangements are contemplated for the transport from the landing place to the army, of supplies of ammunition, food, water, etc., over a tough country with very few roads in it?
>
> Unless details such as these, and there are probably others, are fully thought out before the landing takes place, it is conceivable that a serious disaster may occur.[220]

---

220 Ibid, p164.

In the midst of the Dardanelles affair Maurice was invited to visit the Western Front as a guest of General Robertson, chief of staff of the BEF, to give the War Council a first-hand account of its situation. Visiting Ypres and Ploegsteert in the guise of a serving officer of the Royal Marine Artillery, he heard many opinions from senior soldiers, as well as Robertson's belief that Sir John French was always wanting to do 'reckless and impossible things'.[221] Maurice's position was an extraordinary one: confidante of the King, advisor to the Prime Minister and now intermediary between Churchill and Admiral Fisher, whose relationship had entirely broken down over the control of the Mediterranean force. Indeed it was only an impassioned letter from Maurice that prevented Fisher from resigning over the affair.[222]

On the 21st May 1915 Maurice dined with the Prime Minister and a few others at Downing Street, after which Asquith first discussed the idea of a coalition government, which he formally proposed to the King as being on a 'broad and non-party basis'[223] a few days later. Maurice's advice was, as ever, invaluable, and it was at his instigation that the blockade of Germany was tightened, to the protestation of the USA, though his proposal to devastate the crops of Germany was not taken up for fear of reprisals against France. Churchill, seemingly bracing himself for criticism by the Dardanelles Committee and the House of Commons, asked Maurice for copies of the memoranda that he had written for the Prime Minister on the subject. He received them, but with a letter which stated Maurice's opinion on the matter:

> Personally, I have not the smallest desire to shirk any measure of responsibility which can fairly be attributed to me for the Dardanelles operation. Strategically it has always appeared, and still appears, to me to be the right thing to do. I daresay you noticed in the paper Lord Kitchener circulated and to which you so kindly referred in your letter, that I showed how great an influence the Dardanelles operation had been in bringing Italy into the war. This alone was adequate justification, but I consider the results to be achieved will ultimately be still

---

221 HOLMES R., *The Little Field Marshal: A Life of Sir John French*, 2004, p298.
222 WENTWORTH ROSKILL, p173.
223 JENKINS, 1964, p360.

greater. Never has my conviction on this point been stronger than on my return from France, for I am convinced that unless the Germans can be weakened by diversions elsewhere, such as by the intervention of Italy and Roumania, we can no more force the German lines in front of us than Wellington could force Massena's lines before Torres Vedras.

Nevertheless, I personally never believed in the naval attack, and would have preferred to wait until troops were available. I fully understand your reasons for the naval attack and should probably have done the same if I had been in your position, but from a purely professional point of view I was opposed to it.[224]

In the early summer of 1915 Maurice visited Gallipoli himself, and upon returning was summoned by the King to give a detailed description of the ANZAC operations in Suvla Bay. As autumn approached it became clear that certain individuals were preparing to shed any responsibility for the impending disaster, and indeed on the 5th September Maurice heard from fellow Rugbeian Austen Chamberlain that Lord Kitchener was encouraging the Cabinet to believe that he had been ultimately responsible for the unsuccessful winter campaign.[225] As 1915 wore on however, Maurice's innocence became increasingly apparent, to the extent that by the end of September he had been appointed Secretary to the Dardanelles Committee, which had hitherto been a somewhat confused affair. With Gallipoli evacuated in December his work didn't relent, and on New Year's Day 1916 he was summoned to take minutes of a committee (which included Chamberlain) examining the provision of manpower to the armed forces and munitions work, including by possible conscription. Such duties took up much of his time in the early months of that year as the Asquith coalition began to crumble.

By the end of November 1916 Asquith's position as Prime Minister was untenable. The growing pressure of the inquests into the Dardanelles and Mesopotamia campaigns (following the British surrender at Kut al Amara at the end of April) entirely overshadowed the work of the coalition

224 WENTWORTH ROSKILL, p183.
225 Ibid, p213.

government, and Maurice believed that it never recovered.[226] Asquith was exhausted, and that had been compounded by the death of his son Raymond at the Battle of Flers-Courcelette in September. With public confidence further undermined by the equivocal success of Jutland and the horrifying casualties of the Somme, a powerful triumvirate of David Lloyd George (Secretary of State for War), Sir Edward Carson, and Bonar Law (Colonial Secretary), gathered at the Hyde Park Hotel and devised what was to become the War Cabinet: a council of five members, with complete executive authority over the fighting of the war. On the afternoon of Wednesday, 6th December 1916, the three men met with the King at Buckingham Palace, and at 1900 Lloyd George was asked to form a government. Asquith left Downing Street three days later.

This new form of government required a new form of administration, and one individual was clearly the right person for the job. Alongside administering the Dardanelles Committee and War Council, during 1916 Maurice had been awarded the KCB by King George V and the Légion d'Honneur by the government of France. On the same day as Maurice was knighted by the King, he arranged for the monarch to be given a demonstration of the 'Caterpillar' – the first prototype tank – by Ernest Swinton before they dined at the Army and Navy Club at a dinner in Maurice's honour. With such recognition it was clear that he was trusted not only by Asquith, but across the political spectrum and, indeed, by Britain's allies, and his installation as Cabinet Secretary was swift:

> By the 9th it was "off with the old love and on with the new" and I spent the whole day with the new "War Cabinet", the completion of the minutes keeping me at the office until 9pm. I now find myself secretary, not of the War Ctee, but of the Cabinet, which consists of Lloyd George, Lord Curzon, Mr Henderson, Lord Milner and Bonar Law. An odd turn of the wheel indeed to take place within 7 days![227]

Astonishingly, until this moment no minutes had ever been kept of Cabinet decisions, and Maurice had both the inclination and ability to

---

226 JENKINS, p411.
227 WENTWORTH ROSKILL, p529.

mould his appointment to his own shape. Such was the trust in him that no one challenged his development of the appointment, and in 'Draft Rules of Procedure', written for the War Cabinet, he summarised the duties of the Secretariat as

1. To record the proceedings of the War Cabinet.
2. To transmit relevant extracts from the minutes to departments concerned with implementing them or otherwise interested.
3. To prepare the agenda paper, and to arrange the attendance of ministers not in the War Cabinet and others required to be present for discussion of particular items on the agenda.
4. To receive papers from departments and circulate them to the War Cabinet or others as necessary.[228]

Maurice then effectively constructed the procedures and established the precedent used by the Cabinet Office to this day. As soon as he was appointed he produced a thirty-page memorandum summarising every theatre of the war, demonstrating to its members just why he had been appointed to such a crucial position. This document did not merely set out the situation as it stood but gave Maurice's own opinion on the best course of action in every case. The diplomat Lord Vansittart wrote of him,

> ...and it was Maurice Hankey, who progressively became secretary of everything that mattered... He grew into a repository of secrets, a Chief Inspector of Mines of information. He had an incredible memory... [of] an official brand which could reproduce on call the date, file, substance of every paper that ever flew into a pigeon-hole. If St Peter is as well served there will be no errors on Judgement Day.[229]

Such a position was far from an enviable one in a country at war; the members of the War Cabinet were largely inexperienced in such matters, and to Maurice seemed more interested in amassing coteries of offices

228 NAYLOR, 1984, p27.
229 WENTWORTH ROSKILL, p355.

and secretaries than in the minutiae of Cabinet business. When Asquith asked whether he might have copies of War Cabinet minutes, Maurice's characteristic diplomacy was temporarily eclipsed by the draw of an old friendship:

> My own position is singularly detestable. Necessarily from my position and knowledge I am the linch-pin, more or less, of the new government. They have to turn to me on every occasion and on every kind of subject. I do not altogether like this after serving you so long, but as a patriotic Englishman I am bound to, and intend to strain every nerve to make the new machine a success, and indeed to like and respect my new chiefs, so far as in me lies. But my loyalty to a new Prime Minister is a loyalty to the country, and does not abate by one jot my personal loyalty to you.[230]

Over the course of 1917 Maurice, it may be argued, forged the shape of modern cabinet government. Never before had the Cabinet had agendas prior to meeting, nor had its decisions been recorded or its minutes filed, and the innovation impressed the King, who on several occasions remarked that he had never previously been fully informed of his government's decisions.[231] As ever, Maurice recognised the potential weaknesses of the system, in this case the continued friction between the War Cabinet, the Secretary of State for War and the First Lord of the Admiralty. Though they were in regular attendance to provide advice to the new executive body, as early as Boxing Day 1916 Maurice noted,

> The new War Cabinet are really up against it, as they don't believe in Robertson's "Western Front" policy, but they will never find soldiers to carry out their "Salonica" policy.[232]

As the concept of cabinet minutes was novel to the system of British government, it also lay with Maurice to determine the style and degree of detail to be recorded. The principle of collective ministerial responsibility

---

230 Ibid, p341.
231 NAYLOR, p19.
232 Ibid, p30.

led him to conclude that individual opinions should not be recorded unless they were expressed by an expert on the subject matter (he used the example of Lord Curzon on India to illustrate this point). Such an approach meant that when copies of the minutes were disseminated to departments the opinions of individual cabinet members could not be discerned, and the political struggles of the great characters of state were kept from wider view. Lord Curzon himself initially objected, asking Maurice's assistant Amery why he didn't feature more prominently in the proceedings, but as the new secretariat's role became more established, that of Maurice became ever more vital to its operation. It was at his suggestion, for example, that the Prime Minister terminated the long-standing tradition of sending a hand-written account of the Cabinet business to the King. Though the latter's private secretary objected it was Maurice's opinion that held sway, and such accounts have never returned.

Maurice's position at the heart of government meant that no secrets of the British war machine escaped his notice, and his strategic view, coupled with a still-expanding encyclopedic knowledge of military affairs, meant that his advisory role became ever more indispensable to both the King and the Prime Minister. It was at his suggestion that the idea of a convoy system was pushed upon a reluctant Admiralty in the face of mounting merchant shipping losses to U-Boats in 1917.[233] Such power rested safely in his tactful and deferential hands, and as peace approached in 1918 the novel system of government had achieved a great deal of regularity, so much so that it was inconceivable that the Prime Minister could contemplate a return to the amateurish administration of the past. When the Armistice arrived, Maurice was bedridden at home in Surrey by the Spanish flu that was sweeping the country with such terrible efficiency, but he made a lucky recovery, and in January 1919 sailed again for France, only this time to serve as secretary to the British delegation at the Paris Peace Conference at Versailles.

It was perhaps inevitable that Lloyd George should seek Maurice's service as Cabinet Secretary in his peace-time government following the general election of December 1918. Indeed he continued to serve in that role with distinction until 1938, and upon his retirement that year he was ennobled in the 1939 New Year's Honours List as Baron Hankey of The Chart in the County of Surrey. His later career was no more

---

233 HANKEY M.P.A., 1961, pp 641-51.

impressive, as he became one of the few civil servants to be appointed as a government minister. Having been a trusted and reliable advisor to six prime ministers he was appointed as Minister Without Portfolio in fellow Rugbeian Neville Chamberlain's War Cabinet of 1939. When Chamberlain was replaced by Winston Churchill in 1940 Maurice was appointed Chancellor to the Duchy of Lancaster, but was left out of Churchill's War Cabinet, serving instead as Paymaster General. Outside government, Maurice continued to be widely acknowledged as a towering figure in British political life, and a perpetual source of invaluable advice to politicians of all parties. He died, aged 85, at home on the 26th January 1963.

Having been intended for a life at sea, the Hankey family could not possibly have predicted the enormous influence that Maurice would have, and continues to have, on the British political landscape. He was almost solely responsible for the creation and development of modern cabinet government, and for the refining of the role of the civil service as the country emerged from the somewhat amateur administrations of the previous century. Two of his three brothers died in the service of their country, but from the safety and comfort of Whitehall Gardens Maurice did more than any of them to further the national interest and the efficient prosecution of the greatest war that the world had ever known.

The Cawley Brothers (School House)

Sir Frederick Cawley, Bt, later the 1st Baron Cawley, was a successful Lancashire cotton merchant who served as Member of Parliament for the town of Prestwich between 1895 and 1918.[234] A Justice of the Peace, Privy Counsellor, and Chancellor of the Duchy of Lancaster in the coalition government of Lloyd George, his ennoblement will have come as no surprise to his contemporaries. Away from the pressures of Westminster he raised four sons at Berrington Hall near Leominster; all four boys attended Rugby School, arriving at School House between 1890 and 1896 under the guidance of head masters John Percival and Herbert James, the former of whom was notorious for his vigorous attacks on 'idleness and loafing' and his extraordinary insistence that boys' football shorts be secured below the knees with elastic. Of Sir Frederick's four sons, three were to die in the war, two of whom, Oswald and Harold, were serving Members of Parliament themselves at the time of their death.

Captain Harold Cawley MP

Harold was the second of Sir Frederick and, though he was five years older than Oswald, his education was identical; joining School House in 1891 he also then proceeded to New College, Oxford, where he read History and received a second class degree. It is at this point that their experiences diverge, as Harold was set upon a career in law, and so in 1902 he was called to the bar at Inner Temple and practised for several years on the Northern Circuit. Though he had grown up in Herefordshire and at Rugby, his father's constituency and business were both in Lancashire, so he had spent much time in the county and it was natural for him to stand for a Lancashire constituency when he decided to stand for parliament in 1909 (the year he received his MA). He was elected to represent Heywood in the general election of January 1910, from which Herbert Asquith emerged as Prime Minister, and continued to do so up to his death. It was as a junior MP that Harold served as private secretary to the president of the Board

---

234 Memorials of Rugbeians who Fell in the Great War.

of Education, and then in 1911 to the Home Secretary, the Rt Hon Reginald McKenna[235]. A keen sportsman, Harold was a regular and successful point-to-point rider, winning the Bar Point-to-Point for the last time before mobilising in 1914.[236]

In 1903 Harold had been commissioned into the 2nd Volunteer Battalion of the Manchester Regiment, and transferred to the 6th Battalion in 1913. By the outbreak of war he had been promoted to captain, and as a territorial officer of nearly twelve years' experience he volunteered for active duty as soon as war was declared. On the 10th September he sailed for Egypt as ADC to Major General Sir William Douglas[237], then to the Dardanelles in May 1915, sailing from Alexandria on the 3rd May, with the British ladies of the city providing tea and sandwiches on the quayside as they embarked in the troopship *Derflinger*[238]. It was clear that they were to face heavy action; before they could embark in the *Derflinger* 550 wounded Australian soldiers had to be unloaded, and their first sight when they arrived at the Dardanelles on the 5th was that of HMS *Queen Elizabeth* bombarding Turkish positions ashore. May 1915 was a bloody month for the 6th Manchesters, with repeated attempts to capture the village of Krithia, which had been an objective of the first day of the campaign in April, before they had even arrived to join the battle. The village remained in Turkish hands, and so a renewed assault was planned for the 4th June to allow the advance on Achi Baba which controlled the heights of the peninsula. The officers' mess of the 6th Manchesters was an extraordinarily Rugbeian affair in 1915, with almost a third of the battalion's officers being old boys, and four of them were killed within twenty-four hours at the Third Battle of Krithia[239]: Captains Holt, Kessler and Edgar, and Lieutenant Young[240], with Lieutenant Blatherwick being injured. Such loss only reinforced Harold's desire

---

235 McKenna served as Home Secretary until 1915, when he was appointed Chancellor of the Exchequer.

236 Memorials of Rugbeians who Fell in the Great War.

237 Maj Gen Sir William Douglas KCMG CB DSO (1858-1920).

238 WO95/4316.

239 4th-5th June 1915.

240 Joseph Holt (Whitelaw), Edgar Kessler (Collins), Robert Edgar (Payne-Smith), Edmund Young (Payne-Smith).

to return to his battalion rather than remain at Divisional Headquarters, and he wrote,

> My own battalion has suffered most, and if I had not been on the Staff I should have had little chance of surviving. Most of the men I knew well were killed, but they did as well as I expected, and, as you know, I always expected much... Every combatant Officer who left Egypt with the Battalion has now been killed or wounded, and more killed than wounded. In addition about twelve new Officers have been hit, again mostly killed. As a consequence I am going back to them... I have always felt rather a brute skulking behind in comparative safety while my friends were being killed.[241]

Eventually, on the 8th September, he was allowed to join them in the firing line at Gully Ravine. On the 19th the Manchesters detected and countermined a Turkish tunnel, destroying thirty yards of trench in doing so, having first evacuated their own line. Once the mine was blown, it was Harold Cawley who, with four men, occupied the crater at a distance of only ten yards from the Turkish line, continually harrying the enemy overnight on the 20th September in the face of constant bombs and rifle fire, before withdrawing at dawn. At dusk on the following day the Manchesters again occupied the crater, and what happened next is described in the battalion war diary:

> About midnight there was a suspicion that the Turks were digging towards the crater. Capt. H. T. Cawley, going into the crater to satisfy himself on this point, was killed by a bullet through the temple. He is an irreplaceable loss to the Battn. He displayed most excellent judgement as O.C. firing line.[242]

He was 37 years old. Harold's body was recovered, and buried in Lancashire Landing Cemetery.

---

241 Memorials of Rugbeians who Fell in the Great War.
242 WO95/4316.

As a Member of Parliament, Harold's death was widely felt and deeply suffered; he had long been admired for his courage, both physical and moral, from the days when he developed a reputation in the House of Commons for always representing what he believed to be right, regardless of Liberal Party policy. His death exemplified this same courage in a particularly stark way.

Captain the Hon Oswald Cawley MP

Oswald was the fourth and youngest of the Cawley brothers and was born on the 7th October 1882. He entered School House under Head Master Dr Herbert James in the Advent term of 1896, and in 1900 went up to New College, Oxford, to read History, where he was also the president of the Palmerston Club, a political society[243]. After receiving a second class degree he joined his father's business and began work as assistant manager at the Heaton Mills Bleaching Company, dedicated to bleaching and dying cloth at Blackley, a few miles north of Manchester. Outside his work Oswald was very much devoted to philanthropic work, particularly boys clubs of the kind with which he will have come into contact during his time at Rugby, though in 1911 he also managed to find time to tour much of the world, spending a good deal of time in India and Japan during the course of the trip. In May 1914 he was commissioned as a second lieutenant in the Shropshire Yeomanry, who were quickly mobilised on the declaration of war, marching out of Ludlow on the 8th August. To their disappointment they were sent to join the Welsh Border Mounted Brigade, part of the 1st Mounted Division, the help guard against possible German invasion, based in Flixton, Suffolk. In November 1915 they suffered another disappointment when they were dismounted, but their quiet life on the Suffolk coast was not to last much longer and on the 4th March 1916 they sailed from Devonport in the SS *Arcadian* bound for Egypt. On arrival they found themselves in the midst of the Senussi Campaign, fighting in the western desert and up to the coast at Mersa Matruh. These operations continued for a year, and at Helmieh Camp near Cairo on the 2nd March 1917 they were merged with the 1/1st Cheshire Yeomanry to form the 10th Battalion, The King's Own Shropshire Light Infantry, under the command of the 231st Brigade of the

---

243 THORNTON, 2017, p42.

74th Division. Oswald's newly formed battalion then spent several weeks reorganising and training in infantry tactics before moving to Kantara on the Suez Canal on the 24th March. Finally, on the 2nd April 1917 the battalion entrained at Kantara East with the men accommodated in open cattle trucks for a twenty-two hour train journey to Khan Yunis near Gaza. Ten days later they moved to Deir el Belah and shortly afterwards observed the Second Battle of Gaza, though their own experiences of war remained somewhat passive, remaining in reserve. A member of Oswald's battalion, Lance Corporal Minshall, described what he saw:

> I saw the men walking across the plain before Gaza, every man a hero, they moved forward with splendid steadiness through a shower of shrapnel and high explosives and owing to the open ground many brave fellows dropped, never to rise again as I watched them advance.[244]

The Third Battle of Gaza followed in November 1917, and on the 27th the battalion arrived at Junction Station where two weeks earlier General Allenby had cut the Turkish rail link to Jerusalem, and in December were present at the capture of the city, Allenby's 'Christmas Present' to Lloyd George. Further action followed in the capture of Jericho and on the advance to Nablus, during which Private Whitfield of the KSLI was awarded the Victoria Cross[245].

In January 1918 Oswald's father was raised to the peerage as Baron Cawley and so entered the House of Lords. Oswald was persuaded to stand for his father's former constituency of Prestwich, and won the seat with a large majority, but made it clear before the by-election that if elected he would not remain in the country until the war had ended. Oswald was determined to serve with the 10th KSLI while they were abroad, and so on the 7th May 1918 he travelled with them again, this time to France in response to Germany's 'Spring Offensive', and arrived in Marseilles to travel north by train. In August the 10th KSLI were involved in the Hundred Days Offensive, attacking German positions near Merville when Oswald, recently promoted to captain, was killed leading his company into action. The battalion unwittingly advanced into a trap, wading through high corn towards hidden German machine

---

244 IWM, *Minshall* MSS 86/51/1.
245 10th March 1918.

gun emplacements, which opened fire from short range with devastating effect.[246] The commanding officer wrote to his widowed mother when he was missing but not yet confirmed dead:

> We were on the extreme right of our Corps front and were ordered to conform with an advance by the troops on the left. Your son's Company was on the right, and therefore on the extreme right of the advancing line. It was thought the enemy were moving back and we were to keep in touch and follow them up. We had a very wide front for a Battalion. The enemy lay low, until we were right on their line, and then put down a very heavy barrage behind us and had many machine-guns in front. They counterattacked on the right, and we had many casualties throughout the Battalion, and I regret to say a great number are missing. Your son was hit in the arm, which he got dressed by his Company stretcher-bearers, and then went on and was wounded again the second time in the jaw, and after that we could hear no news, and we had to fall back to our old line. Our men did most awfully well, and I hear your son was seen gallantly leading a charge with his supports, and then a melee ensued. All the Officers were casualties. Your son is one of my best and most reliable Officers. He has only had command of a Company a few weeks, but I look on him as one of the best Company Commanders.[247]

Oswald's mother received many letters from the officers and men of the 10th KSLI, and even from the families of those who had served under him, all agreeing that he was an outstanding leader; as one fellow officer wrote: 'I looked on Oswald as one of the very few friends I had left, and it is a great blow to me. He was one of the very best-living men I have ever met.' His body was recovered and buried nearby, but after the war his family were able to have him exhumed and moved to Nery, and so there he lies alongside his brother John, killed in the village while serving there with the 20th Hussars in September 1914.[248]

---

246 WOOD, 1925.
247 Memorials of Rugbeians who Fell in the Great War.
248 HOLMES, *Riding the Retreat*, 2007, p258.

Sir Edward Goschen (Kilbracken)

Many Rugbeians played significant roles in the Great War, but few were quite so instrumental in its beginnings as Sir William Edward Goschen, Bt, GCB GCMG GCVO. He was the twelfth child and fifth son of German banker Wilhelm Heinrich Göschen, originally of Leipzig, and was born at Eltham on the 18th July 1847. Though entirely of German ancestry, Edward's education was stereotypically English in its style and manner, and in October 1861 the 14-year-old Edward arrived at Rugby and joined the house of the Revd Thomas Jex-Blake, a young master who would go on to be both Principal of Cheltenham College and Head Master of Rugby before his appointment as Dean of Wells in 1891, a post which he held for twenty years. Jex-Blake's house and indeed the wider Rugby school of Frederick Temple's[249] stately headmastership very much suited the teenage Edward, a natural sportsman who excelled in many different disciplines. He played cricket for the school XI and represented Rugby many times at real tennis. The Goschen family had adopted Rugby as their chosen school soon after their arrival in England, and Edward's elder brother George[250] had been Head of School at the time of Dr Tait's resignation as Head Master in 1849, before he left to matriculate at Oriel College, Oxford.

Upon leaving Rugby Edward proceeded to Corpus Christi College, Oxford, where his sporting successes continued, as he twice represented the university at real tennis and five times in first-class cricket matches. Indeed he continued to closely follow the Oxford-Cambridge match for the rest of his life. In 1869, after completing his degree, Edward entered the Diplomatic Service and began a short period of training at the Foreign Office before his first posting, which was to the British Embassy in Madrid. For twenty years he then served as Third, then Second Secretary in Buenos Aires, Paris, Rio de Janeiro, Constantinople and Peking, before his appointment as Secretary to the Legation in Copenhagen in 1888. Such a position of responsibility was an indication that an appointment as ambassador might be possible in the future, but further duties of the same kind followed in Lisbon, Washington (1893-4) and St Petersburg (1894-8), each one at a more important station than the

---

249 Archbishop of Canterbury 1896-1902.
250 Later 1st Viscount Goschen.

last. Lord Salisbury had returned to Downing Street to lead the Unionist coalition government formed in 1895, but also retained the portfolio of Foreign Secretary for himself, and as such appointed Edward to his first ambassadorial post, in Belgrade, in 1899. Serbia was not, at the time, of any particular concern to the British government, but its own political situation was in turmoil. The former King Milan, exiled in 1892, had returned to his homeland to be appointed commander in chief of the Serbian Army by his son King Alexander, and an attempt was made on the former king's life very soon after Edward's arrival in Belgrade. Such excitement was not to last however, as one year later Edward was posted back to Copenhagen, this time as Ambassador of Her Majesty Queen Victoria.

Copenhagen, as the capital of a stable, peaceful state, was something of a dull posting, diplomatically speaking, but in the five years he spent there he at least enjoyed the social opportunities afforded by the appointment. It was also here, in 1904, that he facilitated a meeting between King Edward VII and the Russian diplomat Count Alexander Isvolsky,[251] and it was probably this service which led the King to request that Edward be his new Ambassador to the Imperial Court in Vienna the following year. It might appear odd to appoint the son of a German migrant to the Viennese court, but in 1900 Edward had inherited the estate of Schloss Tentschach in Carinthia from a cousin, which gave him a convenient bolt-hole from the capital. He was now 58 years old and could reasonably have assumed that this would be his last position before retirement, but after three years it became clear that a replacement was needed for Sir Frank Lascelles, who was retiring from the embassy in Berlin after an extremely successful diplomatic career. The Foreign Office's first choice, Sir Arthur Nicolson, was unacceptable to the Kaiser, as he had clearly demonstrated at the Algeciras Conference of 1906 that he would promote French interests over those of Germany.[252] The next choice, Felix Cartwright, was already the British Consul in Munich, but was also rejected as not being enough of a notable public figure, and so eventually the Kaiser was persuaded to accept Edward Goschen as something of a compromise. Regardless of Edward's recent German ancestry, he had always viewed himself as English, and felt

---

251 McLEAN, 2007, p165.
252 MASSIE, 2007, p594.

uncomfortable when his family's past was highlighted; when in 1901 his brother published a biography of their grandfather, a Leipzig publisher, Edward wrote,

> ...for - tho' I oughtn't to – I hate the Germans and dislike being descended from one.[253]

He arrived, however, in Berlin in 1908, in the midst of the Daily Telegraph Affair which led to the resignation of Chancellor von Bülow in June 1909, but soon established excellent diplomatic relations with the new Chancellor, Theobald von Bethmann-Hollweg. The Chancellor and Edward both worked hard to maintain good relations between Britain and Germany over the succeeding years, steering their nations through the Second Moroccan Crisis and the Balkan Crises of 1912-13, but as tensions rose across Europe in 1914 it became clear that the emerging troubles could not be resolved by them alone.

After the assassination of Archduke Franz Ferdinand on the 28th June it was Bethmann-Hollweg and his Foreign Minister, Gottlieb von Jagow, who assured the Emperor of Austria of Germany's unconditional support. Edward himself was on leave in London at the time, ready to watch the annual varsity match at Lords, and was somewhat surprised at the agitation of the Foreign Secretary, Sir Edward Gray, who more fully grasped the gravity of the situation.[254] The July crisis worsened with each day and on the 30th the British government rejected German proposals for British neutrality. On the 3rd August, Albert King of the Belgians refused German demands, and Britain guaranteed military intervention in the event of a German invasion, but exactly that happened on the following morning, with German troops crossing the border and a small detachment demanding the surrender of Liege, though they were repulsed. Sir Francis Villiers, in charge of the British Legation at Brussels, sent a telegram to the Foreign Secretary informing him of the alarming developments, and he asked Edward Goschen, now back in Berlin, to challenge the German government on their intentions. By violating Belgian neutrality they had contravened the 1839 Treaty of London and, though they insisted that it was to prevent a French advance towards Germany through Belgium, the

---

253 DOCKRILL and McKERCHER, 2002, p27.
254 OTTE, 2014, p142.

French government in Paris had confirmed that they had no intention of doing so only a week earlier. Berlin had not responded to an identical request from the Foreign Office. Edward hurried to see Herr von Jagow and asked in the name of the King whether the German government would respect Belgian neutrality. Von Jagow, in a sad tone, informed him that the answer must be no, since German soldiers had already crossed the border. When Edward asked whether they could not still withdraw, he was informed that Germany saw the situation as one of life and death, as they wished to make as quick and decisive blow against France as possible, and a more southerly advance, avoiding Belgian territory, would be a far slower operation, allowing both the preparation of a French defence and the further build-up of Russian troops to the east, dividing the demands upon the German army.

That afternoon, with no indication of a German withdrawal, the Foreign Secretary sent a further telegram to Edward Goschen asking him to deliver a final ultimatum to the Imperial government. He again hurried to see von Jagow, and later described the meeting to Sir Edward Grey:

> I again proceeded to the Imperial Foreign Office and informed the Secretary of State that unless the Imperial Government could give the assurance by 12 o'clock that night that they would proceed no further with their violation of the Belgian frontier and stop their advance, I had been instructed to demand my passports and inform the Imperial Government that His Majesty's Government would have to take all steps in their power to uphold the neutrality of Belgium and the observance of a treaty to which Germany was as much a party as themselves.[255]

Von Jagow said that, however distant the deadline, his answer must remain the same, but expressed his deep regret and disappointment at the situation, though he entirely acknowledged that the British government could hardly have done otherwise. It was now 7pm on the 4th August, and Edward requested to be allowed to see the Chancellor one final time. His request was granted, and he found von Bethmann-Hollweg in an extremely agitated state; he felt that the impending horror was the fault

---

255 VON MACH, 1916, p485.

of Britain, who would go to war over a 'scrap of paper' (the Treaty of London), and implored Edward to ask the Foreign Office to reconsider in light of the probable consequences of their ultimatum. This, for the British government, was a point of honour:

> I hinted to his Excellency as plainly as I could that fear of consequences could hardly be regarded as an excuse for breaking solemn engagements, but his Excellency was so excited, so evidently overcome by the news of our action, and so little disposed to hear reason that I refrained from adding fuel to the flame by further argument.[256]

Both agreed that one of the greatest elements of the tragedy was that such a situation should arise just when relations between the two countries were at their best, but Edward realised that there was nothing further to be done, and returned to the British Embassy. At 9pm Herr von Zimmermann, the Under-Secretary of State called on Edward, and asked whether his demand for the British diplomats' passports was a declaration of war. Though of course he could not say that it was, Edward highlighted that very few such situations had not resulted in war, and that the midnight deadline still stood. Once Zimmermann left, Edward himself left the embassy, by the back door so as not to be seen crying. Midnight came and passed with no further communication from the Kaiser or his government, and no withdrawal of German troops from Belgium, and so a state of war existed from that point, as the British newspapers declared at breakfast the next morning.

Berlin was Edward's final foreign appointment with the diplomatic service, but during the war he founded and administered the Sir Edward Goschen Fund which provided assistance to British subjects interned in Germany. He died aged 76 on the 20th May 1924 at home at Lennox Gardens, Chelsea. Most of Edward's career was spent as a diplomat of an unassailable empire, travelling the world as an envoy of a Queen who was almost a mythical figure to many of her colonial subjects, yet he was instrumental in the beginning of a war which none could quite have foreseen in its scale. He was the human face of British policy, making a last-minute attempt to prevent war while honouring his nation's duty.

---

256 Ibid.

The Reverend Rupert Inglis (Cotton)

Rupert Inglis, country rector and beloved military chaplain, was also the oldest rugby international to be killed in the Great War. He was born at Hanover Square in London on the 17th May 1863, the seventh and youngest child of Major General Sir John Inglis KCB – 'the Defender of Lucknow' in the Indian Mutiny (who died seven months before Rupert was born) – and his wife the Hon Julia Thesiger, daughter of the Lord Chancellor, the first Baron Chelmsford. After initial education at Lindley Lodge School, at Higham-on-the Hill, Leicestershire, Rupert entered Rugby School in 1877, joining the house of Mr H. Lee-Warner, three years into the headmastership of the Revd Thomas Jex-Blake. An old Rugbeian, former assistant master and housemaster himself, Jex-Blake was steeped in the ways of Rugby, and was very much at home after having resigned as Principal of Cheltenham College to take up the helm of the school that had shaped him for most of his life. Inglis was a natural sportsman and was invited to join the XV in 1879, only two years after he arrived at the school, playing almost entirely amongst and against boys older than himself. Rugby Football was not his only sporting strength however, and in his last year, 1881, he played for both the football XV and Cricket XI.[257]

In the Michaelmas term of 1881 Rupert matriculated at University College, Oxford, to read History, and it was inevitable that his Rugby pedigree would lead him towards the university club. That did indeed happen, and he played as a forward in the famous Oxford XVs of 1883 and 1884, seeing the first varsity try hat-trick (by C.G. Wade for Oxford in 1883), and the controversial adoption of colours by the players in 1884 against the wishes of the university boat clubs. The following year, Rupert received his degree from the university and began training for ordination at Ely Theological College, being ordained Deacon in 1889. He had not neglected his chosen sport however; he continued to play for Blackheath and in 1886 played for England three times, against Wales, Ireland and Scotland, remaining unbeaten in all three fixtures.

After ordination Rupert held short curacies in Helmsley and Basingstoke before being appointed rector to the small Kentish

---

257 Memorials of Rugbeians who fell in the Great War.

village of Frittenden in 1900, and in the same year, on the 11th June, he married Helen Gilchrist, with whom he had three children. Interestingly his middle child John (known as 'Tommy') became Vice Admiral Sir John Inglis KBE CB and served as Director of Naval Intelligence between 1954 and 1960. Rupert's parish was very much a rural one, largely devoted to growing hops and fruit, but as war approached he couldn't help but be influenced by international affairs. Frittenden is a very small village to this day, but still twenty-three of its young men gave their lives in the war, including two sets of brothers, and it was as they, in their ones and twos, joined the army that Rupert began to feel his conscience pulling him in the same direction. Though he was now 50, he felt that he had much to give, and so soon after the declaration of war he volunteered his services as a chaplain, and at the beginning of July 1915 found himself on a ship to France as chaplain to the forces, 4th class. His unusual decision to serve in such a capacity had given rise to much discussion in the village, to whom he had tried to explain his motives, and on the 7th July, less than a week after arriving at the front, he wrote a passionate explanation to his parishioners:

> Dear Parishioners,
>
> I think most of you will understand how I come to be writing from France. I have felt that in this great crisis of our nation's history, everyone ought to do what he can to help. I have said this both publicly and privately, but it has been hard to tell people that they ought to leave their homes, to go out into strange and new surroundings, to endure discomforts and danger – perhaps to face death – it has been hard to tell people that this was their duty and then to remain comfortably at home myself. So that is why I have left you for an indefinite period.
>
> I am proud, very proud of what Frittenden has done. I know how hard it has been for many of the soldiers to leave their homes and their families and occupations; but the harder it has been, the greater the credit and reward.
>
> I need not tell you that Frittenden will be constantly in my thoughts and that it will make things easier for me here if I hear that everything is going on well in the Parish.

> I ask for your prayers. I ask you to pray that I may be a help to those to whom I have to minister out here. That God will bless and keep you all, is the prayer of

> Your Affectionate Rector,
> Rupert E. Inglis[258]

On his arrival in France Rupert was confronted by the horrors of modern, mechanised warfare, serving first in No. 23 General Hospital, Étaples, followed by No. 21 Casualty Clearing Station at Corbie, near Albert, where he saw first-hand the horrific injuries and terrible deaths of those brought back from the front-line trenches. He was shocked a week after arriving to be confronted by one of his own parishioners, Lance Corporal Jim Stone, brought in with a leg full of shrapnel, and in his next letter Rupert begged his wife not to tell anyone in the village that the leg would probably have to be amputated. He had been blown up while bringing in injured soldiers from his unit, the 1st Battalion Queen's Own Royal West Kent Regiment. At first he was optimistic, but soon gangrene set into the many wounds in his leg, and on the 21st July Rupert wrote:

> I am very sad to-day as poor Jim Stone died at 3. He was going on so well, but this morning the nurse came and told me gangrene had set in, and that he was to have his leg amputated at 10 o'clock. I went in and stayed with him till he went to the operating theatre - he was very bright and wonderfully plucky. I went to see him as soon as he was brought back. He was partially conscious. I think he knew me, but he only lived an hour. He was a fine chap and I had got to like him. He seemed to be quite a link with home...[259]

Today Jim Stone's name appears on the village war memorial, alongside Rupert's own.

The days in the hospital and CCS were an alternating experience of horror and hope for Rupert; no sooner had he written to tell of the

---

258 INGLIS H., *Rupert Edward Inglis: Chaplain to the Forces, Rector of Frittenden*, 1920, privately published.

259 Ibid.

patients' delight at the delivery of a gramophone or some board game, but he was then describing his sadness at the realisation that those whom he saw paralysed might live for many more years in that condition. Even so, Rupert's letters show a stoic determination and gentle compassion that made him, from the start, an extraordinarily dependable figure upon whom the wounded could call and rely. One of his most memorable early letters recalled an occasion on which he was asked to write about a situation which would lead to one of the legends of the Western Front: Toc H:

> I have just had to write a long letter to the Bishop of Winchester, as the man who was with his son Gilbert, when he was killed, was brought into this Hospital. As the man has both his arms wounded they asked me to send all particulars. I heard from the brother Neville Talbot who is a Chaplain at the front. He crept out after dark and found his brother's body close up to the German Trenches.[260]

The Revd Neville Talbot was awarded the Military Cross for that action, but it was the all-ranks club, named 'Talbot House' after Gilbert by its founder the Revd Philip 'Tubby' Clayton, which was to be the enduring effect of the Gilberts in Belgium, with its famous sign above the door, 'All rank abandon, ye who enter here.'

Rupert long believed that he was about to be sent out to a brigade near the front, and so it happened in November that he joined the chaplains of the 6th Infantry Brigade, coincidentally with Neville Talbot. In many ways this removed him from much of the horror, and his letters give fewer examples and less detail of the injured and dying men to whom he ministered, but soon enough his work took him to the field ambulances near Albert, and Rupert found himself once more in the work to which he had, almost, become accustomed:

> A man often suffers a lot anticipating he is going to be hurt, and by talking to him and interesting him you can often take his mind off—about all sorts of things, cricket, football, boxing - Captain Moore always helps along and joins in. The other day we had a Welshman who had some

---

260 Ibid.

very painful wounds. As a rule Welshmen do not stand pain very well, but this man was very keen on football, so he and I and Moore carried on a violent discussion about football and the man got through it splendidly, and I went off to another man. Then Moore found he had something more to do to the Welshman, so he came over and said "Come along - my local anaesthetic - I want you to talk some more football."[261]

And so 'The Rector', as he had become known, lived a stilted existence between dugouts, tents and huts, sometimes accompanying the battalion to which he was attached on route-marches, sometimes ministering to the dying in field ambulances and, whenever possible, organising concerts and other entertainments for the men, not taking his clothes off nor washing for days at a time, as the routines of trench life dictated. It was, as he wrote home '…a curious sort of life for a respectable old country Rector to be leading'. By this time Rupert was serving with the 1st King's Shropshire Light Infantry, 1st Buffs, 2nd York and Lancasters and 8th Bedfords, and the brigade moved south for the great offensive of the Somme, the guns of which could be heard back in Frittenden. As the battle wore on Rupert's concern for the troops under his care remained apparent; he sent home a skull-cap which the KSLI wore inside their helmets to soak up the sweat and asked that 1,500 copies be made to be given to the Buffs. In the greatest discomfort on the Western Front he gave little thought to his own living conditions, but continually struggled to improve the lot of those around him. Rupert's last letter was posted on the 17th September 1916 and in it he described how, in the aftermath of battle, his job was to lead the stretcher bearers taking the wounded from KSLI HQ to the dressing station, but that Captain Thomas Ingram RAMC, leading the parties collecting the wounded from no man's land, had disappeared and was feared to have been killed or captured when working near the German lines in the dark. He had indeed, it was later discovered, been shot the previous day. His last words home were, 'In a few minutes will be off to the Dressing Station. I shall probably be back early to-day.'

---

261 Ibid.

What happened next was described to Mrs Inglis by Neville Talbot, who wrote to her on the 20th September as soon as he had ascertained the events leading to Rupert's death:

> Unknown to the Headquarters of his Brigade and to the Battalions in the Brigade, your husband went out on Monday afternoon with a party of stretcher bearers headed by Captain Moir. Moir and your husband somehow got separated and your husband fell in with another party which had been sent out by the Sherwood Foresters under Lieut. Mellor. Your husband got the latter party to come and fetch some wounded men whom he had discovered. Whilst they were doing this shelling began and your husband was hit in the leg.
>
> He and Lieut Mellor and a stretcher bearer called Stretton, of the Sherwood Foresters, got into a shell hole and the latter began to bandage the wound. Then another shell landed in the shell hole and killed your husband and Stretton and wounded Mellor dangerously. I got this information from Sgt. Rodgers (since killed in action) of the Sherwood Foresters who was with Lieut. Mellor's party. He had got into a neighbouring shell hole and came over and saw that your husband had been instantaneously killed. He and the rest of the party carried Lieut. Mellor down, and later on he passed through this Dressing Station and is home by now I expect. . . . I have got the spot marked on the map and have reported it to the Brigade. A big burial party was at work all over the ground last night consisting of a Battalion of Divisional Pioneers. I think it is fairly certain they will have carried out the burial. I could not find them this evening, so that I am not sure. I shall find them tomorrow morning. If there is any doubt I and the Brigade staff will not rest till we have seen to the burial. It is not an easy place to get to as it is often shelled, but it shall be managed.
>
> That is my story - I am afraid it is too long and involved, but I have felt that you would like to know all I know .... He has evidently been working rather as a free lance and has helped with the finding of wounded belonging not only

to his own Battalion but to others in the Division. I cannot overstate the sorrow there is to-day in his Brigade. "They simply loved him," so said several officers and men in the Shropshires to me to-day.

He has fallen doing gallant work for others. …. you will, I believe, feel the glory of such a death - simply met in saving others. Yours, ours, is the loss, not his. He has passed on as the faithful friend and servant of others. He is loved and mourned throughout the Division. I was much with him further north and we were great friends …. You must not blame anyone. The Brigadier and staff were absorbed in the fighting. They and one of the Battalion Commanders, Colonel Murray of the Shropshires, had tried to restrain him, but the need of those poor lads lying out wounded hour after hour could not be denied. He has glorified his profession and his Master ….[262]

Rupert Inglis, chaplain 4th class, 53 years old, was buried by members of the 1st Battalion, the Cheshire Regiment, and though it was marked with a simple wooden cross, the continued shelling meant that its position was soon lost. The letters of condolence which arrived at Frittenden Rectory are marked by their universal and sincere admiration for the man who could very easily have stayed at home safely ministering to the families of those fighting at the front, but who could not allow his parishioners to serve their country without him, and who could not encourage others to risk their own lives without leading by example. As General Nicholson, Base Commander at Calais, wrote, 'Of him it can be truly said, "Greater love hath no man than this, that he gave his life for his friends."'

---

262 Ibid.

THE VICTORIA
CROSS

Lieutenant Frank de Pass VC (School Field)

Frank Alexander de Pass was born on the 26th April 1886 at his parents' London home, 2 Kensington Garden Terrace, to a Sephardi Jewish family who had fled persecution in Spain in the 1660s and who had lived in west London for over two hundred years since. His father, Sir Eliot de Pass, had six children, a large house and a successful business, E A de Pass & Co, specialising in the import of sugar and coffee from Jamaica. That was where he had met his wife and Frank's mother Beatrice, and they had married in Kingston on the 29th August 1883. Frank's early education was at the Abbey School, an imposing building with large grounds in Beckenham, Kent, which had opened in 1866. From there he duly passed on to Rugby School in 1901. He joined Brooke House (now School Field), where he was welcomed by his housemaster William P. Brooke, his wife Mary and his two sons, Rupert and Alfred. Rupert and Frank quickly became good friends, but neither could have known that a few short years later the headstone of Frank's grave would bear words taken from one of Rupert's poems.

In 1904 Frank took the entrance examinations for the Royal Military Academy, Woolwich, and, being placed third on the list of successful candidates, began his military career as a promising young artillery officer cadet. After a year and a half of training, in January 1906 Frank was commissioned as a second lieutenant in the Royal Field Artillery, but there were great changes ahead. Promoted to lieutenant in 1909, he accompanied his battery to India shortly afterwards and was entranced by the sights and sounds of his new surroundings, so much so that by August he had applied to transfer to an Indian cavalry regiment, the 34th Prince Albert Victor's Own Poona Horse. Raised in 1817, the regiment had a distinguished history, having most recently fought in the Boxer Rebellion at the turn of the century. The change, for a 23-year-old lieutenant whose career had barely taken him outside London up until then, must have been astounding, but it was one to which Frank adapted quickly and wholeheartedly. His love of polo meant that he quickly made his mark in his new regiment, and his new uniform, with its large gold, red and blue striped turban and sash, made a dashing change from the khaki serge of the artillery. The Poona Horse were known for their polo playing abilities; indeed in 1896 the newly arrived 4th Hussars bought an entire polo stable from them in Bombay in order to kick-start their sporting prowess in India, ably aided by a young polo-mad subaltern, Winston Churchill. Frank learned Hindi and Persian extraordinarily quickly, and so in 1913 was appointed Orderly Officer to General Sir Percy Lake who had recently relieved Sir Douglas Haig as Chief of the General Staff in India. As such, Frank accompanied General Lake to GHQ in Calcutta and Simla, the winter and summer capitals of the British Raj, and was able to see much more of his newly adopted country than his regimental contemporaries. Such an appointment was a clear indication of the esteem in which he was held by his superiors, and so it was only the declaration of war in 1914 that led him to stand down to rejoin his regiment in Secunderabad.

At 2330 on the 9th August 1914, the Poona Horse received orders to mobilise[263] along with the 7th Dragoon Guards and the 20th Deccan Horse, as the 9th (Secunderabad) Cavalry Brigade and part of the 2nd Indian Cavalry Division. The Regiment's feverish preparations are recorded in the war diaries, recalling officers from attachments across India, arranging for those on leave in England to rejoin their squadrons en-route at Port Said (including Captain Grimshaw, commanding D Squadron, of which Frank was an officer), and finding 72 extra horses from the 26th Light Horse and 45 men from the 33rd before they proceeded to Bombay. Frank took charge of Captain Grimshaw's kit, and the entire regiment left Secunderabad by three trains on the 7th September. After arrival in Bombay they bought extra horses to replace the regiment's camels which couldn't be taken to Europe and, after an inspection by Major General Phayre, Frank embarked in the SS *Ranee*[264], in Division A of the Indian Expeditionary Force's convoy, guided by the cruiser HMS *Fox*[265], for the long journey west. The regimental orders, issued by the adjutant Captain Elphinston and preserved with the war diaries, provide a fascinating glimpse of Edwardian Indian military routine, detailing the duties of the British and Indian officers of the day, which parts of the ship were restricted to officers, and much more, even that permission to smoke was to be given by the trumpet call 'Charge'! Interestingly,

---

263 WO 95/1187/4.

264 Built in 1906 for the North German Lloyd Line and seized by British authorities in 1914.

265 Second Class Cruiser of the Astraea Class, launched in 1893 and broken up in 1920.

as well as the usual rations of rice, onions, garlic, chilies, turmeric and potatoes, opium was also issued to those on board on request, at the rate of twenty grains per man per day. In his diary, Grimshaw recalled a conversation with Frank onboard the *Ranee*:

> Curiously enough, when on board ship sharing the same cabin, de Pass told me he had no sense of fear about anything.[266]

By the 7th October 1914 the convoy had passed through the Suez Canal and sailed for France, escorted by the French battleship *Bouvet*. On the 15th, after a sea voyage of several weeks, the officers, men and horses of the Poona Horse arrived at Marseilles and, after disembarking the next morning and a delay of a few days due to bad weather, they began their long journey north to the rapidly expanding Western Front by train. Grimshaw's diaries provide a telling account of the unexpected arrival of Indian troops among the British army; at Orleans, for example, he had a terrible row with a major of the RAMC who believed that his warrant officers were more entitled to a spare first class carriage than the Indian officer who held the Viceroy's commission[267]. They arrived in Calais on the 31st October and headed south to the front, quickly reinforcing the beleaguered 2nd (King Edward VII's Own) Gurkha Rifles at Neuve Chapelle and, in something of a baptism of fire (described by the CO of the Gurkhas as 'an inferno of howitzer shells'[268]), they found themselves in action on the same day they arrived in the line. The 2nd Gurkhas' trench north of the village had been largely overrun by the enemy, leaving a gap between the Connaught Rangers on the left and the 9th Gurkhas on the right and, in order to recapture the position, B and C Squadrons of the Poona Horse launched a day-time attack without any artillery support. Tragically, their commanding officer, Lieutenant Colonel Charles Swanston DSO, was killed by a sniper while attempting to ascertain whether any of the Gurkhas still held the front line. Major Malloy, an officer of the regiment, wrote on the following day,

---

266 GRIMSHAW, 1986, p48.
267 GRIMSHAW, p28.
268 WO 95/1184/4.

> It was at this point that the regiment suffered the loss of our gallant Colonel, shot in the right side whilst using his field glasses, and whose death was reported to have been instantaneous.[269]

The regiment remained under constant fire until withdrawn by the order of the brigade major at approximately 0200. The heavy shelling prevented the immediate recovery of Colonel Swanston's body, but it eventually was, and he lies buried in the Rue de Petillon Cemetery, a short distance from Neuve Chapelle.

The following couple of weeks were rather quiet by comparison, including inspections by both the elderly Field Marshal Lord Roberts (only a few days before his death) and the Prince of Wales, but on the 21st November Flanders was blanketed in snow and the Poona Horse were back in action two days later at the Defence of Festubert, one of the very first attacks on an established trench system, during which the allied forces were pushed west between the villages of Festubert and Givenchy-lès-la-Bassée. D Squadron, including Frank and under the command of Captain Grimshaw, occupied trenches that had recently seen heavy fighting and were still filled with corpses. Grimshaw's diary records his horror at realising that he was standing, not on sandbags as he had thought, but on the body of a young Pathan soldier, killed as they arrived in the line; 'I thought of that youth in his home in the hills of India, probably the pride of his parents, and then to see him thus trampled into the mud like another piece of mud, of no more account than a piece of offal.'[270] Daylight only brought more horror, as the mutilated remains of many members of the 7th Dragoon Guards, who had lately occupied the trench, appeared with the dawn.

It was during this action that Frank de Pass was to lose his life; the following is taken from a handwritten report by Captain Grimshaw, which remains with the regiment's war diary in the National Archives:

> On arrival in the trenches at 4am 23rd [Nov 1914] it was discovered that the enemy had driven a sap up to the parapet of that part of the trench allocated to the Poona Horse. The

---

269 Ibid.
270 GRIMSHAW, p39.

enemy had blown in the parapet and a breach of about 8 feet existed leaving the trench exposed to rifle fire from the sap. A troop was told off to hold the breach, pending daylight when a careful infraction could be made, with rules to construct a traverse at once, to cover themselves from rifle fire. Lt de Pass asked permission to have the defence of this breach placed under his orders. The request was granted. As soon as it was daylight the O.C. Detach. Poona Horse inspected the breach and in order to ascertain what was in the sap called for a volunteer to enter and proceed along it towards enemy lines. Abdullah then volunteered and entered the sap. He returned and reported that enemy had erected a sandbag traverse about 20 yards from the trenches at a point where the sap makes its first bend, and that a man with a rifle was at a loop hole.

At 8am the enemy commenced throwing bombs into our trenches from their side of the loopholes traverse. They continued all day and caused some casualties – early on morning of 24th Lt de Pass placed a charge of gun cotton in enemy gun loop and fired the charge completely demolishing the enemy traverse and rounding off the bend sufficiently to expose, for some yards, the sap to our rifle fire. In doing this enemy threw a bomb at Lt de Pass' party which fortunately missed and exploded behind them.

This action of Lt de Pass stopped all bomb throwing by enemy during 24th and the effect can better be gauged by the fact that there was only 1 casualty that day compared to 6 the day before, and 9 the next day when, under cover of darkness night of 24/25 enemy replaced their loopholed sandbag traverse. The same day Lt de Pass, accompanied by a Trooper (name not known) of 7TH DGs went out in broad daylight and brought in a Sepoy of 58th Rifles, who was lying wounded in rear of our trenches, about 200yd distance.

Lt de Pass did not ask permission to do this and did it on his own initiative when paying a visit to 7th DG defences.

Lt de Pass again volunteered to enter enemy's sap and blow up the traverse but permission was refused.

About 3pm 26th the bomb throwing by enemy became worse and Lt de Pass went to head of sap to supervise to our defences which had not been previously repaired. He endeavoured to shoot the enemy sniper through a loop hole and in doing so got shot himself through the head.

I consider that Lt de Pass' conduct was most intrepid and that his actions were a magnificent example to the men of the detachment.

R Grimshaw Capt
D Sqn Poona Horse

The nature of Frank's death tells us much about his character; his bravery had been noted since his initial cavalry training[271], and time after time he volunteered for the most arduous and dangerous of duties, never expecting his men to accept those tasks in his place. One might presume that such dangers would be shared within the squadron, but Frank was determined that he should lead by example and, in doing so, gave his troopers the ultimate example of duty. When refused permission, he still attempted the most terrifying of responsibilities, even in broad daylight, borrowing two men from the 7th Dragoon Guards to attempt to destroy the enemy sap once again. This final time, he was shot through the centre of his forehead and killed instantly. His body was taken to a mortuary in Béthune, and Captain Grimshaw wrote in his diary the next day,

I felt an unpleasant pang when I stood beside poor 'Bumpty's' body. That lifeless clay was all that was left of his brilliant accomplishments. It was only with an effort that I could bring myself to search his pockets. It was soon over and, giving his hand one last press, I left the room feeling very wretched.

Lieutenant Frank de Pass of the Poona Horse was subsequently buried in Béthune Town Cemetery at 1630 on the 7th December 1914, in heavy rain and in the presence of Lieutenant General Sir Pratap Singh, former Maharaja of Idar, and Lieutenant General Sir Michael Rimington, commander of the Indian Cavalry Corps. As his coffin was

---

271 Ibid, p49.

155

lowered into the grave British artillery could be heard beginning a new bombardment in the distance, giving the mourners no opportunity to forget the conflict, however temporarily. After the war his permanent tombstone bore the words of his old friend Rupert Brooke: 'loved, gone, proudly friended'. Neither did his extraordinary gallantry go unnoticed, particularly after he was first recommended for further recognition by Captain Grimshaw and the acting CO of the Poona Horse, Lieutenant General Cooper, who wrote to the brigade major, 'there is no doubt he acted with great gallantry and boldness throughout a trying time.'[272] He was awarded the Victoria Cross, gazetted on the 18th February 1915, with a citation that stated,

> For conspicuous bravery near Festubert on the 24th November, in entering a German sap and destroying a traverse in the face of the enemy's bombs, and so subsequently rescuing, under heavy fire, a wounded man who was lying in the open. Lieutenant de Pass lost his life on this day in a second attempt to capture the sap which had been retaken by the enemy.

Frank was the first Jewish winner of the Victoria Cross, and for the same action the medal was awarded to Naik (Corporal) Darwan Singh Negi, of the 39th Garhwal Rifles, a little further down the line. Sadly, his father was too ill to collect the Victoria Cross at Buckingham Palace, and so it was delivered to his home by the Royal Mail; it is now held by the National Army Museum along with his sword, tunic and turban. Throughout his career Frank was perhaps typical of a British Indian cavalry officer: a dashing polo player who probably never expected to be involved in a major conflict, but who had a great deal of respect and admiration for the men who served under him, men whom he loved and cared for, and whom he led with unparalleled bravery.

---

272 WO 95/1184/4.

Captain John Norwood VC (Bradley)

John Norwood was the only son of John and Lucy Norwood of Pembury Lodge, New Beckenham, but surprisingly little is known of his childhood. The family had lived in Kent for centuries, having settled in the Isle of Thanet after the Norman Conquest, but there was very little military experience in the few generations leading up to John's birth. His mother died at Bromley in 1890, when John was 12, but his father, a successful hop merchant, had sent him to the Abbey School, founded by the Revd Lloyd Philips in 1866 and, by the time of John's arrival, a highly respected prep school. He arrived at Rugby in 1891, in Donkin's House (now Bradley), under the supervision of Arthur Donkin, who taught at Rugby for an extraordinary forty-five years. Perhaps the highlight of his school career came in the Trinity term of 1894 when he was a member of the Shooting VIII who won the Ashburton Shield, the highest prize available in school shooting, at Bisley. The competition had been begun by Rugby, Eton and Harrow in 1861, with Rugby winning the first annual competition, though the shield itself was not ready[273]. The 1894 victory, in which John scored 46, gave him the privilege of wearing the school coat of arms on the sleeve of his rifle corps uniform. To win the Ashburton was a significant achievement in the life of a Rugbeian, and the winning VIII were celebrated by the town as well as the school:

> The Bisley VIII fetched the Ashburton Shield on Saturday, the 21st of July. The Corps met the VIII at the station with School and Town Bands, and the horses were taken out and selected members of the School dragged the bus up to the Close. Electric lights had been fitted up outside the School House. There Dr Percival, Lieut. Drake, Capt. Barnard and Mr Thompson addressed the crowded meeting.[274]

In the autumn of the same year John matriculated at Exeter College, Oxford, though he soon decided upon a military career instead, and in 1899 was commissioned as a university candidate in the

---

273 The silver shield, still awarded today, was given by Francis Baring, 3rd Lord Ashburton, in 1861.

274 HARRIS, 1960, p9.

5th (Princess Charlotte of Wales') Dragoon Guards, sailing to join the regiment at Sialkot in India. There were in fact two Old Rugbeians who joined the regiment that year; the other, Maurice Black, was killed while serving with the Royal Flying Corps in 1917[275]. One of John's early actions was to organise an extraordinary long-distance solo hunting trip to Kashmir in search of the ibex, a much-prized quarry. He left by train to Rawalpindi and then headed north by tonga, a sort of light carriage. Accompanied by a 'tiffin coolie' (cook), a footman, several porters/guides and a Hindustani textbook for communication, they struggled through the snow, meeting very few other Europeans apart from the Count of Turin, son of the King of Spain and a most prolific hunter. Reaching Shigar, John pitched a tent on the polo pitch and was entertained by the Maharajah and his thirty wives[276], though he was suffering from altitude sickness. The hunting itself was not hugely successful, but the experience of tracking the ibex across the scree and glaciers of Kashmir was an exhilarating one. When he returned to his camp on the 10th September he found that a telegram had caught him up, telling him to return at once to Sialkot as the regiment had been ordered to stand ready to move at short notice. With war in South Africa imminent John was full of excitement and wrote in his diary, 'Hooray! Hooray! When the deuce will it dawn? Dear old Kruger.'[277] Even so, with his kit scattered between Shigar and Sialkot, with nothing clean and little training completed, John was worried that he might be left behind; but he need not have had any such concerns.

The 5th Dragoon Guards left Sialkot on the 20th September 1899 under the command of the famous Lieutenant Colonel Robert Baden-Powell, bound for Table Bay, and a somewhat different kind of conflict than they might have expected in India. After a rough crossing from Bombay, the transport of a regiment of cavalry to Ladysmith on a narrow gauge railway was no easy task, but it was in South Africa that John's fame was to be found, and he soon saw action in the 5th Dragoon Guards' cavalry charge at the Battle of Elandslaagte on the 21st October. After the preliminary exchange of artillery fire and an attack by the infantry

---

275 Major Maurice A Black RFC (Whitelaw's House) was shot down over enemy lines on the 11th February 1917.

276 MURPHY, 2017, p67.

277 Ibid, p71.

of the Gordon Highlanders, D Squadron, plus a squadron from the 5th Lancers, charged the Boers in extended line, then wheeled and again charged the survivors, killing large numbers with sword, lance and revolver. As it was cold and wet John joined the charge in his raincoat, with a cardigan tied around his neck to keep the water out – 'a splendid charging kit for a dragoon!', as he later wrote to Colonel Gore.[278] John stayed on the battlefield all night, with a group of prisoners, as it was too dark to find their way back to camp. The success of that victory didn't last, and within ten days Ladysmith was under siege; between then and the 28th February 1900 the city was surrounded by Boer forces and the railway line to Durban was cut, though the last bullet-riddled train to get through contained both Major General French and his chief of staff Major Douglas Haig, but leaving behind the officer in command, Lieutenant General Sir George White. Early in the siege the defending forces were able to send patrols out into the hills which surround the town, and it was on one of these that John Norwood's actions brought him to the attention of his superiors and, ultimately, the sovereign. In the words of his citation,

> On the 30th October, 1899, this Officer went out from Ladysmith in charge of a small patrol of the 5th Dragoon Guards. They came under a heavy fire from the enemy, who were posted on a ridge in great force. The patrol, which had arrived within about 600 yards of the ridge, then retired at full speed. One man dropped, and Second Lieutenant Norwood galloped back about 300 yards through heavy fire, dismounted, and picking up the fallen trooper, carried him out of fire on his back, at the same time leading his horse with one hand. The enemy kept up an incessant fire during the whole time that Second Lieutenant Norwood was carrying the man until he was quite out of range.[279]

John had dismounted to help Private Mouncer, who had been shot through the throat, and when carrying him back he was joined by Private

---

278 Ibid, p85.
279 *London Gazette*, 27th July 1900.

Sibthorpe who helped him carry the injured man to safety. When under cover again John reported Mouncer's action, but neglected to mention his own part in the heroic action, and it was only when the latter was questioned that the true nature of events became apparent. Indeed his squadron commander's report stated, 'It is against the expressed wish of 2nd Lt Norwood that I report his share in this act of gallantry.' John was awarded the Victoria Cross for his actions that day and Private Mouncer was awarded the Distinguished Conduct Medal. Once the siege was famously lifted by General Redvers Buller, with John seeing the relieving column from his hospital bed while suffering from typhoid, the 5th Dragoon Guards remained in South Africa, but in light of his illness John was given four months' leave on the 27th March 1900, and sailed for Southampton in the SS *Gascon*. There he was met by his sister Amy, and it was at her house in Chelsea in May that he received a letter from the Queen's Equerry stating,

> I have to acquaint you that the Queen has been pleased to signify her gracious intention to personally confer upon you the decoration of the Victoria Cross early in the week commencing 20th instant. The exact date and hour will be notified to you in a further notification.[280]

John was not to receive his decoration personally from the Queen however: by the week of the 20th he was already on his way to rejoin his regiment in South Africa, and by the time he returned the Queen had died, so instead it was presented to him by Lord Roberts. By the 22nd June he was at the Imperial Hotel at Pietermaritzberg waiting to transfer to the Cavalry Depot, and served for a further two years in South Africa, receiving a mention in dispatches in the course of many more minor actions before the regiment returned to India. In 1904 the 5th Dragoon Guards were to return to South Africa, but without Lieutenant Norwood, who moved to Simla to serve as adjutant to the Calcutta Light Horse and Chota Nagpur Rifles, with promotion to captain. A staff appointment in an Indian regiment was a routine career move for an officer of John's seniority, and a sign of promise, as the British adjutant in such a regiment had greater responsibilities even than those serving

---

280 MURPHY, p107.

in the same positions in the UK. For example, he was responsible for the selection and training of all of those who were to receive the Viceroy's Commission. These Indian officers were excellent horsemen who owned their own horses and equipment, as did the Sowars serving beneath them in irregular regiments such as the Calcutta Light Horse. It was while serving in Simla, the summer home of the British Indian government, that John became reacquainted with Lillian Collen, the daughter of Sir Edwin Collen, Secretary to the Government of India Military Department. The couple were married at All Saints', Malabar Hill, on the 5th March 1904, with their first child, also John, following in July 1905.

Further service in South Africa and London separated John from his family, and he was growing tired of army life. He had approximately £20,000[281] invested in his father's former company, the hop dealer Wigans, and that was easily enough to support the Norwoods, so in June 1909 he resigned his commission after an eventful ten years' service, to find employment with Garton, a sugar merchant in London and Southampton. That wasn't to last however, and when war began in 1914 he mobilised with the 2nd County of London Yeomanry. However, as a distinguished former officer of a regular regiment, John was attached to the 5th Dragoon Guards, and happily rejoined his old regiment. Indeed, Colonel Ansell of the 5th DG was so keen to have him back that a Rolls Royce was sent to collect him, and on the 15th August John entrained with B Squadron at Farnborough bound for Southampton, from where they sailed for Le Havre on the SS *Cestrian* the following day. On the night of the 23rd it was known that German infantry were close and advancing, so the regiment spent the night digging trenches, with their horses tied up in a field on the Mons–Valenciennes road, but their defences were of little use when the enemy attacked at 5am, giving John his first taste of action in twelve years. For four days the cavalry attempted to cover the French and Belgian retreats, and somewhere in the confusion of retreating troops and fleeing civilians in Solesmes, John and Lieutenant Lechmere, together with the regiment's signalmen, were separated from the rest of the unit and did not manage to rejoin them until Monday the 31st August. The war diary for the following day is typical of the somewhat light-hearted tone evident at the time,

---

281 Ibid, p147.

but also of the heavier fighting in which the 5th DG suddenly found itself involved:

> Partridge shooting begins!
> A very thick misty morning. The ball opened with half-a-dozen shells bursting over the village [Nery]. Immediately all was bustle. Everybody ran to the lines to saddle up, under shell and rifle fire. "C" Squadron was ordered to hold the houses facing E. "A" and "B" Squadrons were quickly collected, and galloped, under Colonel Ansell, to the N. with the object of turning the German right flank. In the centre of the village the 11th held the outskirts facing E. while the Bays maintained their position at the S. end, though they lost many officers and men wounded, and over 200 horses, by shell fire. Their lines were exposed to the fire of two batteries at a range of about 700 yards. "L" Battery, Royal Horse Artillery, suffered most of all. All their officers and men who were in the battery were killed or wounded except Major Sclater-Booth, commanding, the Battery Sergeant-Major, and their French interpreter. The two latter were left at the end of the fight, still serving a gun. Captain Bradbury, Royal Horse Artillery, had a leg shot off and carried on doing his duty until his other leg was carried away by a shell, when his only request was that he might be carried to the rear, in order that his men might not hear him groaning. All the gun team horses were found shot and lying in their teams.[282]

This action is also significant in Rugbeian history, as the officer who was killed leading the effort to regain control of the Bays' stampeding horses under extremely heavy fire was Major John Cawley of the 20th Hussars, brother to the two Cawley brothers who feature elsewhere in this book, and who was himself an old boy of School House. Lieutenant Colonel Ansell, the commanding officer, was also shot, with his last words being that the troopers tending to him should return to fight, leaving him to die. After such a chaotic introduction to modern warfare, the 5th DG spent almost a week without any direct enemy contact, though looted shops and

---

282 WO95/1109/2.

abandoned artillery pieces were evidence of their recent activity. Finally at 2.30am on the 8th September the regiment advanced, as the lead regiment of the 2nd Cavalry Brigade covering the advance of the 1st Army Corps. The fluid nature of warfare in these opening weeks of the war meant that the regiment was ranged across a wide area, with B Squadron on the right of the line, C Squadron in the centre and A Squadron on the left as they advanced towards the small village of Launoy-Beaufort and down through the woods towards the River Morin. John, newly appointed to the command of B Squadron, scouted ahead and reported that the village of Sablonnières across the river was lightly held, so the decision was made that he would take three troops, along with Captain Partridge, and three troops of A Squadron, to cross the river and attack the village from the east. The river was unfordable however, so the six troops of cavalry were forced to approach Sablonnières by the main road from the south, in full view of the German infantry occupying the village and in trenches immediately north of the river. They were brought into action in a water meadow before they even reached the bridge, and with no cover available casualties were quickly taken. It was here that Captain John Norwood VC was shot and killed, on the day of his 38th birthday, along with Captain Partridge, Sergeants Gough, Nunn and Coole, and Privates Wisdom and Fishlock.[283] Sergeant Nunn, who had served with John in South Africa, later described the event to an enquiry. John's horse had been shot from under him by machine gun fire, and Nunn was injured:

> …when the said John Norwood ran to me and assisted as far as possible and then started running to obtain the aid of one of the Medical Corps to attend to me, when I saw the said John Norwood shot dead, a bullet having gone through his neck and killed him. I saw the body of the deceased put into a cart and taken away to be buried and afterwards learned from Sergeant Hadida of the 5th Dragoon Guards that he had buried him in a suitable place.[284]

The village was quickly taken by the majority of the regiment coming up in support of the decimated advance troops, but it was too late for John,

---

283 Ibid.
284 MURPHY, p172.

who became the first Victoria Cross winner to be killed in the Great War. His last letter to his wife had ended,

> I think that the French in everything but their frontline troops are rotten and I still think that our true allies should be the Germans. My dislike of the Frenchman has increased. I have had to shoot one of my horses. Dearest, I simply adored your dear letter and the eye picture of the family prayers. It was too much for me altogether. I am so glad and thankful. Ever dearest, your loving and devoted John.[285]

In July 1915 his body was moved to Sablonnières New Communal Cemetery, overlooking the water meadow where he fell. He left behind his wife Lilian, daughter Diana and sons Robin and John, aged 9, who later became a group captain in the Royal Air Force. Robin also joined the RAF and served as a Spitfire pilot in the Battle of Britain.

Early in the Great War the deaths of Old Rugbeians were still an unwelcome novelty in the school, and were announced in chapel by the Head Master, Dr David. In subsequent years the sheer number of casualties meant that this practice stopped, to be replaced by a termly 'Call Over' service, but the death of such a well-known figure only a month after the conflict began did little to temper the militaristic tendencies of the teenage boys of Rugby. That, unfortunately, took a great deal longer.

---

285 Ibid, p165.

Lieutenant Robert Vaughan Gorle VC (Bradley)

Robert Vaughan Gorle is a somewhat enigmatic figure, about whom little information is available. He was born at 67 Victoria Road South, Southsea, on the 6th of May 1896, the only son of Major Henry Gorle of the Army Service Corps, who went on to win the DSO in South Africa, and his wife Edith. Robert's mother died when he was 8, and it was about that time that his education began, at Wells House School in Great Malvern, where Sir Edward Elgar was the music master. In 1910 Robert entered Dickinson's House (now Bradley) at Rugby School, an impressive crenellated building on Barby Road, opposite School Field, where Rupert Brooke and Frank de Pass had lived a few years before, but Robert was not to have a long Rugbeian career. Only a year later the Gorle family emigrated to the Transvaal, and so Robert left the school in 1911 to live on his father's farm, and his education was completed in South Africa. When war was declared he returned to England, and on the 15th of May the 19-year-old Robert was gazetted as a second lieutenant in the Royal Field Artillery. His battery was attached to the 31st Division, 50th Brigade, serving in France from the end of 1915.

In 1918 Robert had been promoted to temporary lieutenant, and by late September he was in command of A Battery, 50th Brigade Royal Field Artillery, and as part of the fourth Battle of Ypres they were retaking ground held by Germany continually since 1914. At 0615 on the 1st October they reached the village of Ledeghem, west of Courtrai, and the 12th Royal Scots captured the railway station, but the Germans still held the village itself. It was a hard-fought day, and one in which the RFA's 18 pdr guns were in close support to the infantry. Robert was awarded the VC for his actions on that day, and his citation read,

> For most conspicuous bravery, initiative and devotion to duty during the attack on Ledeghem on 1st October, 1918, when in command of an 18-pounder Gun working in close conjunction with the infantry. He brought his gun into action in the most exposed positions on four separate occasions, and disposed of enemy machine guns by firing over open sights under direct machine-gun fire at 500 to 600 yards' range. Later, seeing that the infantry were being driven back

by intense hostile fire, he, without hesitation, galloped his gun in front of the leading infantry, and on two occasions knocked out the enemy machine guns which were causing the trouble. His disregard of personal safety and dash were a magnificent example to the wavering line, which rallied and re-took the northern end of the village.

The whole village was finally taken two weeks later. The advance continued, and six weeks later the war came to an end, and Robert's battery returned to England. He received his Victoria Cross from King George V at Buckingham Palace on the 19th of June 1919, accompanied by his father, before they both returned to Africa, and Robert settled on a farm near Fort Jameson, Northern Rhodesia (now Zambia). In 1924 he married Ruth Thomas, and they had three children. In 1928 he was appointed as Sergeant at Arms and Librarian to the Legislative Assembly of Southern Rhodesia (now Zimbabwe), and continued in these duties until his death from yellow fever on the 9th of January 1937 while on a trip to Durban. He was buried there, in the Stellawood Cemetery. His family sold his Victoria Cross in 1993 and it was returned to the UK where it is on display in the Lord Ashcroft Gallery of the Imperial War Museum.

Lieutenant Colonel Christopher Bushell VC DSO
(School House)

Christopher Bushell was in many ways a quiet and unassuming boy when he arrived at School House from his family home of Hinderton Lodge at Neston, Cheshire, in 1901. Born on the 31st October 1888, his father Reginald was a Liverpool merchant and JP who died in 1904 when Christopher was 16, after which his mother Caroline moved the family to their London house in Knightsbridge. Life in School House in Christopher's time was quite an experience; until the 1960s the Head Master was also Housemaster of School House, and under the able direction of Dr Herbert James the house, and indeed the school, flourished. Dr James led a rather extraordinary career, being headmaster successively of Rossall School, Cheltenham College and Rugby, before ending his working life as President of St John's College, Oxford, so it's no wonder that in 1926, at a dinner in his honour, the Foreign Secretary described the elderly academic as 'one of the greatest and most forceful characters who had ever devoted his life to education.'

Though as a schoolboy Christopher didn't particularly stand out in either sport or academic work (he certainly didn't represent the school in any teams), he matriculated to read Modern History at Corpus Christi College, Oxford, in Michaelmas term 1906, and there he developed into a leading member of the college, largely through his involvement with the boat club. He had never rowed before his arrival in Oxford, but took to the sport extremely quickly and rowed in the 1st VIII in all three years of his undergraduate career. It is therefore no surprise that he became Captain of Boats in his third year, leading the college to ninth on the river in 1909, the highest that Corpus had placed since the 1880s.

After receiving his BA in History, Christopher decided upon a career in Law, and was received at the bar at the Inner Temple on the 17th November 1911. His chambers at 2 New Square, Lincolns Inn meant that he could still live at home with his mother, but the 23-year-old Christopher was also in search of adventure, and so he applied to join the Special Reserve of Officers, and on the 8th May 1912 was gazetted as a second lieutenant in the 1st Battalion the Queen's (Royal West Surrey Regiment). Alongside his legal and military commitments, Christopher's social conscience was very much in evidence, as he served both as treasurer to the Rugby Clubs in Notting Hill and on the committee of the

Cavendish Society; both of these organisations served to run boys clubs that were designed to encourage working class boys in Christian values and to help them to develop skills and attributes which would help them to find work. Army life suited the young barrister who was otherwise confined to the city and so, when war was declared in August 1914, and no one could have foreseen the horror to come, Christopher was one of the first reserve officers to volunteer for foreign service.

With the regiment's 1st Battalion, the newly-promoted Lieutenant Bushell took part in the retreat from Mons. At 7.10am on the 14th September 1914 the battalion marched off to escort the brigade's artillery near the village of Paissy, in the Aisne. As they attempted to pass the village, with companies in extended line, they came under considerable rifle and machine gun fire from German troops, and when enemy artillery fire also began to be focussed on them the commanding officer made the decision to withdraw. One officer was killed and nine were injured,[286] including Christopher, resulting in an eleven-month period of convalescence in England. During this time he married Rachel Lambert, daughter of the Rev E. Lambert of Wye, Kent, in August 1915, and they had one daughter; after the horror of Mons the pleasures of a quiet summer in the country was an extraordinary contrast. Once recovered, on the 15th October the same year, he was appointed ADC to Major General Herbert Landon, commanding the newly formed 33rd Division, and accompanied him to France. In June of 1916 Christopher was appointed staff captain to the 100th Brigade, serving in this important position throughout the subsequent Battle of the Somme.

When the battle abated, Christopher was appointed temporary (later confirmed) commanding officer of the 7th Battalion of his former regiment, and was created a Companion of the Distinguished Service Order in the New Year's List 1918, 'For continued gallantry and devotion to duty on numerous occasions', but it was in March 1918, as a 29-year-old temporary lieutenant colonel, that he was to take part in the action for which he received the highest of gallantry awards. The battalion was operating in the vicinity of the St Quentin Canal, around the village of Vendeuil, approximately ten miles south of St Quentin itself. At 2300 on the 20th, after a few days rest behind the lines, orders were received to stand to in support of the 7th Buffs, in anticipation of an expected attack the next

---

286 WO95/1280/1.

morning, which was to become the German Spring Offensive of 1918. At 0445 the German artillery barrage began, but when the sun rose there was a thick mist, and it was only when that cleared that it became apparent to Christopher and his battalion that the enemy had broken through the line on both of their flanks. Sporadic action continued throughout the day, until the 7th Queen's withdrew across the canal by platoons to Frieres Wood at 0400 the next morning, after almost twenty-four hours of fighting.

After establishing defensive positions on the 22nd, the next day Christopher led C Company of the 7th Queen's in support of two battalions of French troops effecting a counter-attack back across the canal. The subsequent action for which he was awarded the Victoria Cross is best described by the citation from the *London Gazette* of the 30th April 1918:

> For most conspicuous bravery and devotion to duty when in command of his battalion. Lt Col Bushell personally led C Company of his battalion, who were co-operating with an Allied regiment in a counter-attack, in face of very heavy machine gun fire. In the course of this attack he was severely wounded in the head, but he continued to carry on, walking about in front of both English and allied troops encouraging and reorganising them. He refused even to have his wound attended to until he had placed the whole line in a sound position, and formed a defensive flank to meet a turning movement by the enemy. He then went to brigade headquarters and reported the situation, had his wound dressed, and returned to the firing line, which had come back a short distance. He visited every portion of the line, both English and Allied, in the face of terrific machine-gun and rifle fire, exhorting the troops to remain where they were, and to kill the enemy. In spite of his wounds this gallant officer refused to go to the rear, and had eventually to be removed to the dressing station in a fainting condition. To the magnificent example of energy, devotion and courage shown by their Commanding Officer is attributed the fine spirit displayed and the keen fight put up by his battalion not only on the day in question but on each succeeding day of the withdrawal.[287]

---

287 *"No. 30667". The London Gazette (Supplement).* 30th April 1918.

The medal was awarded by HM King George V at Buckingham Palace on the 11th May 1918, and Lieutenant Colonel Bushell VC DSO continued to lead the 7th Queen's throughout the rest of the German Spring Offensive. Much of the summer proved to be a wet affair, and by early August the battalion's trenches were filled with mud, but the casualties were few as the next big attack was planned and orders disseminated. It was in this attack near Morlancourt that Christopher was killed. The battalion's war diary is surprisingly terse on the occasion, simply stating,

> 8th – Day of Great attack - & success of Battalion. Objectives, result and casualties are given in attached report. Lt. Col. C. Bushell V.C. D.S.O. fell in action.[288]

The attached report, detailing battalion actions between the 8th and the 10th August, gives a little more detail; the 7th Queen's formed up at 0340 and attacked at dawn. The report continues:

> 0700 – Commanding Officer went forward with his runner to deal with the situation. Gathering all available men together he led them CROYDON TRENCH to the assault and captured CLONCURRY TRENCH between CULGOA and CLOUD SUPPORT. He had sent for Tank assistance but the Tank had only proceeded 50 yards along CLONCURRY TRENCH from BRAY-CORBIE Road when operation had been completed. The Commanding Officer then proceeded along Trench to organise and cheer the men. On his way to the Tank to give orders to the Tank Commander for the next movement he intended to make, the Commanding Officer was fatally sniped while carrying out this missive.

> 0830 – The Commanding Officer's runner reported to Battalion HQ that the Commanding Officer had been seriously hit. Lt. Col. A. L. Ransome, D.S.O., M.C, 7th BUFFS was placed in command of all troops of the Brigade in the forward area.[289]

---

288 Surrey History Centre, QRWS/17/1.
289 Ibid.

In his letter of congratulations after the attack, Brigadier General E.A. Wood DSO, commanding the 55th Infantry Brigade, wrote, 'In particular I wish to extend my sympathy to the Officers, Warrant Officers, N.C.O.s and men of 7th Queens on the loss of their most beloved and gallant Colonel,"[290] but such a brief line can hardly express the loss felt at the death of an officer who had served with such bravery and dedication for almost the entire war, being killed only three months before the Armistice, leaving his wife and daughter in Kent. As Christopher was killed in the trench it was possible to recover his body, which was buried at Querrieu British Cemetery, nine miles south of Albert. In death, as in life, Christopher Bushell proved to be an extraordinary example of leadership to all.

---

290 Ibid.

Lieutenant Geoffrey Cather VC (Cotton)

Geoffrey St George Shillington Cather was, by the accounts of all those who knew him, a shy, quiet and earnest boy, who was never particularly prominent in any sphere of school life, and so none of his companions in Wilson's House (now Cotton) could have imagined that he would be awarded the highest award for valour in the armed forces of his country. Geoffrey was born at 55 Christchurch Road, Streatham Hill in south-west London, on the 11th October 1890, to Robert Cather, a tea merchant, and his wife Margaret, and grew up in the family home Redroofs, in Limpsfield, a leafy Surrey village in the shadow of the North Downs. Both of his parents, however, were originally from Northern Ireland, and most of Geoffrey's childhood holidays were spent with his maternal family in Portadown, though his education was to be spent in England. After several years at Hazelwood prep school near his home, Geoffrey entered Rugby School in 1905, but after a quiet school career he left upon the death of his father at the early age of 48 in 1908, and entered the company of which his father had been a director – Joseph Tetley & Co, tea merchants. It was also at that time that his military career began, as Geoffrey joined the Artists' Rifles as a private soldier in 1909, and led a quiet middle-class life, as a tea buyer's assistant in Surrey, playing golf at Limpsfield Chart Golf Club, and attending the Drill Hall on parade nights with his local volunteer unit.

In 1911 Geoffrey's quiet life was to change significantly, as he heard that Tetley intended to send him to work in their New York office, so he resigned from the Artists' Rifles and sailed for the USA early in 1912. He didn't return home until April 1914, spending just over two years in both New York and Canada, returning as the clouds of war gathered over Europe. When the conflict began Geoffrey left Tetley and joined the 19th Battalion (2nd Public Schools), Royal Fusiliers. This was one of five battalions raised solely for those who had attended public schools, many of whom were retired officers who wished to serve in the ranks, but in May 1915 Geoffrey was gazetted in the 9th Battalion, Royal Irish Fusiliers as a second lieutenant, and after joining his new unit in Seaford, Sussex, he sailed for Le Havre with the 36th (Ulster) Division in October. In fact, there were three members of the same family sailing with the 9th Battalion that day, as Geoffrey was joined by his cousin, Lieutenant Tom Shillington, and uncle,

Captain David Shillington (commanding D Company)[291], father and son from Portadown. Tom would later be killed in Flanders in 1918[292], though his father survived the war. Geoffrey's background in business and administration proved to be of great use when he was appointed assistant adjutant only four weeks after arriving in France, and adjutant to the battalion a month later.

The first six months of 1916 were, compared to many, a quiet time for the 9th RIF; after lots of battalion and divisional training in the villages north of Amiens, Geoffrey's unit took possession of the line on the east bank of the River Ancre. No major movements occurred for several months, but in June it was clear that a large scale attack was in preparation – what would become the first day of the Battle of the Somme. On the 22nd the battalion practised the attack behind the trenches at Varennes for the last time, and the next morning entered the Hamel section of the front line; the following days saw a bombardment of the German lines which made the imminence of the attack clear to both sides. For five days, 18 and 60 pdr guns, and even the great 15-inch howitzers, pounded the wire protecting the German defences, and after observing the fire and sustaining minimal casualties the 9th, RIF were withdrawn for twenty-four hours rest in Mesnil before the day of the attack, though further enemy shellfire on the village resulted in seven further casualties. The war diary for the following day simply states the preparations for what was to become perhaps the most infamous day of the war:

> Battn. to HAMEL trench line for the assault on enemy trenches tomorrow morning – Z Day.[293]

At midnight the battalion left Mesnil and marched through the dark, across the river and the remains of the Arras to Amiens railway line, and by 0300 they were in position for the attack, with the first wave out in the mud of no man's land, only 150 yards from the German front line. A nerve-wracking four and a half hours followed, but at 0730 the tension

---

291 WO 95/2505/2.
292 Lt Thomas Graham Shillington died on the 18th August 1917 of wounds received two days earlier and is buried in Brandhoek Military Cemetery.
293 WO 95/2505/2.

reached a crescendo as whistles sounded along the line and the advance began; the commanding officer's report described it thus:

> The 1st wave suffered little loss getting through our wire, lanes in which had been previously cut, but during the advance to the Ravine casualties were numerous, more especially on the left, from M.G. fire on the flanks. The 2nd wave suffered more severely crossing our wire, and also came under M.G. fire from the flanks. The majority of the officers of the 2 left Companies were casualties before reaching the Ravine, where the two leading waves were reorganised in one line and the advance continued.
>
> The 3rd and 4th waves were caught by a severe M.G. fire both frontal and flanking, and also by an artillery barrage which the Germans had now placed between our wire and the Ravine, and were practically annihilated. Some 150 yards from the German line the assaulting line again came under heavy M.G. fire and suffered severely: notwithstanding this, small bodies of men of the right and the two left Companies reached the German wire and charged the trenches, in places the Germans held up their hands to surrender, but realising there were no supporting troops resumed the contest until there were only a handful of our men left.
>
> The Right Centre Company appears to have suffered less severely, and was seen to penetrate the 3 German lines and a small body of them was reported to have reached BEAUCOURT STATION.
>
> Owing to the intensity of the fire only 1 runner got through, he came from the Left Centre Company Commander, from a spot about 30 yards short of Ravine, with the message "Cannot advance without support".
>
> The supporting platoon of 12th R.I.R. was sent out but was wiped out.[294]

The report paints a bleak picture, yet the RIF made greater progress than almost any other battalion on the first day of the Somme; a report which uses words such as 'annihilated' and 'wiped out' was, ironically, one of

---

294 Ibid.

the most successful to be submitted that day. Even so, as successful as the attack was, the lack of support on either flank meant that the foremost sections of the 9th RIF, far ahead of the battalions on either side, had to withdraw as darkness approached and Bavarian reinforcements arrived from the north-east. As adjutant, Geoffrey had remained at Battalion HQ, and so survived both the attack and the withdrawal, as had his cousin Tom and uncle David, though they had been in the thick of the fighting and officer casualties were heavy. Under cover of night the surviving officers of the battalion regrouped to consider their position, but it was clear that there were many, many casualties still alive in no man's land, unable to reach their own lines either because of injury or the heavy enemy fire which greeted any visible movement. Geoffrey could not sit idly by listening to their cries, and so with the battalion's intelligence officer, Captain William Menaul, he crawled slowly and quietly out of the line and towards the noise of the casualties. By midnight he had personally brought in three of them, and at first light the two men headed out again, risking their lives with every slight movement. Geoffrey took water to the dying and moved survivors closer to the British line, from where they could be collected by stretcher bearers. This continued for two and a half hours, until yet another burst of machine gun fire rang out, and both men fell. William Menaul was severely injured, but Geoffrey was dead by the time he was brought back to the line. He was hurriedly buried close to where he fell, but his grave was lost in the course of the five months' fighting that followed, and he remains there today, somewhere near the Ulster Tower on the road from the River Ancre to Thiepval. His death took the number of officer fatalities in the battalion that day to a horrifying eight out of fifteen who took part in the attack. Tom Shillington was also wounded.

News of Geoffrey's selfless action and heroic sacrifice soon spread, and his commanding officer, Lieutenant Colonel S.W. Blacker, recommended that he receive a posthumous award. It was clear to the battalion that something significant was deserved, and the chaplain wrote to Geoffrey's mother:

> I was always greatly attached to him by the high-mindedness
> and unselfishness of his nature, and the longer I lived with
> him the stronger the bond between us seemed to grow...
> He was one who lived on a very high level, and yet he
> was always in full sympathy with his fellow creatures,
> and ready at all times to extend a kindly hand... His loss

to the Battalion is indeed great, as he was especially fitted for the position of Adjutant, not only by his good mental gifts, but also by the sweetness and gentleness of his nature, which contributed not a little to the efficiency and splendid comradeship which pervaded all ranks… He has left behind with us all the happiest of memories, and by his noble self-sacrificing death, the highest of examples… We all very much hope that his name will be added to the list of gallant heroes who have gained the V.C.[295]

The *London Gazette* of the 8th September 1916 carried the news that 'His Majesty the KING has been graciously pleased to award the Victoria Cross to the undermentioned', and the citation described Geoffrey's feats of bravery on that terrible July day:

For most conspicuous bravery. From 7 p.m. till midnight he searched 'No Man's Land,' and brought in three wounded men. Next morning at 8 a.m. he continued his search, brought in another wounded man, and gave water to others, arranging for their rescue later. Finally, at 10.30 a.m., he took out water to another man, and was proceeding further on when he was himself killed. All this was carried out in full view of the enemy and under direct machine gun fire and intermittent artillery fire. He set a splendid example of courage and self-sacrifice.[296]

On the 31st March Margaret Cather, who had lost her husband and now her son, received Geoffrey's Victoria Cross from the King at Buckingham Palace. After her death it passed to Geoffrey's brother, who gave it to the Royal Irish Fusiliers Museum in Armagh, where it remains today. Geoffrey Cather was an unlikely war hero; a quiet, meticulous, golfing tea-merchant from Surrey, yet when he found himself in the heat of battle the strength of his character drove him on, determined to lead his battalion by example in the hardest of times. For that he lost his life, but it did not go unnoticed.

---

295 Memorials of Rugbeians who fell in the Great War.
296 Ibid.

In Memoriam

3,252 Rugbeians served in the Great War, of whom 687 were killed: this represents twenty-one per cent of the total, almost twice the national average and this clearly demonstrates the extraordinary scale of Rugby's personal and institutional contribution to the national war effort. That such a huge number should die is partially explained by the large proportion who served as junior officers, and were therefore very much in the thick of the action at every turn, in every theatre of the war. As an example, when the 6th Battalion of the Manchester Regiment landed at Gallipoli in May 1915 eight of their officers were old boys of the school, and five of them were to be killed before that battalion withdrew, including Captain Harold Cawley, the MP for Heywood in Lancashire. The arrival of peace in 1918 brought an end to the deaths, but not to the grief, and the school had a need to commemorate its sacrifice in addition to the individual memorials scattered across the country. Indeed, such thoughts had already been in the collective mind of the school community for a while, and on the 4th April 1917 a committee had met in London to establish the Rugby War Memorial Fund. Three principal aims were established:

i) The erection of a permanent Memorial at Rugby of Rugbeians who have fallen in the War.
ii) Provision for enabling the sons of Rugbeians who have fallen or been incapacitated in the War to be educated at Rugby.
iii) Application of surplus funds for the purpose of enabling the sons of other Rugbeians who have suffered financially through the War to be educated at Rugby, preference being given to the sons of those who have served in the War.

The initial request for funds raised an astonishing £50,000 from the friends and families of those who had died, partly in general donations and partly in the form of amounts intended to provide for the third aim in the shape of exhibitions and scholarships in memory of particular individuals, as well as two prizes (the latter in memory of Rupert Brooke). The huge sum also allowed work to begin after the Armistice on two permanent memorials – a chapel and a stone cross. Both were designed by Sir Charles Nicholson Bt (O.R. 1881-86), and the cross was unveiled outside New Big School (now the Macready Theatre) on the 19th June 1920. It remains the site where the school's cadets gather at 11am each Armistice Day, while the whole-school events of Remembrance Sunday take place in the Chapel. The biggest single expenditure by the fund was in the building of a new chapel, the Memorial Chapel, a restrained and elegant building which sits at the edge of the pitch known as Pontines, next to the great Butterfield bulk of the principal school chapel, to which it is joined by a vestry and a short cloister. It is built of stone in the form of a Greek cross, and the dominating feature of the interior is the four large windows, one on each face of the building. The building material was deliberately chosen to contrast with the coloured brick of the main chapel, so that there was no possibility of it being mistaken for a simple extension. Each element of the building was paid for by the family of a Rugbeian who had lost his life in the war, and in such a way the grief of individuals helped to commemorate all those who had died, and continues to do so.

The altar, also of stone, stands before a reredos containing a central pieta, with statues of St Peter and St Nicholas representing the Navy on the left, and St Alban and St Martin representing the Army on the right. Both altar and reredos were the gift of Colonel and Mrs D. Mason-McFarlane, in memory of their son, Captain Carlyon Mason-McFarlane of the 2nd (Queen's Own) Hussars, who was killed in Egypt on the 5th September 1916 while serving as a company commander with the Imperial Camel Corps and leading a raid on an enemy-held oasis. His commanding officer described him as 'the very type of a British cavalry officer'. The four flanking statues were given by Mr and Mrs G. Compton in memory of their son Cyril, a lieutenant in the 3rd Battalion, The Queen's Own (Royal West Kent) Regiment. He was killed on the 23rd July 1916, aged 19, leading his platoon in an attack on the German-held village of Guillemont, in the Somme, and his body was never recovered.

178

The four great windows of the chapel, and the altar service book, were given by W.B. Gair (O.R. 1869-72) and his wife in memory of their son, Second Lieutenant Henry Gair of the Dorsetshire Regiment, killed at Bretoncourt Mill, Pas de Calais, on the 15th May 1918. The windows contain many elements of Rugbeian imagery, and in the north window there is an image of Henry Gair himself, kneeling in prayer with his sister, who served as a nurse throughout the war. The windows of the cloister and ante-chapel were given by the same family as the great memorial lectern, perhaps the most memorable item in the chapel. Wilfred Littleboy had been an influential figure in Rugby life, as a star player in the XV and senior Cadet Officer in the OTC when he left the school in December 1914 to join the Royal Warwickshire Regiment. His death was described to his parents by a letter from one of his fellow officers:

> The Battalion had orders to attack Polderhoek Chateau, near Gheluvelt, which was strongly defended, being shell-proof (reinforced concrete) with a 'pill-box' on right and left. The ground in front was swept by machine-gun fire. Littleboy went forward with his Platoon in line in the first wave. He was hit in the leg, but he went on and was hit again and killed. The Battalion lost heavily, 13 Officers killed, wounded and missing.[297]

He was 21.

The lectern is built of oak, inlaid with walnut, holly and ebony, standing on eight carved oak columns. It contains eight chained volumes which give brief biographies and a photograph of all those from the school who were killed in the war, and is surmounted by the figure of a second lieutenant in service dress (modelled on Wilfred Littleboy himself), his head bowed in remembrance. Unfortunately the bronze original was stolen several years ago, but it has been replaced by a very good resin copy to deter further theft. In the centre of the chapel's floor is the stone of remembrance, inscribed with the text of the King's Scroll, which was sent to the next of kin of all those killed in the war; it was given in memory of Lieutenant Leslie Pierson of the East Yorkshire

---

297 Memorials of Rugbeians who Fell in the Great War.

Regiment by his mother. A 'boy of shy, retiring and gentle disposition at school', he was killed aged 20, leading a patrol on the front line near Hebuterne in October 1916. His body was never recovered.

The Bible, given for use in the chapel, was donated by Mrs A.R. Windle in memory of her only son, Lieutenant John Iles of the South Staffordshire Regiment, killed in the great attack in Loos on the 25th September 1915. He was shot through the head after saying to his platoon, 'I am going on.' The altar desk on which the Bible rests was given in remembrance of Second Lieutenant Leonard Cook MC, of the Royal Lancaster Regiment, killed instantly with two others on the 7th of July 1917 when a shell hit their dugout as they discussed a trench raid planned for later that night. He was 20 years old and had only returned from leave that afternoon. The vases were given by the Revd and Mrs F.G. Oliphant in memory of their son Second Lieutenant Marcus Oliphant of the Norfolk Regiment, killed at Suvla Bay, Gallipoli, on the 12th of August 1915. A friend wrote of the moment of his death:

> I can see him now, patient in pain, calm in the disorder and insisting that he was quite all right, when he was almost done. Great, noble, pure and heroic! I go ahead and thank God that I could have known such a splendid soul.[298]

Finally, the chalice veils and burses provided for the chapel were embroidered in remembrance of three friends in the same year group of St Hill's house: Vincent Wing (Royal Field Artillery), Charles Cutcliffe Hyne (Irish Guards) and Charles Potts (The Cheshire Regiment). After four years growing up together, all died in the service of their country, Vincent Wing in somewhat unusual circumstances:

> Colonel Hippolyto, the Commander of the Portuguese Artillery, and his Staff were inspecting the gun positions. The Germans found the range and shelled them. The first shell set fire to a barn which was the men's billet, killing and wounding several of them. Wing, who was off duty and ill in bed, did not stop to dress, but ran into the barn, where he helped to save the wounded, showing "great bravery

---

298 Ibid.

and a total disregard of personal danger" under heavy shell fire. The Portuguese Staff, with the Officers and men of the Battery, then moved to a detached section, and, when Wing joined them, he was called up and congratulated by Colonel Hippolyto, who insisted on his wearing his cloak, which the Portuguese Staff Officer was carrying. Wing thanked him, but said he could not wear it as it had a Colonel's badge on it. Colonel Hippolyto thereupon stepped forward, saluted Wing, and said, "Then I will make you a Portuguese Colonel for the day," and put the cloak on him. He then helped to dress the wounded, when a shell fell in a gun-pit close by, killing him and five of the men. He was buried at La Gorque Cemetery, Estaires, wearing the cloak, by the Colonel's special request, and covered with the Portuguese Flag as well as the Union Jack. The Portuguese attach much importance to their Flag, and this is believed to be the first instance, since the Peninsular War, of the Portuguese Flag being placed over an English soldier's body.[299]

The Memorial Chapel is an extraordinary place in an extraordinary school. Its cool, quiet atmosphere encourages reflection, and the names of those from the Great War on the walls have since been joined by those killed between 1939 and 1945 and those who died in Korea in the 1950s. It is used regularly for services of all kinds, but remains, in its very existence, a great reminder to modern Rugbeians of the sacrifices of those who have gone before them.

As well as the Memorial Chapel there was an addition to the main chapel during the war which, while not intended as a memorial, certainly served as such, and that is the bell. Known as 'The Boomer', it weighs 3¼ tons, and was given in memory of the Revd Charles Elsee[300], housemaster, and was donated by his children after his death[301]. By coincidence, that meant that it was raised in the tower over the summer holiday of 1914, and so was ready for use in the first term after war was declared. It was decided that, with an increasing number of Rugbeians

---

299 Ibid.
300 Master 1860-89.
301 WILSON, 1923, p10.

serving abroad, it would be rung every day at noon, as a moment for the school to pause in thought and prayer for those in danger. It is such a large and loud bell, situated as it is at the top of the High Street, that much of the town soon began to join the moment's quiet each day, and this continued until the Armistice was signed in 1918. Today the bell is still regularly rung: it calls the school to chapel four times a week, and marks the start of morning break each day, though few will now realise or remember the bell's original function during the four years of the Great War.

Among the 3,252 Rugbeians who served in the war, 3,128 honours were awarded. This included four Victoria Crosses, 199 appointed to the Distinguished Service Order and 449 Military Crosses, as well as many other British awards and others from sixteen different countries. In May 2017, as part of the events to commemorate the 450th anniversary of the founding of the school, a bronze plaque was placed in the Temple Speech Room to honour all those Rugbeians who have been awarded the Victoria and George Crosses, unveiled by Major General Andrew Keeling (O.R., Tudor), before the CCF was inspected on the Close by Lieutenant General Tim Radford (O.R., Cotton), who also presented the contingent with new banners. The annual commemoration of all those killed in conflict from Rugby School is an impressive occasion: the two hundred cadets of the CCF line the 'Porridge' in front of School House as the rest of the school and many parents and visitors arrive at the chapel, where the 'Levée' (school prefects) read out the list of the names of the dead, which takes almost an hour to complete as the chapel fills. This act stands long in the memory of today's Rugbeians. The service includes a sermon by a serving chaplain of the armed forces, and the Corps of Drums play in New Quad as the congregation moves to Old Big School for refreshments. In ways such as this those men commemorated in this book, and the hundreds more listed in the Memorial Chapel, are not forgotten in the school which shaped them and which they in turn helped to shape. The sentiment remains which was preached by Canon William Temple O.R. (later Archbishop of Canterbury) in the school on the 21st June 1919:

> No doubt when we think of the friends that we have lost, it is of different names that each finds his memory most full. But here, as at all other great schools in England, we

stand at a place made sacred for ever by the steady stream of boys who, throughout the war, went forth to danger and endurance without shrinking and without parade, taking the step that others call heroic in the same temper in which they would have done whatever else might have come next in the ordinary course of duty.[302]

---

302 Memorials of Rugbeians who Fell in the Great War.

Postscript by the Head Master

Just consider the majestic and sombre names that were given to the collective battles of 1914 to 1918: World War I, the Great War, even The War to End all Wars. There is now hardly anyone alive in Britain who remembers it. Yet, it has a special place in the national memory.

The physical and psychological horrors that were endured by those who fought, the shocking numbers of dead and wounded, the accounts of bravery, honour, and unquestioning duty – they continue to pierce the heart. It was a war that changed the course of global history, especially in Europe, and presaged huge social upheaval in Britain. And every year in November we still wear its symbol – a badge in the shape and colour of the red poppies that grew out of the mud of Flanders.

Every year, Rugby School – like so many institutions, great and small, across the country – holds a special service to commemorate the dead of that war. World War I is history to the students who fill our splendid Victorian chapel. For them it is an extraordinary episode which precipitated major political change and economic depression across the world and in which an unimaginable sixteen million people lost their lives.

It may be a chapter of history for our students, but they are reminded every year that among the casualties were four staff and 683 pupils from Rugby, some of the latter joining the army and going to war within weeks of leaving school. Sitting in the chapel, the twenty-first century students think about the enormity of that long-ago war, affecting – as it did – nearly every family in Britain, probably including their own. They look up and see the memorial to Rupert Brooke, an Old Rugbeian whose glorious poetry survives and will continue to do so.

What sadness the then Head Master must have felt as he read out the casualty list every week, and how understandable it was that, as the number grew, he abandoned the practice. How moved the boys must have been when the chapel bell rang out every day at noon – for nearly four years – signalling them to stop work and take a moment to reflect on those from their own school – boys who might have sat at the same desks or slept in the same beds, and who probably played rugby on The Close – who were fighting for their country hundreds of miles away.

When our students attend the Remembrance Day service – and they all attend, whatever their nationality, age or religion – they are visibly moved. At the beginning of the order of service there is a poem by H.C. Bradby, an Old Rugbeian, but also the successor to Rupert Brooke's father as Housemaster of School Field. His son, Daniel Bradby, was killed serving with the Rifle Brigade on 9th April 1917.

> Can you not see them? One by one they file
> In front of us; each, as his name is read
> As this last sad Call-Over of the dead
> passes in long procession down the aisle.

We still see them in the aisles. The long roll of honour of those Rugby students who died is read out as the girls and boys arrive in chapel, and they know that many of those unlucky, ordinary boys who lost their lives were not much older than they are.

It is their ordinariness, their bad luck, that makes the loss even more profound. I am reminded of the story of Louis Stokes, the son of a vicar (and an amateur antiquarian) who grew up in the vicarage of St Paul's in Cambridge with his parents, three sisters, two servants, three cats and a dog called Pickles. The family could only just afford the fees when he joined the school in 1911; he was delighted with the presents of a penknife, a picture of Napoleon and a pot of jam for his fifteenth birthday, and once, in the LXX, walked home to Cambridge because he didn't have enough money for the train fare. He won prizes for poetry but failed to get an academic scholarship; he was occasionally in trouble – for imitating his housemaster's voice when saying grace, or laughing at a boy who chose to play hockey with some girls and whose parents then complained. There was no military tradition in his family, and he had to persuade the Head Master, Dr David, to encourage his father to allow him to join the Officer Training Corps, as it was called then. The choice of the Royal Marines was suggested by Dr David because he thought it might be fun to go to sea! When Louis was killed he had only been in France for a few months. His character, attitude and circumstances were the same as many of the boys and girls who, all those years later, listen to the reading of the names during our Remembrance Day service.

'Laying down your life for your country' is a concept that is difficult for most young people now to understand. They are, mostly, happily global in their outlook – politically, economically, socially and emotionally – and are, mostly, mistrustful of extreme nationalism, abhorring the violence to which it can lead. Patriotism may flare during a sporting competition, but it is usually good natured.

There will never be another war like the Great War. It changed the world. Every community in Britain was touched. A generation of young men was lost, the impact on those who survived was huge. At Rugby School we continue to remember it and mark its end not only because the big events of history should not be forgotten and suffering on this scale should not be ignored, but also to remind us of the need to make the world a better place and to recognise the importance of trying to do so. Human beings start wars. And human beings end them.

The necessary qualities of a wise and good human being include selflessness, kindness and fairness; caring for someone who may not be as lucky as you; recognising the importance of team spirit. These are qualities that we continue to encourage at Rugby School. They are qualities that will carry you through life, whether you were called to fight in 1914 or lucky enough, more than 100 years later, to be living in peace.

Peter Green
Rugby School

Appendix One

Rugbeians who fell in the Great War

Name	Rank	House	Unit	Date of Death	Decorations
Abell, W.H.	Maj	School House	4th Bn, Middlesex Regiment	23/08/14	
Ackroyd, T.N.	Lt	Donkin	1st Bn, Bedfordshire Regiment	23/04/17	
Acton, C.A.	Maj	School House	9th Bn, Royal Welch Fusiliers	25/09/15	
Adam, R.W. W.	Sgt	School House	11th Bn, 3rd Inf Bde, Australian Imperial Force	25/07/16	
Akerman, C.S.A.	Maj	Scott	Royal Engineers	26/09/15	
Alcock, E.	Lt	Collins	Royal Field Artillery	20/08/17	MC
Allen, W.L.	Maj	Elsee	2nd Bn Border Regiment	25/10/14	DSO
Amphlett, R.F.	2nd Lt	Michell	8th Bn Worcestershire Regiment	05/04/17	
Anderson, R.C.	Capt	Wilson	1st Bn Black Watch	27/09/15	
Anderson, J.R.H.	Lt	Wilson	2nd Bn Cameron Highlanders	11/05/15	
Armitage, A.C.	2nd Lt	G.F. Bradby	1st Bn The Queen's (Royal West Surrey) Regiment	21/07/15	
Armitage, G.D.	2nd Lt	School House	11th Bn East Surrey Regiment	06/08/15	
Armitage, S.R.	Lt	Stallard	Army Service Corps	11/05/17	
Armstrong-Lushington-Tulloch, G. de M.	Lt	Donkin	1st Bn Connaught Rangers	05/11/14	
Arnold, F.F.W.	Capt	Whitelaw	1st Bn Suffolk Regiment	23/05/15	

Name	Rank	House	Unit	Date of Death	Decorations
Aston, R.M.	Lt	Steel	2nd Bn Duke of Cornwall's Light Infantry	15/03/15	
Bailward, T.	Lt	Collins	26th Light Cavalry, Indian Army	29/04/15	
Baird, J.F.M.	Capt	Michell	9th Bn Argyll & Sutherland Highlanders	10/09/17	
Baker, D.S.	Lt	Donkin	Royal Engineers	23/07/16	
Baker, G.T.	Lt	H.C. Bradby	5th Bn The Buffs	07/01/16	
Baker, R.D.	Maj	Steel	1st Bn East Lancashire Regiment	13/08/15	
Ball-Acton, R.T.A.	Maj	School House	2nd Bn The King's Own (Yorkshire Light Infantry)	22/05/16	
Bannatyne, D.A.	Lt	School House	9th Bn The Royal Scots	01/08/18	
Barber, V.L.	Lt	Dickinson	Royal Air Force	24/05/18	
Barclay, R.H.M.	2nd Lt	Donkin	3rd Bn King's Royal Rifle Corps	14/09/14	
Barrett, J.H.	Sgt	Stallard	5th Bn Royal Sussex Regiment	11/05/15	
Barrow, G.S.	Capt	Brooke	Royal Field Artillery	26/12/18	OBE
Beachcroft, W.G.	2nd Lt	School House	3rd Bn The King's Own (Royal Lancaster Regiment)	31/07/17	
Beatson, R.S.M.	Lt	Michell	6th Bn The King's Own (Yorkshire Light Infantry)	02/07/16	
Beattie, M.A.	Maj	Whitelaw	Royal Garrison Artillery	13/02/20	DSO
Beausire, C.E.	2nd Lt	School House	12th Bn The London Regiment	14/02/15	
Bell, J.C.	LCpl	Stallard	1st Bn Black Watch	03/09/16	
Bengough, J.C.	Capt	Stallard	Gloucestershire Yeomanry	26/02/16	
Benham, J.R.	2nd Lt	Whitelaw	Royal Field Artillery	04/05/15	
Bennett, C.T.	Capt	Stallard	3rd Bn The Queen's Own (Royal West Kent Regiment)	23/07/16	

Name	Rank	House	Unit	Date of Death	Decorations
Bennett, P.D.	Capt	Donkin	5th Bn Royal Warwickshire Regiment	24/02/19	
Bennett, A.S.	Lt	Michell	9th Bn Leicestershire Regiment	14/07/16	
Bernheim, G.E.	Eng Vol	Donkin	2eme Regiment d'Artillerie	05/10/15	Croix de Guerre
Bevington, C.C.	2nd Lt	Steel	Royal Air Force	22/05/18	
Bevir, C.E.F.	Lt	School House	Royal Field Artillery	29/09/15	
Bickersteth, S.M.	Lt	Steel	13th Bn The Prince of Wales's Own (West Yorkshire Regiment)	01/07/16	
Bignell, G.	Capt	School House	2nd Bn Bedfordshire Regiment	15/07/16	
Birch, E.W.	Lt	Brooke	4th Bn The Duke of Wellington's Regiment	17/01/17	MC
Bishop, N.F.W.	2nd Lt	School House	5th Bn The Prince of Wales (North Staffordshire Regiment)	13/10/15	
Black, M.A.	Maj	Whitelaw	5th Dragoon Guards	11/02/17	
Blackwell, C.	2nd Lt	Steel	4th Bn The Royal Fusiliers	20/07/15	
Blake, E.A.C.	Maj	Whitelaw	2nd Bn Durham Light Infantry	20/10/14	
Blandy, C.M.	Capt	Stallard	Royal Field Artillery	08/04/16	
Blathwayt, H.W.	Maj	Whitelaw	Royal Field Artillery	30/11/17	
Bliss, F.K.	2nd Lt	Wilson	Royal Field Artillery	28/09/16	
Boddy, G.G.D.	2nd Lt	School House	4th Bn The Royal Fusiliers	27/03/16	
Bodvel-Roberts, H.O.	Lt	Collins	7th Bn The London Regiment	18/11/15	MC
Bolton, F.W.	Capt	School House	9th Bn The London Regiment	18/06/16	
Bond, A.D.	2nd Lt	Whitelaw	5th Bn York and Lancaster Regiment	22/05/16	
Bonham-Carter, N.	2nd Lt	Bowden-Smith	The Household Battalion	03/05/17	
Bowden-Smith, W.A.C.	Capt	Town	4th Bn The Royal Fusiliers	27/08/14	

Name	Rank	House	Unit	Date of Death	Decorations
Bowen, C.E.L.	Lt	Stallard	British East Africa Police	01/12/14	
Bowyer, J.W.	Capt	School House	13th Bn The Rifle Brigade	10/04/17	
Boyd, E.F.	2nd Lt	Wilson	1st Bn Northumberland Fusiliers	20/09/14	
Boyd, H.A.	2nd Lt	Stallard	2nd Bn Royal Inniskilling Fusiliers	07/09/14	
Bradby, D.E.	Capt	School House	9th Bn The Rifle Brigade	09/04/17	
Bradley, E.J.	Pte	Steel	5th Bn The London Regiment	05/12/14	
Breul, O.G.F.J.	Lt	H.C. Bradby	Royal Engineers	16/10/17	MC
Brierley, H.J.	Lt	Steele	9th Bn Lancashire Fusiliers	06/08/15	
Brook, A.C.	2nd Lt	School House	5th Bn Manchester Regiment	04/06/15	
Brooke, W.A.C.	2nd Lt	Brooke	8th Bn The London Regiment	14/06/15	
Brooke, R.C.	Sub Lt	Brooke	Hood Bn, Royal Naval Division	23/04/15	
Brooks, F.C.	2nd Lt	G.F. Bradby	Royal Flying Corps	17/08/17	
Browett, A.L.T.	Capt	Donkin	7th Bn Royal Warwickshire Regiment	05/07/16	
Brown, A.C.	2nd Lt	Wilson	11th Bn South Staffordshire Regiment	02/07/16	
Brown, J.C.D.	2nd Lt	School House	5th Durham Light Infantry	27/04/15	
Brown, P.L.	Capt	Collins	2nd Bn Lincolnshire Regiment	09/08/15	
Browne, W.C.D.	Sub Lt	Collins	Hood Bn, Royal Naval Division	04/06/15	
Brunton, D	Capt	Steel	2nd Bn Honourable Artillery Company	09/10/17	
Buckley-Roderick, A.W.N.	Lt	G.F. Bradby	4th Bn Welsh Regiment	09/08/15	
Buckley-Roderick, H.	Capt	Collins	Welsh Guards	01/12/17	

Name	Rank	House	Unit	Date of Death	Decorations
Buckley-Roderick, J.V.T.	Lt	G.F. Bradby	1st Bn Coldstream Guards	21/08/18	
Buist, C.E.	Capt	Wilson	Royal Garrison Artillery	21/10/17	MC
Bullivant, R.P.	Capt	Payne-Smith	1st County of London Yeomanry	26/09/18	MC
Burdekin, G.E.	2nd Lt	Stallard	3rd Sherwood Foresters	26/01/15	
Burnyeat, H.P.	Lt Col	School House	Royal Horse Artillery	30/10/18	
Burridge, A.C.	LCpl	Payne-Smith	East African Mounted Rifles	25/09/14	
Burt-Marshall, W.M.	Capt	Brooke	2nd Bn Argyll and Sutherland Highlanders	17/11/14	
Bush, J.W.	2nd Lt	Town	2nd Bn Royal Scots Fusiliers	28/09/15	
Bushell, C.	Lt Col	School House	7th Bn The Queen's (Royal West Surrey Regiment)	08/8/18	VC, DSO
Butler, L.G.	Capt	School House	3rd Bn The Rifle Brigade	21/08/16	
Sutton, V.C.W.	2nd Lt	Whitelaw	20th Bn The London Regiment	14/09/18	
Cadle, L.M.	Capt	Stallard	18th Bn Australian Infantry	14/05/18	
Caffyn, H.H.	Capt	School house	1st Bn The Prince of Wales (North Staffordshire Regiment)	22/03/15	
Cairnes, W.J.	Capt	St Hill	Royal Air Force	01/06/18	
Calderon, G.L.	Lt	School House	9th Bn Oxfordshire and Buckinghamshire Light Infantry	04/06/15	
Calderon, F.E.	Pte	School House	2nd Bn, 1st Bde, 1st Canadian Contingent	03/04/16	
Calrow, W.R.L.	2nd Lt	School House	1st Loyal North Lancashire Regiment	07/10/14	
Cameron, H.W.L.	Lt	Michell	1st Bn Queen's Own Cameron Highlanders	14/09/14	

Name	Rank	House	Unit	Date of Death	Decorations
Campbell, T.L.	2nd Lt	Brooke	8th Bn Argyll and Sutherland Highlanders	01/03/17	
Campbell, D.	Capt	School House	2nd Bn Black Watch	18/05/15	
Campbell, N.D.	Lt Col	Brooke	8th Bn Argyll and Sutherland Highlanders	12/04/18	
Campbell, A.C.	Maj	Steel	11th Bn The Royal Scots	03/04/18	DSO
Carnduff, K.M.	Capt	Steel	Royal Engineers	11/01/16	
Carrick, L.S.	Lt	Brooke	49th Bn Canadian Infantry	15/09/16	
Carver, C.C.	Lt	G.F. Bradby	Royal Field Artillery	23/07/17	
Cather, G. St G.S.	Lt & Adjt	Wilson	9th Royal Irish Fusiliers	02/01/16	VC
Cator, E.P.D.	Capt	G.F. Bradby	Royal Engineers	11/04/18	
Cawley, J.S.	Maj	School House	20th Hussars	01/09/14	
Cawley, H.T.	Capt	School House	6th Bn Manchester Regiment	24/09/15	MP
Cawley, The Hon O.	Capt	School House	Shropshire Yeomanry	22/08/18	MP
Cay, A.J.	Lt	Steel	Worcestershire Yeomanry	23/04/16	
Chamberlain, J.	Capt	Steel	3rd Bn South Wales Borderers	14/05/17	MC
Chambers, A.J.F.	2nd Lt	St Hill	Warwickshire Yeomanry	11/08/16	
Champion, E.O.	2nd Lt	H.C. Bradby	11th Bn South Lancashire Regiment	11/06/17	
Chaning-Pearce, W.T.	Capt	Stallard	Royal Army Medical Corps	01/10/17	MC
Chaworth-Musters, P.G.	Lt	Collins	1st Bn King's Royal Rifle Corps	12/01/15	
Chaworth-Musters, P.M.	Capt	G.F. Bradby	Royal Field Artillery	18/07/17	MC
Chaworth-Musters, R.	Capt	G.F. Bradby	12th Bn King's Royal Rifle Corps	10/10/18	MC
Christie, W.C.	Maj	Elsee	1st Bn Royal Warwickshire Regiment	13/10/14	

Name	Rank	House	Unit	Date of Death	Decorations
Chrystal, G.G.	Lt	Donkin	9th Bn Argyll and Sutherland Highlanders	25/05/15	
Churchman, C.H.	Capt	Michell	6th Bn Suffolk Regiment	03/05/17	
Churchward, P.A.	Sapper	Steel	Royal Engineers	29/09/18	
Clark, E.A.	2nd Lt	Dickinson	Royal Flying Corps	20/03/18	
Clarke, W.H.	2nd Lt	School House	3rd Bn Worcestershire Regiment	12/03/15	
Colbeck, L.G.	2nd Lt	Staff	Royal Field Artillery	03/01/18	MC
Colebrook, G.B.	2nd Lt	H.C. Bradby	1st Bn The Queens (Royal West Surrey Regiment)	26/07/15	
Collin, F.S.	Bvt Maj	Steel	Royal Engineers	17/03/20	
Collins, P.	Capt	Michell	7th Bn The Rifle Brigade	30/07/15	
Collins, P.G.F.	Lt	Brooke	6th Bn Duke of Cornwall's Light Infantry	18/08/16	
Combe, S.B.	Lt	Whitelaw	North Irish Horse	30/09/14	
Compton, C.H.	Lt	Wilson	3rd Bn The Queen's Own (Royal West Kent Regiment)	23/07/16	
Cook, P.H.	LCpl	Stallard	17th Bn The King's (Liverpool Regiment)	30/07/16	MM
Cook, F.R.	Lt	Whitelaw	Royal Flying Corps	22/02/18	
Cook, L.N.	2nd Lt	Stallard	3rd Bn The King's Own (Royal Lancaster Regiment)	07/07/17	MC
Corbould-Warren, J.D.	Off Cdt	Hawkesworth	Royal Military Academy Sandhurst	07/07/17	
Cowie, G.	2nd Lt	School House	Royal Flying Corps	22/10/17	
Cowley, G.E.	Maj	Michell	10th Bn The London Regiment	18/06/18	
Cracroft, R.B.	Lt	School House	3rd Bn East Yorkshire Regiment	10/07/16	
Crawley-Boevey, E.M.	Capt	Morice	1st Bn Royal Sussex Regiment	24/12/14	
Cropper, T.A.	2nd Lt	St Hill	Royal Field Artillery	19/04/18	
Cruickshank, A.H.P.	Capt	Brooke	32nd Sikh Pioneers	28/04/15	

Name	Rank	House	Unit	Date of Death	Decorations
Cumming, L.R.	Lt	Stallard	1st Bn Black Watch	14/09/14	
Cunliffe, T.H.W.	Capt	Michell	1st Bn Lancashire Fusiliers	04/06/15	
Curran, N.W.	Lt	Whitelaw	5th Dragoon Guards	04/10/16	MC, Croix de Guerre
Currie, J.H.	Lt	Dickinson	3rd Bn Hampshire Regiment	25/08/18	
Curtler, F.G.O.	Lt	Donkin	2nd Bn Worcestershire Regiment	21/10/15	
Curwen, G.C.	2nd Lt	H.C. Bradby	16th Bn The London Regiment	23/06/18	
Curwen, C.N.	Lt	Brooke	18th Bn KRRC	15/09/16	
Cutliffe Hyne, C.G.H.	Lt	St Hill	2nd Bn Irish Guards	21/11/16	
Dangar, C.H.	Cond.	Steel	French Red Cross	22/04/20	
Dashwood, W.J.	Lt	School House	Grenadier Guards	02/08/17	
Davenport, L.M.	2nd Lt	Wilson	3rd Bn Royal Irish Fusiliers	06/09/16	
Davenport, F.M.	Capt	Stallard	1st Bn Oxfordshire and Buckinghamshire Light Infantry	24/11/15	
Davey, The Hon. A.J.	Asst Director	School House	War Office	10/10/18	CBE
Davie, B.G.	Lt Col	School House	8th Bn The London Regiment	24/12/17	
Davies, C.H.	2nd Lt	Collins	9th Bn The Welsh Regiment	17/01/16	
Davies, G.	2nd Lt	Stallard	24th Bn The London Regiment	01/05/15	
Davies, O. St L.	Lt Col	Bowden-Smith	6th Bn Manchester Regiment	05/04/18	
Daw, H.W.B.	Sub Lt	Michell	Royal Naval Volunteer Reserve	28/03/17	
Dawkins, Sir C.T.	Maj Gen	Elsee	General Staff	04/10/19	KCMG, CB
De La Rue, T.	Capt	School House	The King's Own (Royal Lancaster Regiment)	28/07/17	
De Pass, F.A.	Lt	Brooke	Poona Horse	25/11/14	VC
Denton, G.C.	Maj	Stallard	12th Pioneers, Indian Army	09/10/16	

Name	Rank	House	Unit	Date of Death	Decorations
Dewar, I.D.	Capt	School House	5th Bn, Queen's Own Cameron Highlanders	16/03/16	
Dickinson, R.F.B.	Capt	Steel	Liverpool Scottish	16/06/15	
Dickinson, A.P.	Capt	Steel	Liverpool Scottish	01/06/18	MC
Dixon, C.M.	Maj	Bowden-Smith	16th Lancers	05/11/14	
Dobell, C.M.	Lt	G.F. Bradby	1st Bn Royal Welch Fusiliers	30/05/18	
Dobie, J.J.	Capt	Steel	3rd Hussars	30/09/18	DSO, MC
Donald, W.F.M.	Capt	Michell	9th Bn Highland Light Infantry	19/09/18	MC
Donkin, H.A.B.	Pte	Dickinson	1st Bn The Queen's (Royal West Surrey Regiment)	22/12/16	
Douglas, A.G.	Capt & Adjt	Whitelaw	14th Bn The London Regiment	30/11/17	MC
Dove, P.M.	Maj	Scott	2nd Bn Sherwood Foresters	15/05/15	
Dowson, O.J.	Capt	H.C. Bradby	4th Bn Royal Berkshire Regiment	03/05/17	
Duckworth, E.	2nd Lt	Dickinson	2nd Bn Lancashire Fusiliers	07/08/15	
Dugdale, The Revd R.W.	Chaplain	Collins	Royal Army Chaplains' Department	23/10/18	MC
Dunlop, L.L.B.	2nd Lt	Michell	11th Bn Cheshire Regiment	09/05/17	
Dunlop, W.E.B.	2nd Lt	Michell	1st Bn The Border Regiment	19/05/17	
Edgar, R.G.	Capt	Payne-Smith	6th Bn Manchester Regiment	04/06/15	
Egerton, C.C.	Lt	Whitelaw	2nd Bn Duke of Wellington's Regiment	18/04/15	
Ellice, A.R.	2nd Lt	Steele	4th Bn Grenadier Guards	29/09/16	
Ellice, A	Capt	Steel	5th Bn Queen's Own Cameron Highlanders	18/10/16	
Elphick, W.R.	2nd Lt	Town	108th Infantry, Indian Army	07/06/16	

Name	Rank	House	Unit	Date of Death	Decorations
English, R.C.	Lt	Stallard	Army Service Corps	25/07/16	
Esdaile, A.J.	Capt	Steel	3rd Bn Devonshire Regiment	07/11/18	
Esson, W.	Maj	Donkin	Royal Marine Light Infantry	27/04/16	
Evelegh, R.C.	Capt	Whitelaw	2nd Bn Oxfordshire and Buckinghamshire Light Infantry	19/09/14	
Evers, H.L.	Capt	Payne-Smith	8th Bn Worcestershire Regiment	01/11/18	MC & Bar
Fagan, N.	2nd Lt	School House	6th Bn The Rifle Brigade	20/07/16	
Fargus, F.A.B.	Lt	Brooke	9th Bn The London Regiment	01/01/15	
Field, A.W.	Capt	School House	Royal Flying Corps	09/01/18	
Fielding-Johnson, H.G.	Cpl	Steel	Royal Engineers	23/08/14	
Firth, P.R.	2nd Lt	Dickinson	Royal Air Force	17/10/18	
Fitzgibbon, B.N.R.	Lt	Town	6th Bn Royal Irish Regiment	20/08/16	
Fitzroy, M.A.	Capt	Steel	4th Bn Seaforth Highlanders	16/04/15	
Fleming, E.C.	Maj	Payne-Smith	Royal Field Artillery	18/07/17	MC
Ford, R.N.	Maj	Michell	3rd Bn The Royal Fusiliers	06/01/18	MC
Forrester, P.H.	2nd Lt	Stallard	8th Bn Black Watch	11/10/15	
Forshall, J.	Lt	Wilson	Royal Field Artillery	12/04/18	
Foster, The Revd Canon K.G.	Chaplain	Whitelaw	Royal Army Chaplains' Department	27/02/18	
Fowler, G.H.	Lt Col	Morice	8th Bn Sherwood Foresters	15/10/15	
Fox, C.A.N.	Capt & Adjt	School House	2nd Bn Worcestershire Regiment	25/09/17	MC
Francis, B.H.	2nd Lt	Michell	3rd Bn The Royal Scots	04/02/15	
Franklyn, Sir W.E.	Lt Gen	School House	General Staff	27/10/14	KCB
Fraser, W.	Capt & Adjt	Morice	19th Bn The King's (Liverpool Regiment)	30/07/16	

Name	Rank	House	Unit	Date of Death	Decorations
Fraser, J.H.	Lt	Steel	2nd Bn Gordon Highlanders	30/10/14	
Frecheville, W.R.	Capt	Whitelaw	Royal Engineers	08/01/20	
Freeman, N.W.	Maj	Donkin	Royal Field Artillery	21/03/18	MC
Gaddum, R.C.S	2nd Lt	Michell	14th Bn The Royal Fusiliers	11/09/16	
Gair, H.B.	2nd Lt	Collins	4th Bn Dorsetshire Regiment	15/05/18	
Gamlen, R.A.W.	Capt & Adjt	St Hill	4th Bn Worcestershire Regiment	30/11/17	
Garrett, H.F.	Capt	School House	6th Bn East Yorkshire Regiment	22/08/15	
Garrett, S.	Capt	Brooke	4th Bn Suffolk Regiment	12/03/15	
Garrett-Smith, L.	2nd Lt	Collins	Royal Engineers	31/07/15	
Gatacre, J.K.	Maj	School House	Probyn's Horse	12/10/14	
Geddes, A.F.	2nd Lt	Wilson	2nd Bn Royal Scots Fusiliers	16/06/15	
Geddes, J.	Capt	Morice	79th Cameron Highlanders (Can.)	23/04/15	
Gilkison, D.S.	Capt	Donkin	2nd Bn Cameronians	30/09/14	
Gilkison, J.D.R.	Lt	Donkin	1st Bn Argyll and Sutherland Highlanders	26/08/14	
Gilliat-Smith, A.	Lt	Whitelaw	Royal Engineers	01/11/14	
Glover, R.H.	2nd Lt	School House	Royal Field Artillery	25/09/17	
Godfrey, W.J.	2nd Lt	Stallard	1st Bn Black Watch	03/09/16	
Godman, L.	Lt Col	Morice	Royal Field Artillery	30/09/17	DSO
Goldie, G.H.	Lt	Brooke	1st Bn Loyal North Lancashire Regiment	14/09/14	
Goold Adams, J.	Capt	School House	1st Bn Prince of Wales' Leinster Regiment	04/05/15	
Gore Browne, H.T.T.	2nd Lt	School House	6th Bn Royal Rifle Corps	23/08/16	
Gotch, R.M.	Capt & Adjt	School House	7th Bn Sherwood Foresters	01/07/16	
Graham, F.N.	Capt	Donkin	11th Bn Royal Warwickshire Regiment	16/11/16	

RUGBEIANS IN THE GREAT WAR

Name	Rank	House	Unit	Date of Death	Decorations
Graham, C.E.	Maj	Town	2nd Bn The Border Regiment	01/07/17	
Grant, A.	2nd Lt	Wilson	1st Bn Royal Scots Fusiliers	03/09/18	
Grantham, E.R.H.	2nd Lt	Stallard	3rd Bn Northumberland Fusiliers	31/03/17	
Gray, P.W.	2nd Lt	School House	Royal Field Artillery	09/05/17	
Gray, R.H.	Lt	H.C. Bradby	Royal Horse Artillery	02/12/17	MC
Greany, J.W.	Capt & Adjt	Whitelaw	5th Bn Wiltshire Regiment	05/04/16	DSO
Greener, L.L.	Capt	Stallard	6th Bn Royal Warwickshire Regiment	05/12/17	MC
Greg, A.T.	Capt	G.F. Bradby	Royal Flying Corps	23/04/17	
Greg, R.P.	2nd Lt	G.F. Bradby	4th Bn Cheshire Regiment	03/05/18	
Grierson, F.V.	Lt	Whitelaw	5th Bn King's Own Scottish Borderers	14/02/22	
Grubb, L.E.P.	2nd Lt	Town	2nd Bn King's Own (Yorkshire Light Infantry)	15/11/14	
Grundy, G.S.	Pte	Collins	1st Bn Honourable Artillery Company	14/04/15	
Gubbins, L.R.	2nd Lt	School House	New Zealand Field Artillery	23/04/18	
Guinness, E.C.	Capt	Michell	2nd Bn Royal Irish Regiment	11/09/20	DSO
Gumming, C.L.	Lt	Town	Royal Air Force	31/01/19	
Gurney, K.G.	2nd Lt	Donkin	5th Bn Gloucestershire Regiment	17/12/17	
Hadden, A.	Lt	Collins	53rd Sikhs, Indian Army	08/03/16	
Hadden, F.J.	Lt	Elsee	42nd Sqn, Remount Service	05/05/16	
Hadrill, A.W.	Lt	Michell	9th Bn Lincolnshire Regiment	12/08/15	
Hales, A.J.S.H.	Capt	School House	1st Bn Wiltshire Regiment	05/07/16	MC

Name	Rank	House	Unit	Date of Death	Decorations
Hall, R.H.	Capt	Brooke	Royal Field Artillery	12/07/12	
Hall, F.R.	Pte	Town	11th Bn The Royal Fusiliers	03/05/17	
Hamblin, W.E.	Lt	Brooke	Royal Engineers	05/05/16	MC
Hamilton-Johnston, E.C.R.	Lt	Donkin	2nd Bn King's Own Scottish Borderers	01/09/18	
Hancock, R.E.	Lt	School House	1st Bn Devonshire Regiment	29/10/14	DSO
Hancocks, W.	Lt	Wilson	7th Bn Worcestershire Regiment	09/10/17	
Handfield-Jones, N.M.	2nd Lt	Stallard	Royal Field Artillery	25/09/15	
Handford, H.B.S.	Capt	Steel	8th Bn Sherwood Foresters	14/10/15	
Handford, E.F.S.	Lt	Steel	8th Bn Sherwood Foresters	14/10/15	
Hankey, D.W.A.	2nd Lt	Collins	3rd Bn Royal Warwickshire Regiment	12/10/16	
Hardy, R.L.	Capt & Adjt	Donkin	8th King's Royal Rifle Corps	24/08/17	
Harrison, G.	2nd Lt	G.F. Bradby	Machine Gun Corps	01/07/16	
Harrison, J.M.	Lt Col	Whitelaw	Royal Army Service Corps	10/03/19	
Harrowing, J.S.	Capt	Whitelaw	2nd Bn Royal Warwickshire Regiment	04/05/17	MC
Harvey, W.	2nd Lt	Collins	3rd Bn The King's (Liverpool Regiment)	25/09/15	
Harvey, J.	Capt	Brooke	7th The King's (Liverpool Regiment)	17/03/15	
Harvey, G.	Lt	Michell	2nd Bn Grenadier Guards	27/03/18	
Harwell, F.L.	Capt	Brooke	16th Bn The London Regiment	29/04/17	
Haslam, B.J.	Maj	Town	Royal Engineers	26/08/18	DSO
Hays, F.R.	Lt	School House	24th Bn Australian Infantry	05/08/16	
Heape, J.S.	LCpl	H.C. Bradby	16th Bn Middlesex Regiment	01/07/16	
Heath, R.M.	2nd Lt	Donkin	9th Bn Somerset Light Infantry	16/09/16	

Name	Rank	House	Unit	Date of Death	Decorations
Heath, J.L.	Lt	Wilson	1st Bn King's Own Yorkshire Light Infantry	01/10/15	
Heberden, A.C.	2nd Lt	Payne-Smith	6th Bn King's Royal Rifle Corps	10/07/17	
Hemingway, R.E.	2nd Lt	School House	8th Bn Sherwood Foresters	14/10/15	
Henderson, N.W.A.	Lt	School House	1st Bn Royal Scots Fusiliers	10/11/14	
Henderson, M.W.	Lt Col	School House	9th Bn Black Watch	25/09/15	
Henderson, E.F.S.	Maj	Collins	2nd Bn Leicestershire Regiment	06/01/16	
Hendriks, A.M.	Capt	Collins	5th Bn Royal Fusiliers	25/05/15	
Henty, A.F.	Capt	School House	11th Bn Middlesex Regiment	04/03/16	
Hepburn, R.P.	2nd Lt	Wilson	Royal Engineers	03/08/17	MC
Herbert, M.C.N.	Lt	Donkin	1st Bn Gloucestershire Regiment	02/01/15	
Herbert-Stepney, H.A.	Maj	Michell	1st Bn Irish Guards	07/11/14	
Hess, A.F.	Maj	Brooke	8th Bn West Yorkshire Regiment	14/07/16	
Heywood, G.G.	Pte	Steel	1st Bn Honourable Artillery Company	12/03/15	
Hicks, B.P.	Lt	Brooke	8th Bn Royal Berkshire Regiment	25/09/15	
Higginbotham, C.E.	Maj	School House	2nd Bn Northamptonshire Regiment	10/03/15	
Higgins, P.C.	Capt	Donkin	Nigeria Regiment	22/09/17	
Hill, P.G.P.	Maj	Brooke	1st Bn Australian Infantry	09/06/15	
Hill, H.	Bvt Lt Col	School House	Royal Welch Fusiliers	10/09/16	MVO, DSO
Hillerns, H.W.O.	Maj	Steel	Royal Field Artillery	14/04/17	
Hilton, M.V.	Col	J.M. Wilson	7th Bn East Lancashire Regiment	20/10/15	
Hind, J.F.M.	Lt	Brooke	9th Bn Sherwood Foresters	27/09/16	

APPENDIX ONE

Name	Rank	House	Unit	Date of Death	Decorations
Hipwell, H.R.	2nd Lt	Collins	4th Bn Seaforth Highlanders	23/04/17	
Hirst, H.	Capt	Stallard	4th Bn King's Own (Yorkshire Light Infantry)	24/06/15	
Hobart-Hampden, G.M.A.	Lt	Brooke	Royal Flying Corps	17/09/17	
Hobson, L.F.	2nd Lt	Stallard	4th Bn Yorkshire and Lancashire Regiment	11/07/15	
Hobson, A.F.	Maj	Stallard	Royal Engineers	28/08/16	DSO
Hodgkinson, A.	Capt	Wilson	3rd Bn Royal Warwickshire Regiment	01/07/16	
Hodgson, G.G.	Lt	Stallard	2nd Bn Royal Berkshire Regiment	09/05/15	
Hodgson, J.S.R.	Lt	School House	2nd Bn Dorsetshire Regiment	25/03/17	
Holland, V.E.	Capt	Collins	7th Hussars	08/11/18	
Holt, J.	Capt	Whitelaw	6th Bn Manchester Regiment	04/06/15	
Homan, R.W.	Capt	Wilson	1st Bn The Buffs	11/08/15	
Honey, G.H. Le S.	2nd Lt	School House	4th Bn King's Royal Rifle Corps	21/10/16	
Hopkinson, E.H.	Lt	Donkin	1st Bn Cambridgeshire Regiment	02/06/15	MC
Hornby, W.	2nd Lt	Whitelaw	17th Bn The King's (Liverpool Regiment)	12/10/16	
Hornby, G.P.	Lt	Whitelaw	3rd Bn Suffolk Regiment	08/05/15	
Horsey, A.M.	Surg. Pr.	Wilson	Royal Naval Volunteer Reserve	09/08/17	
Hoskyns, H.C.W.	Maj	Collins	2nd Bn Lincolnshire Regiment	25/09/15	DSO
House, M.H.	2nd Lt	G.F. Bradby	8th Bn The Rifle Brigade	03/05/17	
Howden, G.B.	2nd Lt	G.F. Bradby	2nd Bn Duke of Cornwall's Light Infantry	08/05/16	
Hoyle, H.K.	2nd Lt	School House	5th Bn Lancashire Fusiliers	07/05/15	
Hoyle, G.M.	Lt	Donkin	3rd Bn Sherwood Foresters	09/08/15	

Name	Rank	House	Unit	Date of Death	Decorations
Hoyle, J.B.	Lt	Donkin	7th Bn South Lancashire Regiment	01/07/16	MC
Huddart, L.H.L.	Lt	Steel	Nigeria Regiment	05/02/17	
Hughes, E.R.G.	2nd Lt	H.C. Bradby	2nd Bn Oxfordshire and Buckinghamshire Light Infantry	25/09/15	
Hughes, N.A.	Capt	School House	11th Bn The Welsh Regiment	18/09/18	
Hughes, G.	Lt	Brooke	1st Bn Grenadier Guards	05/08/18	
Hunter, W.C.	2nd Lt	Town	Royal Garrison Artillery	29/10/15	
Hunter, A.G.B.F.	Off Cdt	Donkin	Officer Cadet Battalion, Cambridge	16/12/18	
Hunter, D.H.K.	Lt Col	Donkin	Royal Field Artillery	17/08/21	
Hurlbutt, C.	Lt Col	Bowden-Smith	5th Royal Welch Fusiliers	15/03/17	
Hutchinson, J.S.	Capt	Michell	2nd Bn South Lancashire Regiment	26/08/14	
Iles, J.O.	Lt	School House	1st Bn South Staffordshire Regiment	25/09/15	
Inglis, J.A.P.	Lt	Collins	Royal Engineers	25/09/15	
Inglis, Revd R.E.	Chaplain	Lee-Warner	Army Chaplains' Department	18/09/16	
Isaacson, C. de S.	Capt	Town	East Africa Protectorate Forces	11/06/17	MC
Isham, J.V.	2nd Lt	School House	5th Dragoon Guards	03/06/16	
Jackson, B.W.	Capt	Whitelaw	2nd Bn King's Royal Rifle Corps	13/09/14	
James, B.A.	Capt	Whitelaw	13th Bn Middlesex Regiment	18/08/16	
Jennison, J.L.	2nd Lt	Donkin	15th Bn West Yorkshire Regiment	03/05/17	
Jervis-Smith, E.J.	Maj	Steel	Royal Field Artillery	05/10/20	
Jobling, J.B.	Capt	Michell	Labour Corps	04/11/18	
Johnson, A.L.	Capt	Wilson	5th Bn North Staffordshire Regiment	14/10/18	

Name	Rank	House	Unit	Date of Death	Decorations
Johnson, R.T.	Captain	Morice	5th Bn North Staffordshire Regiment	13/10/15	
Johnson, E.	Pte	School House	16th Bn The Queen's (Royal West Surrey Regiment)	12/04/18	
Johnston, E.J.F.	Capt	Michell	1st Bn Royal Scots	12/04/15	
Johnstone, J.C.	Pte	Michell	2nd Bn Honourable Artillery Company	23/04/17	
Johnstone, H.N.	2nd Lt	Michell	8th Bn West Yorkshire Regiment	01/06/21	
Jones-Bateman, F.	Capt	G.F. Bradby	3rd Bn Royal Welch Fusiliers	04/11/18	
Judge, W.S.	2nd Lt	St Hill	Royal Field Artillery	26/07/16	
Keen, A.W.	Maj	G.F. Bradby	Royal Flying Corps	02/09/18	MC
Keller, R.L.	Capt	Michell	Royal Air Force	15/08/18	MC
Kelly, H.H.	Capt	Stallard	Royal Engineers	24/10/14	
Kennedy, T.G.	Lt	Steel	Royal Field Artillery	28/03/18	
Ker, W.	Lt RN	School House	Royal Naval Division	13/11/16	
Kessler, E.	Capt	Collins	6th Bn Manchester Regiment	04/06/15	
King, R.N.	Capt	Donkin	1st Bn Lincolnshire Regiment	01/11/14	
Kittermaster, A.N.C.	Capt	School House	9th Bn Worcestershire Regiment	05/04/16	
Knapp-Fisher, S.B.	2nd Lt	Stallard	3rd Bn North Staffordshire Regiment	06/10/14	
Knight, J.O.C.	2nd Lt	Steel	6th Bn The Queen's (Royal West Surrey Regiment)	30/11/17	
Knight, J.H.	Col	Whitelaw	5th Bn North Staffordshire Regiment	13/10/15	
Knox, J.V.	Lt	Steel	Royal Flying Corps	04/01/18	
Laird, W.	2nd Lt	Stallard	5th Bn Coldstream Guards	01/12/17	
Lamb, J.	2nd Lt	Michell	Royal Engineers	17/10/17	
Lambert, K.	Capt	Steel	1st Bn King's Own (Yorkshire Light Infantry)	09/05/15	

Name	Rank	House	Unit	Date of Death	Decorations
Langdon, W.M.	Capt	Whitelaw	10th Bn Cheshire Regiment	21/05/16	
Langham, C.R.	Capt	Stallard	5th Bn Royal Sussex Regiment	16/08/17	
Latimer, H.	2nd Lt	Steel	3rd Bn The Queen's (Royal West Kent Regiment)	03/07/16	
Le Mesurier, A.E.	2nd Lt	Wilson	6th Gurkha Rifles, Indian Army	09/03/17	
Le Mesurier, H.	2nd Lt	Wilson	9th Bn King's Royal Rifle Corps	24/08/16	
Le Motée, E. de A.	Major	Michell	General Staff	27/09/15	DSO
Leadbetter, A.E.G.	Maj	Michell	Royal Horse Artillery	04/08/17	
Leckie, J.H.	Lt	Donkin	1st (Royal) Dragoons	13/05/15	
Lee, P.W.	Capt	School House	Royal Field Artillery	11/10/17	
Leech, N.B.	Capt	Brooke	10th Bn East Yorkshire Regiment	10/05/17	
Leechman, C.B.	Lt	Donkin	3rd Hussars	23/09/14	
Lees, G.O.	Capt	Whitelaw	Royal Highlanders of Canada	24/04/15	
Leeson, A.N.	Lt	Whitelaw	Royal Flying Corps	22/10/17	DSO
Leigh-Pemberton, T.E.G.	Lt	Collins	13th Bn London Regiment	11/01/15	
Leresché, A.S.	2nd Lt	Steel	7th Bn West Yorkshire Regiment	03/09/16	
Lester, E.G.	Lt	Whitelaw	102nd Bn Canadian Infantry	25/06/17	
Levin, W.F.	Maj	School House	6th Wellington Mounted Rifles, NZEF	25/12/15	
Levinstein, G.E.	Lt	Brooke	26th Bn Manchester Regiment	12/10/16	
Lewthwaite, C.G.	Michell	Michell	Royal Field Artillery	29/07/17	MC
Lindeck, R.E.	Rfn	Wilson	2nd Bn Rifle Brigade	27/05/18	
Lindsay, B.W.	Capt	School House	Royal Field Artillery	22/11/18	
Lindsay, C.T.	Lt	Town	Army Service Corps	28/04/16	
Linnell, W.H.	Sapper	Town	Royal Engineers	08/04/18	
Lister, H.H.H.	Lt	Town	2nd Bn Royal Warwickshire Regiment	04/15/17	

Name	Rank	House	Unit	Date of Death	Decorations
Little, D.L.	2nd Lt	Town	Royal Air Force	21/06/18	
Littleboy, W.E.	Lt	School House	16th Bn Royal Warwickshire Regiment	09/10/17	
Lloyd, R.A.H.	2nd Lt	Hardwich	Royal Air Force	10/10/18	
Lloyd, E.A.C.	Lt	Collins	3rd Bn Scots Guards	31/07/17	
Lomax, S.H.	Lt Gen	Hutchinson	General Staff	10/04/15	CB
Loveday, H.D.	Pte	Donkin	4th Bn Oxfordshire and Buckinghamshire Light Infantry	13/08/16	
Loveitt, A.P.C.	2nd Lt	G.F. Bradby	7th Bn Royal Warwickshire Regiment	26/07/16	
Loverock, H.G.	2nd Lt	Town	Warwickshire Yeomanry	04/08/16	
Low, G.H.	Pte	Stallard	14th Bn London Regiment (London Scottish)	01/11/14	
Lowe, H.S.	Lt	Michell	2nd Bn Worcestershire Regiment	21/10/14	
Lucas, K.	Capt	School House	Royal Flying Corps	05/10/16	FRS
Lupton, M.	Capt	Collins	7th Bn West Yorkshire Regiment	19/06/15	
Lupton, L.M.	Lt	Collins	Royal Field Artillery	16/07/16	
Lupton, F.A.	Maj	Collins	8th Bn West Yorkshire Regiment	19/02/17	
Lupton, C.R.	Capt	G.F. Bradby	Royal Air Force	09/05/18	DSC & Bar
Lutyens, C.J.L.	Lt	Steel	Royal Field Artillery	03/10/17	
Macarthur-Onslow, A.W.	Capt	Steel	16th Lancers	05/11/14	
Maccunn, F.J.	Capt	Brooke	6th Bn Queen's Own Cameron Highlanders	26/09/25	
Macgregor, C.A.	2nd Lt	Whitelaw	9th Bn Gordon Highlanders	25/09/15	
Mackinnon, R.L.	Capt	Donkin	4th Bn Gordon Highlanders	15/04/21	
Mackinnon, W.	Capt	Stallard	14th Bn London Regiment (London Scottish)	11/05/17	
Mackinnon, D.	Lt	Stallard	1st Bn Scots Guards	09/10/17	

Name	Rank	House	Unit	Date of Death	Decorations
Maclehose, J.C.	2nd Lt	School House	16th Bn Rifle Brigade	14/02/17	
Maclehose, N.C.	Lt	Whitelaw	8th Bn London Regiment (Post Office Rifles)	26/05/15	
Macmaster, D.C.D.	Lt	G.F. Bradby	6th Bn Queen's Own Cameron Highlanders	25/09/15	
Manly, E.C.J.	Lt	Dickinson	Royal Garrison Artillery	18/07/17	
Mann-Thomson, W.D.	Lt Col	Scott	Royal Horse Guards	22/10/18	
Mantle, A.	Lt	St Hill	7th Bn London Regiment	22/05/17	
Marshall, J.	Lt	Brooke	9th Bn London Regiment	26/09/17	
Marshall, R.B.	Lt	Brooke	1st Bn East Surrey Regiment	14/09/19	
Mason, E.W.	Lt	Wilson	South African Artillery	12/08/17	
Mason-Macfarlane, C.W.	Capt	Steel	Imperial Camel Corps	05/09/16	
Mather, N.	2nd Lt	Scott	10th Bn The King's (Liverpool Regiment)	09/08/16	
Maton, L.E.L.	Capt	Steel	1st Bn Devonshire Regiment	09/05/17	MC
Maxwell, W.	2nd Lt	Collins	20th Bn London Regiment	16/09/16	
McDougall, D.A.H.	2nd Lt	Wilson	1st Bn Seaforth Highlanders	09/05/15	
McKenzie, K.B.	Capt	Payne-Smith	123rd Outram's Rifles, Indian Army	25/09/15	
McMaster, H.	Maj	Collins	Royal Field Artillery	02/12/17	DSO, MC
Meiklejohn, K.F.	Lt	Brooke	1st Bn Queen's Own Cameron Highlanders	25/09/14	
Melly, H.P.E.M.	2nd Lt	G.F. Bradby	1st Bn The King's Own (Royal Lancaster Regiment)	01/06/16	
Menzies, W.A.	2nd Lt	Wilson	Royal Garrison Artillery	14/06/17	
Merk, J.W.A.	Lt	G.F. Bradby	6th Gurkha Rifles, Indian Army	14/04/16	
Messer, A.E.	Capt	Wilson	5th Bn King's Royal rifle Corps	17/02/16	

Name	Rank	House	Unit	Date of Death	Decorations
Michell, J.C.	Capt	Michell	12th Lancers	28/08/14	
Miley, M.	Lt	Steel	Royal Field Artillery	30/12/15	
Millar, A.K.	2nd Lt	Payne-Smith	10th Bn East Surrey Regiment	29/07/16	
Millar, A.L.	Capt	Stallard	6th Bn The Rifle Brigade	01/04/18	
Millar, G.H.	Capt	Payne-Smith	Roya Air Force	29/04/18	
Miller, G.L.	2nd Lt	School House	Royal Engineers	14/09/14	
Miller, W.R.	2nd Lt	Whitelaw	1st Bn Grenadier Guards	15/09/18	
Miller-Hallett, S.A.	2nd Lt	Michell	2nd Bn South Wales Borderers	11/07/16	
Mills, A.C.	Capt	H.C. Bradby	Royal Air Force	08/08/18	
Mills, R.N.F.	Capt	Brooke	Royal Flying Corps	21/09/17	
Mitchell, J.S.	2nd Lt	School House	Royal Flying Corps	05/10/16	
Moir, J.E.	Maj	Whitelaw	Hodson's Horse, Indian Army	26/01/17	
Molson, E.E.	Lt	Steel	3rd Bn Royal Scots	01/04/15	
Mond, F.L.	Capt	Brooke	Royal Air Force	15/05/18	
Montagu, R.H.	Lt	Collins	8th Bn Hampshire Regiment	21/09/17	
Morgan, J.W.R.	2nd Lt	Michell	4th Bn Royal Dublin Fusiliers	01/07/16	
Morris-Davies, C.T.	Capt	Town	6th Bn Royal Warwickshire Regiment	02/07/16	
Morris, H.	2nd Lt	Wilson	5th Bn Middlesex Regiment	28/09/15	
Morton, W.R.	Capt	Donkin	8th Royal Warwickshire Regiment	04/04/17	
Moule, H.E.	Maj	Collins	4th Gurkha Rifles, Indian Army	21/05/15	
Moyna, E.G.J.	Capt	Stallard	7th Bn Royal Scots Fusiliers	26/09/15	
Muir, B.L.	Capt	Stallard	Army Service Corps	04/11/18	
Munby, E.J.	2nd Lt	Scott	Royal Engineers	31/01/15	
Murchison, K.B.	2nd Lt		8th Bn Seaforth Highlanders	22/08/17	

Name	Rank	House	Unit	Date of Death	Decorations
Murray, A.S.	2nd Lt	School House	8th Argyll and Sutherland Highlanders	22/03/18	
Nash, W.F.	Lt Col	Bowden-Smith	The Border Regiment	28/12/15	DSO
Newstead, G.P.	Lt Col	Whitelaw	Sierra Leone Battalion, West African Frontier Force	04/03/15	
Newton, H.G.T.	Capt	School House	13th Hussars	25/04/17	
Nicholls, E.C.H.R.	Lt	H.C. Bradby	Royal Air Force	20/09/18	
Nicholson, B.L.	Lt	Brooke	Royal Field Artillery	24/07/15	
Noakes, S.B.	Capt	Whitelaw	Army Service Corps	30/12/17	
North, K.C.	Lt	Brooke	4th Hussars	31/10/14	
Norton, B.G.	LCpl	Town	Royal Engineers	11/02/19	
Norway, F.H.	2nd Lt	Brooke	2nd Bn Duke of Cornwall's Light Infantry	04/07/15	
Norwood, J.	Capt	Donkin	5th Dragoon Guards	08/09/14	VC
Nye, R.R.	Capt	Steel	3rd Bn Royal Scots	17/12/15	
O'Brien, D.	Lt	Steel	Royal Field Artillery	26/09/17	
O'Meara, L.A.	2nd Lt	Steel	3rd Bn East Lancashire Regiment	06/02/17	
Oakley, M.F.	Lt	School House	Royal Air Force	03/07/18	
Oke, R.W.L.	Capt	Stallard	3rd Bn Royal Berkshire Regiment	25/09/15	
Oliphant, M.F.	2nd Lt	Steel	5th Bn Norfolk Regiment	12/08/15	
Orr, R.C.	Capt	Brooke	3rd Bn Somerset Light Infantry	19/12/14	
Oswald, W.D.	Lt Col	Donkin	5th Dragoon Guards	30/04/16	DSO
Ozanne, E.G.	Capt	Donkin	3rd Bn Royal Fusiliers	14/02/15	
Parry N.C.	Lt	Stallard	3rd Bn York and Lancaster Regiment	27/07/15	
Parry, F.A.	Maj	Stallard	16th Royal Warwickshire Regiment	27/09/18	MC

Name	Rank	House	Unit	Date of Death	Decorations
Pattinson, H.L.	Capt	Payne-Smith	3rd Bn Royal Fusiliers	04/08/15	
Pattison, W.L.H.	Sub Lt	Whitelaw	Royal Naval Air Service	17/03/18	DSC
Pattullo, H.J.	Lt	School House	Royal Field Artillery	29/09/18	
Peace, H.K.	Lt	Steel	3rd Bn York and Lancaster Regiment	16/10/14	
Pearson, S.J.	Capt	School House	8th Bn West Yorkshire Regiment	15/08/16	
Penn-Gaskell, W.	Capt	Whitelaw	25th Bn Manchester Regiment	12/10/16	
Pepperday, G.A.G.	LCpl	Town	2nd Public Schools Bn Royal Fusiliers	28/01/16	
Pepperday, L.J.D.	Pte	Town	1st Bn Honourable Artillery Company	13/08/15	
Percival, A.J-B.	Lt Col	School House	General Staff	31/10/15	DSO
Peto, W.S.	Sapper	School House	Royal Engineers	26/12/17	
Pierson, L.D.	Lt	Wilson	10th Bn East Yorkshire Regiment	30/10/16	
Pillman, R.L.	Capt	Brooke	10th Bn The Queen's Own (Royal West Kent Regiment)	09/07/16	
Pirie, G.L.	2nd Lt	Donkin	Northamptonshire Yeomanry	16/06/15	
Pirie, A.M.	Lt Col	Lee-Warner	21st Lancers, Indian Army	21/11/17	DSO
Pitt, J.M.	Capt & Adjt	Donkin	1st Bn Dorsetshire Regiment	30/10/14	
Podmore, H.	Lt Col	Collins	12th Bn Middlesex Regiment	31/12/17	DSO
Pope, P.G.	Lt & Adjt	Collins	Royal Field Artillery	16/10/17	
Porter, A.B.	Lt	Collins	4th Bn Highland Light Infantry	03/10/15	
Porter, A.G.	Capt	School House	1st Bn Royal Irish Fusiliers	29/10/18	
Porter, H.G.	2nd Lt	Donkin	Royal Garrison Artillery	06/11/16	MC

Name	Rank	House	Unit	Date of Death	Decorations
Potter, D.R.	Capt	Wilson	4th The Queen's (Royal West Surrey Regiment)	21/12/17	
Potts, C.	2nd Lt	St Hill	4th Bn Cheshire Regiment	11/06/17	
Poulton Palmer, R.W.	Lt	School House	4th Bn Royal Berkshire Regiment	05/05/15	
Powell, K.	Pte	Michell	1st Bn Honourable Artillery Company	18/02/15	
Pratt, E. St G.	Brig Gen	J.M. Wilson	General Staff	24/11/18	CB, DSO
Pretty, D.S.	Lt	Brooke	4th Bn Suffolk Regiment	11/05/15	
Prior-Wandesforde, C.B.	Lt	Whitelaw	4th Bn Yorkshire Regiment	27/06/17	
Purves, H. de B.	Maj	Whitelaw	2nd Bn Argyll and Sutherland Highlanders	18/06/16	MC
Purvis, J.R.	Capt	Steel	9th Bn Rifle Brigade	25/09/15	
Quincey, T.E. de Q.	2nd Lt	Steel	6th Bn Rifle Brigade	09/05/15	
Quinn, J.P.C.	Pte	Stallard	1st Bn Honourable Artillery Company	14/11/16	
Rait-Kerr, S.C.	Capt	Donkin	Royal Field Artillery	13/05/15	
Rait-Kerr, W.C.	Capt	Donkin	Royal Field Artillery	10/11/14	DSO
Raley, W.H.	2nd Lt	Steel	5th Bn York and Lancaster Regiment	14/05/15	
Raley, W.H.G.	Capt	Steel	3rd Bn Yorkshire Regiment	15/06/15	
Ramsay, J.R.	Maj	Collins	Royal Field Artillery	06/01/17	
Ranking, Revd G.H.	Chaplain	Michell	Army Chaplains' Department	20/11/17	
Ransom, J.	Capt	Steel	2nd Bn Royal Berkshire Regiment	04/09/19	MC
Ransome, G.C.	Lt	Whitelaw	10th Bn Yorkshire Regiment	15/01/18	
Rathbone, A.R.	Capt	Bowden-Smith	3rd Bn South Lancashire Regiment	24/06/15	
Rawlinson, C.V.	2nd Lt	Michell	3rd Bn Dorsetshire Regiment	22/05/15	
Rayson, W.H.R.	Capt	School House	Royal Field Artillery	27/03/18	

Name	Rank	House	Unit	Date of Death	Decorations
Relton, G.L.	Lt	Wilson	1st Bn East Surrey Regiment	14/09/14	
Rendel, A.J.	Maj	Payne-Smith	Royal Field Artillery	29/06/17	MC
Renny-Tailyour, H.F.T.	2nd Lt	Whitelaw	Royal Engineers	11/11/14	
Reynolds, A.S.	2nd Lt	School House	Royal Field Artillery	24/07/17	
Reynolds, W.K.	Lt	Wilson	3rd Bn Leicestershire Regiment	10/09/15	
Rice, B.N.	Capt	Stallard	10th Bn East Yorkshire Regiment	10/07/17	
Richardson, A.J.B.	2nd Lt	Steel	4th Bn Yorkshire Regiment	04/01/15	
Richardson, J.M.	Lt Col	Arnold	Royal Garrison Artillery	30/03/18	
Richardson, R.S.	Lt	Collins	Machine Gun Corps	01/09/16	
Ridley, C.M.	Capt	Brooke	10th Bn Essex Regiment	31/10/16	
Ridley-Thompson, A.	Pte	Town	Princess Patricia's Canadian Light Infantry	31/10/14	
Rigby, C.N.B.	Lt	Wilson	Royal Marine Artillery	23/04/18	
Rigby, F.J.	Capt	Stallard	3rd Bn Seaforth Highlanders	21/01/16	MC
Ripley, G.E.	Col	Lee-Warner	6th Bn Northamptonshire Regiment	16/10/16	
Ritson, J.A.	Capt	Michell	7th Bn South Lancashire Regiment	23/07/16	
Roberts, J.L.	Lt	G.F. Bradby	6th Bn Leicestershire Regiment	21/03/18	MC
Robson, G.D.	Lt	School Hose	9th Bn King's Royal Rifle Corps	24/08/17	
Robson-Scott, T.S.	Lt	Whitelaw	2nd Bn Royal Scots	14/12/14	
Roe, A.R.M.	Capt	Steel	1st Bn Dorsetshire Regiment	16/09/14	
Romer, M.L.R.	Capt	Wilson	7th Bn King's Royal Rifle Corps	20/09/16	
Roper, W.E.	Capt	Whitelaw	5th Bn The King's Own (Royal Lancaster Regiment)	31/07/17	

Name	Rank	House	Unit	Date of Death	Decorations
Rose, J.C.R.	Lt	School House	2nd Bn Argyll and Sutherland Highlanders	08/11/14	
Ross, H.D.	Pte	School House	29th Bn Royal Fusiliers	20/07/16	
Ross, Revd T.E.	Chaplain	Town	Royal Navy	13/07/18	
Rowden, C.R.	Maj	St Hill	Royal Air Force	20/04/18	MC
Rowlands, C.H.	Cpl	Donkin	Royal Engineers	13/04/18	
Russell-Smith, H.F.	Capt	Brooke	6th Bn Rifle Brigade	05/07/16	
Ruston, C.H.S.	2nd Lt	Donkin	4th Bn The Buffs	04/04/18	
Rutter, E.F.	Maj	Morice	1st Bn East Lancashire Regiment	13/05/15	
Ryley, H.F.B.	Capt	Collins	2nd Bn Loyal North Lancashire Regiment	02/11/14	
Sale, R.C.	Capt	Wilson	1st Bn Herefordshire Regiment	26/03/17	
Salmon, B.B.	2nd Lt	School House	18th Bn Manchester Regiment	09/07/16	MC
Samson, O.M.	2nd Lt	Staff	Royal Garrison Artillery	17/09/18	
Sanders, J.D.G.	Capt	Michell	Royal Flying Corps	06/01/16	
Sanderson, A.K.	2nd Lt	Stallard	5th Bn Middlesex Regiment	25/09/15	
Savage, C.F.	Lt	Collins	10th Bn Northumberland Fusiliers	20/06/17	
Scott, W.D.	Lt	Whitelaw	4th Bn Oxfordshire and Buckinghamshire Light Infantry	22/08/17	
Scott, J.W.	Lt Col	Michell	8th Bn Somerset Light Infantry	23/04/17	DSO
Scott-Gatty, C.C.S.	Maj	Payne-Smith	1st Bn Hertfordshire Regiment	24/07/16	
Scriven, J.B.	Lt Col	Scott	21st Lancers, Indian Army	05/09/15	
Seckham, G.A.	Lt	Michell	2nd Bn East Lancashire Regiment	06/01/15	
Sellman, E.N.N.	Lt	Steel	3rd Bn Gloucestershire Regiment	04/04/18	

Name	Rank	House	Unit	Date of Death	Decorations
Selous, F.C.	Capt	J.M. Wilson	25th Bn Royal Fusiliers	04/01/17	DSO
Selous, F.H.B.	Capt	School House	Royal Flying Corps	04/01/18	MC
Selwyn, G.V.C.	Lt	School House	Royal Field Artillery	25/10/18	
Shairp of Houstoun, N.	Capt	Whitelaw	Ayrshire Yeomanry	13/10/18	MC
Sheriff, K.	2nd Lt	Stallard	3rd Bn The Queen's Own (Royal West Kent Regiment)	23/06/15	
Shirley, A.V.S.	2nd Lt	Donkin	Royal Flying Corps	08/06/17	
Simon, H.	Maj	Whitelaw	Royal Field Artillery	08/09/17	
Simon, V.H.	Maj	Whitelaw	Royal Engineers	05/06/17	MC
Simpson, C.F.B.	Capt	Stallard	9th Bn Durham Light Infantry	03/12/17	
Simpson, A.H.	Lt	Whitelaw	1st Bn Royal Warwickshire Regiment	01/02/15	
Simpson, G.W.A.	Lt	Michell	Royal Army Ordnance Department	25/01/19	
Sinclair, G.J.	Capt	Dickinson	1st Bn Black Watch	18/04/18	
Sissons, N.L.	Lt	Steel	11th Bn East Yorkshire Regiment	09/09/16	
Slacke, C.O.	Capt	Steel	12th Bn East Surrey Regiment	12/11/16	
Slaney, J.C.	Lt	Payne-Smith	Royal Field Artillery	17/02/16	
Smale, J.N.	LCpl	Michell	3rd Bn South Staffordshire Regiment	27/05/15	
Smallwood, F.G.	Col	Green	Royal Garrison Artillery	30/12/19	
Smeathman, J.M.	Lt	Steel	Royal Engineers	24/10/14	
Smeathman, C.	Lt	Steel	1st Bn Leicestershire Regiment	24/10/14	
Smethurst, J.	2nd Lt	Stallard	21st Bn The King's (Liverpool Regiment)	16/09/16	
Smith, F.G.	2nd Lt	Town	Royal Flying Corps	08/02/18	
Smith, W.W.	2nd Lt	Donkin	19th Bn Manchester Regiment	09/07/16	
Smith, H.D.D.	Capt	Stallard	Royal Flying Corps	14/12/15	
Smith, H.L.	Sub Lt	Dickinson	Royal Naval Air Service	24/05/17	

Name	Rank	House	Unit	Date of Death	Decorations
Smith, I.P.	Maj	Brooke	Royal Garrison Artillery	30/11/17	DSO
Smith, G.A.C.	Capt	G.F. Bradby	14th Bn Argyll and Sutherland Highlanders	28/09/18	MC
Smyth, J.	Capt	Collins	2nd Bn Lancashire Fusiliers	08/07/15	
Snelgrove, S.H.	Lt	Brooke	14th Bn King's Royal Rifle Corps	31/07/15	
Snowden, H.J.	Lt	Brooke	1st Bn Hertfordshire Regiment	11/01/15	
Soames, R.E.	Lt	Brooke	8th Bn East Surrey Regiment	01/07/16	
Solly, A.N.	Capt	Michell	Royal Flying Corps	11/08/17	
Spittle, T.S.	Capt	Stallard	1st Bn Monmouthshire Regiment	02/10/17	
Sproat, J.M.	2nd Lt	H.C. Bradby	17th Bn The King's (Liverpool Regiment)	11/07/16	MC
Stanford, J.V.	Lt	G.F. Bradby	8th Bn Seaforth Highlanders	25/09/15	
Staniland, G.	2nd Lt	Michell	4th Bn Lincolnshire Regiment	13/04/15	
Staniland, M.	Capt	Michell	4th Bn Lincolnshire Regiment	29/07/15	
Steel, E.B.	Maj	Morice	Royal Army Medical Corps	23/11/14	
Stehn, A.E.	Capt	Whitelaw	4th Bn Royal Warwickshire Regiment	08/11/18	
Stevenson, F.O.	Pte	Morice	32nd Bn Middlesex Regiment	07/11/18	
Stewart-Richardson, Sir E.A. Bt	Capt	Donkin	3rd Bn Black Watch	28/11/14	
Stiebel, E.A.	Pte	School House	Inns of Court Officer Training Corps	24/08/17	
Stobart, W.	Lt	Michell	Royal Flying Corps	24/08/16	
Stokes, L.M.	2nd Lt	School House	Royal Marine Light Infantry	13/11/16	
Stokes, P.D.	2nd Lt	G.F. Bradby	11th Bn Rifle Brigade	10/04/17	
Stone, R.C.	Lt	Collins	Machine Gun Corps	08/04/17	

Name	Rank	House	Unit	Date of Death	Decorations
Strangeways-Rogers, A.E.F.F.	2nd Lt	School House	3rd Bn Grenadier Guards	04/11/18	
Strauss, V.A.	Lt	Brooke	Royal Flying Corps	27/11/16	
Surtees, W.B.	Capt	Steel	9th Bn West Yorkshire Regiment	28/09/16	
Sutton, E.G.	Lt	Whitelaw	7th Bn Royal Sussex Regiment	08/04/16	MC
Swann, G.H.	2nd Lt	St Hill	Royal Flying Corps	18/10/17	
Swann, H.N.	Capt	Steel	2nd Bn Lincolnshire Regiment	04/04/17	
Swinburne, T.A.S.	Maj	Donkin	Royal Engineers	01/04/18	DSO
Sykes, W.	Lt	School House	Royal Field Artillery	04/04/18	
Tahourdin, P.R.	Lt	Donkin	47th Sikhs, Indian Army	18/04/16	
Tapp, T.A.	Capt	Michell	1st Bn Coldstream Guards	21/10/17	MC and Bar
Tatham, C.	Capt	School House	1st Bn Honourable Artillery Company	18/06/15	
Taylor, C.P.	Capt	Wilson	8th Bn East Yorkshire Regiment	28/10/16	
Taylor, J.C.W.	Lt	Stallard	3rd Bn Sherwood Foresters	09/08/15	
Thomas, R.I.	Lt	Donkin	1st Bn Connaught Rangers	14/09/14	
Thompson, C.B.	Capt	Morice	14th Bn Middlesex Regiment	23/05/16	
Thompson, G.	Lt	Stallard	Royal Garrison Artillery	16/01/15	
Thompson, R.	Lt	Whitelaw	2nd Bn East Lancashire Regiment	23/10/16	
Thompson, A.J.O.	Lt Col	Elsee	4th Bn Australian Infantry	26/04/15	
Thorpe, H.G.	2nd Lt	Town	1st Bn The King's (Liverpool Regiment)	24/03/18	MC
Tindall, H.	LCpl	Donkin	Honourable Artillery Company	16/06/15	
Toller, E.N.	Capt	Donkin	20th Bn Royal Fusiliers	20/07/16	

Name	Rank	House	Unit	Date of Death	Decorations
Tolson, J.	Capt	Michell	6th Bn Sherwood Foresters	28/10/17	
Tomkins, A.G.	2nd Lt	Donkin	3rd Bn Irish Guards	13/09/16	
Townsend, E.T.	Capt	Donkin	5th Bn Highland Light Infantry	08/11/17	
Townsend, R.T.	Capt	Donkin	Royal Flying Corps	30/11/17	
Townsend, T.A.	Capt	School House	Royal Army Medical Corps	24/03/18	MC and Bar
Traill, C.B.	Maj	Stallard	10th Bn East Yorkshire Regiment	28/06/18	MC
Trevelyan, W.	2nd Lt	Whitelaw	4th Bn Rifle Brigade	05/05/15	
Treves, H.T.	Lt	Collins	Royal Naval Division	23/05/15	
Trevor, H.E.	Lt Col	Collins	9th Bn Essex Regiment	11/04/17	
Tripp, D.O.H.	Capt	Collins	3rd Bn Loyal North Lancashire Regiment	18/08/16	DSO
Troup, J.G.	2nd Lt	Stallard	Royal Flying Corps	13/05/17	
Truscott, F.G.	Lt	Michell	Royal Flying Corps	06/04/17	MC
Turner, T.E.	Lt	Donkin	13th Bn London Regiment	09/05/15	
Twist, F.C.O.	2nd Lt	Wilson	18th Bn Manchester Regiment	30/07/16	
Underhill, T.W.	2nd Lt	Steel	8th Bn The Buffs	19/08/16	
Van Gruisen, W.	Lt	St Hill	1st Bn Royal Fusiliers	01/11/16	
Vaudrey, C.H.S.	Capt	Steel	1st Bn Manchester Regiment	02/05/16	
Vaudrey, N.	Capt	Steel	17th Bn Manchester Regiment	01/07/16	
Vaughan, P.C.	2nd Lt	Steel	Royal Garrison Artillery	26/09/17	
Vavasour, L.O.	Lt	Brooke	2nd Bn North Staffordshire Regiment	25/07/15	
Venables, G.R.	2nd Lt	Collins	3rd Bn King's (Shropshire Light Infantry)	07/03/15	
Vertue, A.F.	Cpl	G.F. Bradby	1st Bn Honourable Artillery Company	21/04/15	
Vesey-Fitzgerald, W.H.L.	2nd Lt	Town & Stallard	3rd Bn Devonshire Regiment	14/08/16	
Vincent, J.T.C.	2nd Lt	Stallard	3rd Bn Welsh Regiment	09/05/15	

Name	Rank	House	Unit	Date of Death	Decorations
Voelcker, H.L.	2nd Lt	Wilson	6th Bn South Lancashire Regiment	20/07/16	
Wake, C.B.D.	2nd Lt	Hawkesworth	6th Bn King's Royal Rifle Corps	25/09/18	
Walford, A.E.	Lt	Payne-Smith	2nd Bn Suffolk Regiment	16/08/16	
Walford, G.H.	Maj	Morice	General Staff	19/04/15	
Walker, B.S.	2nd Lt	Michell	5th Bn Cheshire Regiment	10/05/15	
Walker, T.C.	2nd Lt	Michell	5th Bn Manchester Regiment	06/06/15	
Walker, G.H.	Lt	Brooke	Royal Flying Corps	02/18	
Walker, R.W.S.	Lt	Brooke	Royal Army Medical Corps	22/08/22	
Walker, G.W.	Pte	Donkin	16th Canadian Infantry Battalion	22/04/15	
Wallace, J.R.	2nd Lt	School House	1st Bn Royal Scots Fusiliers	22/04/15	
Ward, T.P.	2nd Lt	Dickinson	7th Bn Northamptonshire Regiment	31/07/17	
Waterlow, C.M.	Lt Col	Donkin	Royal Naval Air Service	20/07/17	
Waters, R.R.	Capt	Collins	4th Bn Royal Warwickshire Regiment	24/10/16	
Watson, H.S.	Capt	Stallard	8th Bn Gordon Highlanders	25/09/15	
Watson, C.C.	Lt	Michell	Royal Field Artillery	01/06/17	
Wayman, W.A.	Capt	Wilson	4th Bn Oxfordshire and Buckinghamshire Light Infantry	14/08/16	
Weightman, J.	Sub Lt	Steel	Royal Naval Volunteer Reserve	04/06/15	
Welch, J.S.L.	Lt	H.C. Bradby	12th Bn The King's Own (Yorkshire Light Infantry)	01/07/16	
Welsh, A.R.	Lt	School House	4th Bn Yorkshire Regiment	19/02/16	
Wheatcroft, G.H.	2nd Lt	School House	Royal Garrison Artillery	11/08/15	

Name	Rank	House	Unit	Date of Death	Decorations
Wheatcroft, R.D.	Lt	School House	6th Bn Sherwood Foresters	02/07/16	
Whinney, J.A.P.	2nd Lt	Wilson	Oxfordshire Yeomanry	22/06/17	
Whitaker, F.	Lt	Donkin	Royal Army Medical Corps	28/10/16	
Whitefoord, Revd C.B.	Chaplain	Payne-Smith	Army Chaplains' Department	29/05/18	
Whittall, R.W.L.	2nd Lt	School House	General Intelligence Officer	06/08/15	
Whitting, R.H.	Off Cdt	H.C. Bradby	Royal Military Academy Sandhurst	01/09/18	
Wiggins, W.E.	2nd Lt	Town	Leicestershire Yeomanry	19/08/16	
Willard, K.H.	2nd Lt	Town	Royal Flying Corps	12/10/17	
Williams, V.F.	2nd Lt	St Hill	Royal Flying Corps	02/04/17	
Williams, H.C.	Lt	Brooke	2nd Bn The Queen's (Royal West Surrey Regiment)	18/10/15	
Wilmot, S.D.	Capt	Steel	Royal Garrison Artillery	14/10/18	
Wilson, H.S.	2nd Lt	Staff	8th Bn Worcestershire Regiment	14/09/15	
Wilson, T.W.	Lt	Michell	6th Bn The King's (Liverpool Regiment)	05/05/15	
Wing, V.S.	2nd Lt	St Hill	Royal Field Artillery	10/08/17	
Wintle, F.	Lt Col	Bowden-Smith	87th Punjabis, Indian Army	23/03/16	
Wolley-Dod, D.K.	Lt	School House	12th Bn The King's (Liverpool Regiment)	25/09/15	
Wood, L.I.	Lt Col	Lee-Warner	2nd Bn Border Regiment	16/05/15	CMG
Worthington, S.	Lt	Brooke	Royal Horse Artillery	28/11/17	
Wray, K.C.G.	Capt	Collins	4th Bn South Lancashire Regiment	09/08/16	
Wyley, W.R.F.	Lt & Adjt	School House	Royal Field Artillery	19/09/16	
Young, E.T.	Lt	Payne-Smith	6th Bn Manchester Regiment	05/06/15	

Appendix Two

Casualties by House

Houses are listed here by their modern names. There are certain houses of Rugby School which do not appear on this list as they have opened since the end of the Great War: Dean, Griffin, Rupert Brooke, Sheriff and Southfield. The greater number of casualties from School House reflects the larger number of boys in that house during this period: an average of eighty compared to fifty in the other houses.

Bradley: 69
Cotton: 70
Kilbracken: 77
Michell: 69
School Field: 73
School House: 103
Stanley: 76
Town: 31
Tudor: 58
Whitelaw: 57
Staff: 4

Total: 687

Appendix Three

Places of Burial and Commemoration

Individuals featured in this book who were killed in action are buried or commemorated at the following locations.

Arthur Keen	Terlincthun British Military Cemetery, France, III.A.17.
Christopher Bushell	Querrieu British Cemetery, France, E.6.
Frank de Pass VC	Béthune Town Cemetery, France, I.A.24.
Frederick C. Selous	Isolated Grave, Selous Game Reserve, Tanzania.
Frederick H. B. Selous*	Arras Flying Services Memorial, France.
Geoffrey Cather VC*	Thiepval Memorial, France, Face 15A.
Harold Cawley	Lancashire Landing Cemetery, Turkey, A.76.
Jasper Richardson	Étaples Military Cemetery, France, XXVIII.F.3.
John Norwood VC	Sablonnières New Communal Cemetery, France, 4.
Kenneth Powell	Loker Churchyard, Belgium, II.D.7.
Oswald Cawley	Nery Communal Cemetery, France.
Ronald Poulton Palmer	Hyde Park Corner (Royal Berks) Cemetery, Belgium, B.11.
Rupert Brooke	Isolated grave, Skyros, Greece.
Rupert Inglis*	Thiepval Memorial, Face 4C.

*Grave unknown.

Appendix Four

Old Rugbeians who served as General Officers in the Great War

The following are listed in their final rank, though all reached the rank of at least brigadier general during the war.

- General Sir Thomas Cubitt KCB CMG DSO – Commander of the 38th Division. Later Governor of Bermuda (1931-36) and Colonel Commandant of the Royal Artillery.
- Major General Sir George Forestier-Walker KCB – Chief of Staff of 11 Corps, then Commander of the 21st and 27th Divisions. Ernest Swinton was his fag at Rugby.
- Brigadier General Sir Alexander Gibb GBE CB – Civil Engineer-in-Chief to the Admiralty.
- Brigadier General George Macarthur-Onslow – Commander of the 2nd and 5th Light Horse Brigades. Later commanded the 1st Cavalry Division between 1927 and 1931.
- General Sir Ivor Maxse KCB CVO DSO – Commander of XVIII Corps. Later Inspector General of Training.
- Major General Sir Ernest Swinton KBE CB DSO. Instrumental in the invention of the tank, and Chichele Professor of Military History at All Souls, Oxford between 1925 and 1939.
- Brigadier General Sir Percy Sykes KCIE CB CMG. Commander of the South Persian Rifles.
- Brigadier General John Wigan CB CMG DSO – Commander of the 7th and 22nd Mounted Divisions.

Bibliography

AINSWORTH R.B., *The Story of the 6th Battalion the Durham Light Infantry*, 1919, London: St Catherine Press.

ARMSTRONG G. & GRAY T., *The Authentic Tawney: A New Interpretation of the Political Thought of R.H. Tawney*, 2016, Luton: Andrews Ltd.

ASHBY J., *Seek Glory, Now Keep Glory: The Story of the 1st Battalion Royal Warwickshire Regiment 1914-1918*, 2000, Birmingham: Helion & Company.

BARLOW R.A., & BOWEN H.V., *A Dear and Noble Boy*, 1995, Barnsley: Leo Cooper.

BATESON F.W., *Review of English Studies*, Vol.14, No.54, April 1938.

BROOKE R., *The Collected Poems of Rupert Brooke with a Memoir*, 1919, London, Sidgwick & Jackson.

BROOKER P. & THACKER A., *The Oxford Critical and Cultural History of Modernist Magazines Volume One*, 2009, Oxford: OUP.

BURNS R.M., *Historiography: Politics*, 2006, Abingdon: Taylor & Francis.

BYRNE P., *Mad World: Evelyn Waugh and the Secrets of Brideshead*, 2010, London: Harper Press.

CARPENTER H., *The Brideshead Generation: Evelyn Waugh and Friends*, 1989, London: Weidenfeld and Nicholson.

CHAMBERLAIN A., *The Austen Chamberlain Diary Letters*, 1995, Cambridge: Cambridge University Press.

COOPER I., *Immortal Harlequin: The Story of Adrian Stoop*, 2004, Stroud: Tempus Publishing.

CORSAN J., *For Poulton and England: The Life and Times of an Edwardian Rugby Hero*, 2009, Leicester: Troubadour Publishing.

CRUTTWELL C.R.M.F., *A History of the Great War 1914-1918*, 1934, Oxford: Clarendon Press.

CRUTTWELL C.R.M.F., *The War Service of the 1/4 Royal Berkshire Regiment (T. F.)*, 1922, Oxford: Basil Blackwell.

DAVIE M. (Ed.), *The Diaries of Evelyn Waugh*, 1979, Harmondsworth: Penguin.

DAVIES R., *A Student in Arms: Donald Hankey and Edwardian Society at War*, 2016, London: Routledge.

DELANY P., *Fatal Glamour: The Life of Rupert Brooke*, 2015, Toronto: McGill-Queens Press.

DOCKRILL M.L. & McKERCHER B.J.C., *Diplomacy and World Power: Studies in British Foreign Policy, 1890-1951*, 2002, Cambridge: Cambridge University Press.

DOUIE C., *The Weary Road: Recollections of a Subaltern of Infantry*, 1929, London: John Murray.

DUTTON D., *Austen Chamberlain: Gentleman in Politics*, 1985, Piscataway: Transaction Publishers.

EDWARDS P. and WALLACE C., *Wyndham Lewis: Art and War*, 1992, London: Lund Humphries.

ELLETSON D.H., *The Chamberlains*, 1966, London: Murray.

GALBRAITH J.S. & HUTTENBACK R.A., *Bureaucracies at War: The British in the Middle East in the First World War* in *National and International Politics in the Middle East: Essays in Honour of Elie Kedourie*, ed. Edward Ingram, 2013, London: Routledge

GOUGH P., *A Terrible Beauty: British Artists in the First World War*, 2010, London: Sansom.

GRIFFITH K., *Thank God we Kept the Flag Flying: The Siege and Relief of Ladysmith 1899-1900*, 1974, New York: The Viking Press.

GOLDMAN L., *The Life of R.H. Tawney: Socialism and History*, 2013, London: A&C Black.

GRIMSHAW R., *Indian Cavalry Officer 1914-15*, 1986, Tunbridge Wells: Costello.

HALE K., *Friends and Apostles: The Correspondence of Rupert Brooke and James Strachey, 1905-1914*, 1998, London: Yale University Press.

HANKEY D., *A Student in Arms*, 1917, London: Andrew Melrose Ltd.

HANKEY M.P.A., *The Supreme Command, 1914-1918 Vol. 2*, 1961, London: George Allen & Unwin.

HARDY H.H., *Rugby*, 1911, London: Sir Isaac Pitman and Sons.

HARRIS H.J., *Rugby School Corps 1860 to 1960*, 1960, London: Brown Knight & Truscott.

HARTLEY J., *6th Battalion The Manchester Regiment in the Great War: Not a Rotter in the Lot*, 2010, Oxford: Casemate UK.

HASSALL C., *Rupert Brooke, a Biography*, 1964, London: Faber & Faber.

HASTINGS A., *A History of English Christianity, 1920-1990*, 1991, London: SCM.

HOLLIS C., *Oxford in the Twenties*, 1976, London: Heineman.

HOLMES R., *The Little Field Marshal: A Life of Sir John French*, 2004, London: Weidenfeld& Nicolson.

HOLMES R., *Riding the Retreat: Mons to the Marne 1914 Revisited*, 2007, New York: Random House.

HOPE SIMPSON J.B., *Rugby Since Arnold*, 1967, London: Macmillan.

HUNTER A., *Renaissance of the Rose*, 2010, Fleet: emp3books.

JENKINS R., *Asquith*, 1964, London: Collins.

KEYNES G., *The Letters of Rupert Brooke*, 1967, London: Faber & Faber.

LEACH H. & FARRINGTON S.M., *Strolling About on the Roof of the World: The First Hundred Years of the Royal Society for Asian Affairs*, 2003, London: Routledge.

LEWIS W., *Blasting and Bombardiering*, 1967, Berkeley: University of California Press.

LUCAS F.L., *Journal Under the Terror, 1938*, 1939, London: Cassells.

LUCAS F.L., Letter, *The Weekend Review*, 16 September 1933.

LUCAS F.L., *Review of T.S. Eliot's The Waste Land*, in *The New Statesman*, November 1923.

LUCAS F.L., *The Greatest Problem and Other Essays,* 1960, London: Cassells.

LYON P.H.B., *Songs of Youth and War*, 1918, London: Erskine Macdonald.

MARSH E., Rupert Brooke, A Memoir, 1918, Toronto: McClelland, Goodchild and Stewart Ltd.

MASSIE R. K., *Dreadnought: Britain, Germany and the Coming of the Great War*, 2007, London: Random House.

MCCRERY N., *Into Touch: Rugby Internationals Killed in the Great War*, 2014, Barnsley: Pen and Sword Books.

MCCRERY N., *The Extinguished Flame: Olympians Killed in the Great War*, 2016, Barnsley: Pen and Sword Books.

MALLON B. & BUCHANAN I., *The 1908 Olympic Games: Results for All Competitors in All Events, with Commentary*, 2009, Jerfferson NC: McFarland.

BIBLIOGRAPHY

McLEAN R.R., *Royalty and Diplomacy in Europe 1890-1914*, 2007, Cambridge: Cambridge University Press.

METCALFE N., *Blacker's Boys: 9th (Service) Battalion, Princess Victoria's (Royal Irish Fusiliers) (County Armagh), 1914-1919*, 2012, N.P. Metcalfe.

MICHELL A.T. (Ed.), *Rugby School Register, Volume III, From May 1874 to May 1904*, 1904, Rugby: A.J. Lawrence

MILLER A., *Rupert Brooke in the First World War*, 2018, Oxford: OUP.

MILLER E., *Letters of Donald Hankey*, 1920, London: Fleming H. Revell Company.

MURPHY R., *Captain John Norwood VC*, 2017, Amazon.

O'KEEFE P., *Some Sort of Genius: A Life of Wyndham Lewis*, 2015, Berkeley: Counterpoint.

OTTE T.G., *July Crisis: The World's Descent into War, July 1914*, 2014, Cambridge: Cambridge University Press.

PATEY D.L., *The Life of Evelyn Waugh*, 1998, Oxford: Blackwell.

PETRIE C., *The Chamberlain Tradition*, 1938, London: The Right Book Club.

POULTON E.B., *Ronald Poulton*, 1919, London: Sidgwick & Jackson.

RANSOME A., *The Autobiography of Arthur Ransome*, 1976, London: Century Publishing.

READ M., *Forever England: The Life of Rupert Brooke*, 1997, London: Mainstream Publishing.

RICH N., *Great Power Diplomacy since 1914,* 2003, New York: McGraw-Hill.

ROSE W.K. (Ed.), *The Letters of Wyndham Lewis*, 1963, New York: New Directions.

SCOTT A.J.L., *Sixty Squadron RAF 1916-1919*, 1990, London: Greenhill Books.

SELDON A. & WALSH D., *Public Schools and the Great War*, 2013, Barnsley: Pen and Sword Books.

SIMPSON J.H., *Schoolmaster's Harvest*, 1954, London: Faber & Faber.

SMITH M., *The Secrets of Station X*, National Archives, London, 2011.

STONE W., 'Some Bloomsbury Interviews and Memories', in *Twentieth Century Literature*, Vol.43, No.2, Summer 1997.

SWINTON E.D., *Eyewitness, being personal reminiscences of certain phases of the Great War, including the genesis of the tank, by Major-General Sir Ernest D. Swinton*, 1933, New York: Doubleday, Doran & Co.

SWINTON E.D., *Over My Shoulder*, 1951, Oxford: George Ronald.

TAWNEY R.H., *Religion and the Rise of Capitalism*, 1926, New York: Penguin Books.

TAWNEY R.H., *The Radical Tradition*, 1966, Harmondsworth: Penguin Books.

TERRILL R., *R.H. Tawney and his Times: Socialism as Fellowship*, 1973, Harvard: Harvard University Press.

THORNTON N., *Led by Lions*, 2017, Stroud: Fonthill Media.

VON MACH E., *Official Diplomatic Documents Relating to the Outbreak of the European War*, 1916, London: Macmillan.

WALSTON C., *With a Fine Disregard...: A Portrait of Rugby School*, 2006, London: Third Millennium.

WAUGH A., Fathers and Sons, 2004, London: Headline Publishing.

WAUGH E., *A Little Learning*, 1983, Harmondsworth: Penguin.

WENTWORTH ROSKILL S., *Hankey: Man of Secrets*, 1972, London: Collins.

WILSON W.N., *Rugby School Memorial Chapel*, 1923, Rugby: George Over.

WOOD W. de B., *History of the King's Shropshire Light Infantry in the Great war 1914-1918*, 1925, London: The Medici Society.

WOODWARD D.R., *Field Marshal Sir William Robertson*, 1998, London: Praeger.

WRIGHT E. & LYON B., *Hugh Lyon, a Memoir*, 1993, Berkhamsted: Lawrence Viney.

War Diaries

WO95/1109/2: 5th Dragoon Guards.

WO95/1187/4: 34th Prince Albert Victor's Own Poona Horse.

WO95/1219/3/2: 1st Battalion, Scots Guards.

WO95/1280/1: 1st Battalion, Queen's (Royal West Surrey) Regiment.

WO94/1484/3: 1st Battalion, Royal Warwickshire Regiment.

WO95/1669/1: 22nd Battalion, Manchester Regiment.

WO95/1896/1: 7th Battalion, The Rifle Brigade.

WO95/2049/2: 7th Battalion, The Queen's Own (Royal West Kent Regiment).

WO95/2051/1: 7th Battalion, Queen's (Royal West Surrey) Regiment.

WO95/2505/2: 9th Battalion, Royal Irish Fusiliers.

WO95/2762/1: 1/4th Battalion, Royal Berkshire Regiment.
WO95/2840/2: 6th Battalion, Durham Light Infantry.
WO95/5145/3: 12th Indian Infantry Brigade: 1/5th Battalion, Queen's (Royal West Surrey) Regiment.
WO95/5332/15: 25th Battalion, Royal Fusiliers.

Manuscripts

British Library, IOR/L/MIL/17/15/105.
IWM, Minshall MSS 86/51/1.

Index